GUERRILLA
DATING
TACTICS

GUERRILLA
DATING
TACTICS

Strategies, Tips, and Secrets for Finding Romance

SHARYN WOLF, C. S. W.

A DUTTON BOOK

DUTTON
Published by the Penguin Group
Penguin Books USA Inc., 375 Hudson Street, New York, New York 10014, U.S.A.
Penguin Books Ltd, 27 Wrights Lane, London W8 5TZ, England
Penguin Books Australia Ltd, Ringwood, Victoria, Australia
Penguin Books Canada Ltd, 10 Alcorn Avenue, Toronto, Ontario, Canada M4V 3B2
Penguin Books (N.Z.) Ltd, 182–190 Wairau Road, Auckland 10, New Zealand

Penguin Books Ltd, Registered Offices:
Harmondsworth, Middlesex, England

First published by Dutton, an imprint of New American Library, a division of Penguin
Books USA Inc.
Distributed in Canada by McClelland & Stewart Inc.

First Printing, February, 1993
10   9   8   7   6   5   4   3   2   1

Excerpt from *Lost in the Cosmos* by Walker Percy. Copyright © 1983 by Walker Percy.
Reprinted by permission of Farrar, Straus & Giroux, Inc.

Excerpt from *On a Clear Day They Could See Seventh Place* by George Robinson and Charles
Salzberg. Copyright © 1991 by George Robinson and Charles Salzberg. Used by permission
of Dell Books, a division of Bantam Doubleday Dell Publishing Group, Inc.

REGISTERED TRADEMARK—MARCA REGISTRADA

LIBRARY OF CONGRESS CATALOGING IN PUBLICATION DATA:

Wolf, Sharyn.
   Guerrilla dating tactics : strategies, tips, and secrets for finding romance /
Sharyn Wolf
      p.   cm.
   ISBN 0-525-93570-3
   1. Dating (Social customs)—United States.   2. Courtship—United
States.   I. Title.
HQ801.W79   1993
646.7'7—dc20   92–24100
                                                                                CIP

Printed in the United States of America
Set in Palatino
Designed by Leonard Telesca

For Boots Maleson,
my best date

Acknowledgments

I want to express heartfelt thanks to the following people:

Heide Lange, my smart, wonderful agent, who pushed me farther than I ever would have ventured.

Douglas Stallings, for his original enthusiasm for this project and for his encouragement during the past two years.

Ross Klavan, who was instrumental in helping me shape this book, and gave generously of his wisdom and time. I owe him a great deal.

Alexia Dorszynski, my editor, for her keen intelligence in forging a path to the heart of this book. She has the gift.

Deb Brody, my editor, for her perceptive eye and polished grace in helping to pull it all together. Each moment with her was a pleasure.

David Sparr, Nan Lee, Jonathan Wimpenny, and Jody Watkins for reading drafts, and Lyn Meehan, who offered ongoing support. Michael Mark and Robert Kaplan for their insight. Also, Linda Antoniucci, Alfred Maleson, and Roberta Fabiano for scouting out great stories time and again. Their advice and reassurance meant a great deal.

Sarah Mills, Gary Keske, and Victoria Watson for their creative expertise in helping me to reinvent myself.

Deborah Henson-Conant, a model of personal drive during the writing of this book. She was inspirational.

Charles Salzberg, for his generosity in answering one thousand of my questions about the book business.

Dr. Laura George, for offering me a lens through which to see myself. Her help has been indispensable.

Boots Maleson, my husband. I'll never get to say that time spent on this book took me away from him. He's so busy that he hasn't had a day off since 1964. I thank him for reading chapters, for restoring computer files I deleted, for listening to the constant hum of my anxiety, for his quirky sense of humor, and for his excellent advice.

Jamie Jaffe, Director of Education for the Boston Center for Adult Education, who is a woman of vision, integrity, and strength. Much of what I've learned about the value of Continuing Adult Education to the community I have learned from her.

Deb Leopold, President of First Class in Washington, D.C., a shining light in the field of Adult Education. I want to thank her for her creative spirit and commitment to excellence.

Suzanne Wilson and Jessica Michelson, who offered great enthusiasm, support, and their individual contributions to workshop ideas. Thanks are also due to Carol Petrucelli and the staff of The Learning Exchange and Liz Allen and the staff of The Learning Connection for offering me an ongoing forum for my work.

The entire staff of the Boston Center for Adult Education, for the eight years they have taken registration, set up rooms, promoted my workshops, and continuously made my visits a pleasure in every way.

A book such as this one gets written because people tell the truth about what's delighted, confused, devastated, titillated, disappointed, and thrilled them. Over the years, thousands of workshop participants have done just that. These men and women have been the best teachers any student of human behavior could hope for. Thank you all for your courage, your humor, and your wisdom.

Contents

IV. Countermoves: Maneuvers for When the Tables Are Turned

V. Survival Strategies: How to Protect Yourself While Working Up to the First Date

VI. Coopting Internal and External Conflict: Late-Night Thoughts on Preparing to Date

VII. How to Get More Than Name, Rank, and Serial Number: First Dates

VIII. Sabotage, Insurrection, and
the Double Bind

IX. Reframing Romance for the Nineties:
Tender Treaties

"... it is possible to learn more in ten minutes about the Crab Nebula in Taurus, which is 6,000 light-years away, than you presently know about yourself, even though you've been stuck with yourself all your life."
—Walker Percy, *Lost in the Cosmos*

GUERRILLA
DATING
TACTICS

Introduction

This is an optimistic book for healthy men and women who truly like each other, or who think they could like each other if they could only gather the courage to say hello and then stick around long enough to get something going. If you've found lately that initiating romantic connections seems more complicated than ever, you're not alone. Our world has changed so much that the customary, recognizable code of whom to ask, when to ask, and how to ask for a date ought to be tossed out the window along with everything your parents ever told you about romance. What worked for your parents will frustrate you because it's not the old days anymore, and the old ways just don't cut it.

Contemporary dating needs an overhaul and a manual—complete with an updated map that reflects the territory women and men have gained. The first things to delete from the old manual are the romantic myths that have tracked us throughout our lives. My parents and friends have related them to me. I've repeated them to others, and I bet you've heard them all.

Myth: If it's meant to be, it will happen.
Reality: What would you think if someone said, "If I'm meant to get a raise, I'll get it"?

Myth: It happens when you're not looking.
Reality: No! That's when you get hit by a bus.

Myth: Without immediate chemistry, it's a waste of time.
Reality: The pounding in your heart that signals "Romance ahead" is indistinguishable from the pounding that signals "Danger ahead."

Romantic myths can hurt us. They let us believe that we have no control over our romantic lives. This simply isn't true. Your social life is not up to fate. It's up to you.

For the past nine years, I've led workshops for thousands of single men and women focusing on ways to make it easier in the world of dating: easier to take risks, easier to make a connection once you do meet, and easier to know if the person you have met is relationship material. What these participants have to tell you about what's worked for them may delight, intrigue, and, in some cases, even shock you, but I want you to know that these stories are true stories, told to me by people between the ages of twenty and seventy-five—people from every profession and walk of life you can imagine. Several of these stories are my own. In fact, as I began writing this book, I was struck by the strong personal connections I felt to so much of this material. When I got to Chapter 18, "The Hamlet Syndrome," I came face-to-face with my own ambivalence about commitment. Subsequent to the completion of the chapter, I finally took the leap and married my partner of seven years. So my fiancé, whom I mention in early chapters, is my husband toward the end of the book.

I place the following accounts of action, bravery, coordination, and creativity under the umbrella of Guerrilla Dating Tactics. They show how to be innovative without being shocking. Keep in mind that while the phrase *Guerrilla Dating Tactics* invokes a martial tone, the use of military images in this book is in no way meant to suggest that successful dating requires the attack mode. In fact, I hate the phrase *battle of the sexes,* which evokes winners and losers. As you find yourself more and more comfortable using Guerrilla Dating Tactics, you will create encounters where both parties win.

It won't happen overnight. After all, it took you a lifetime to become who you are at this moment, and your frame of mind can't be changed in one fell swoop. But if it appeals to you to do so, you can challenge your thinking and let go of chronically unproductive outlooks. In other words, you can reframe the way you see yourself in a fashion that will encourage you to try more, dare more, be more. It takes work, but you can even learn to let yourself have more fun. In fact, while the purpose of this book is to reframe you as a risk taker, the goal of this book is to reawaken and nurture the spirit of adventurous fun, an indispensable survival strategy in your search to learn how to find a good date, how to plan a good date, and how to be a good date.

Throughout the book, I have interspersed gender and attempted to balance stories evenly. This is in no way meant to suggest that a Guerrilla Dating Tactic tried by a man cannot be used by a woman, or vice versa. You may choose to modify a technique to fit your style, sexual orientation, or age, but please don't assume that a story you've read is meant only for the gender portrayed there.

In addition to dumping the tired myths, women and men in

the following stories dumped the obsolete games and tired rules. Dating in the nineties calls for an entirely new set of rules, and the first rule is that there are no rules. That does not mean we are left with total chaos, where everything and everyone is up for grabs. What it does mean is that to meet others in this much-altered environment, you must step outside the traditional accepted ways into a new framework that focuses on improvisation, creative thinking, using your environment as a tool instead of a deterrent, and claiming the freedom to act.

If you come away from this book with new ways of looking at yourself, I'll know I've done my job. After all, you've worked too hard to trust your future to magic or an unguaranteed fate. Lift the ceiling off your thinking and focus on the possibilities rather than the limitations.

First, you will want to shatter the most prevalent myth of all:

Myth: I keep looking, but I can't find the right person.
Reality: Stop looking to *find* the right person. Start looking to *be* the right person.

As we begin our journey, let me leave you with three little words:

> UNFASTEN YOUR SEATBELT!

Guerrilla
Dating
Tactics

CHAPTER 1

Guerrilla Dating Tactics

You're at the motor vehicle bureau waiting in Line C when you spot a vibrant brunette waiting in Line A. How can you get from your line to her line without handing her a line?

You're eating dinner alone at the counter of a sushi restaurant when you lock eyes with a guy who's seated with three friends. You'd love to meet him, but unless he approaches you, it's hopeless. He's part of a group!

You've already watched a woman shoot down two men who have asked her to dance. You don't want to be number three, but you'll kick yourself for a week if you don't do something.

You're at your tenants' association meeting, where an invited speaker humorously describes how her ceiling became her floor. Is she married? Living with someone? Do you ask her or hope you see her again . . . next month?

You're running to catch your flight when you drop your purse and everything flies out. The contents are retrieved by Mr. Tall, Dark, and Smiling—but you're already late, late, late.

There are ways to tackle the ongoing dilemma of how to approach someone when time to talk is measured in milliseconds. These are the do-or-die opportunities encountered when you are walking down the street one way and your heart thumps madly at the sight of someone walking down the street the other way. Or when you are perusing the frozen foods and catch sight of someone ethereal pinching a honeydew. Or when you simply must make eye contact with a person seated two rows behind you at the movies. The optimal solution would be the magical appearance of a mutual friend who makes a proper introduction and invites the two of you to join her for lunch. Statistically, you are more likely to find the Dead Sea Scrolls, Part II.

Of course, you could do what you've usually done—nothing.

But that means getting the results you've usually gotten. Besides, you bought this book so you wouldn't have to wonder what to do.

When every second counts, the answer to how to meet that intriguing person rests in developing the spirit, ingenuity, and courage of the guerrilla soldier. Guerrilla soldiers are brave, scrappy troopers who owe their success to spotting unconventional opportunities in out-of-the-way places and making the most of each one. They operate without formal guidelines, flashy uniforms, or a reliance on safety in numbers.

A guerrilla soldier does not have the benefits of high technology or a comfortable environment. He must rely on himself and learn to make do with what is at hand. He must be willing to take charge and make it up as he goes along. He must step outside of the traditional ways of getting things done and invent new ones.

We are going to look at ways to develop such a spirit without taking a single step into a combat zone, because our objective has nothing to do with fighting, overpowering, or manipulating another person.

Do not for one moment think of the people you want to meet as your enemies. The real enemies are *your own doubts,* those nasty little glue-traps on the bottom of your shoes that keep you stuck, and those dust mites in your throat that keep you quiet. Your mission is to disarm the doubts (even if you can't dispel them) and to replace them with practical ideas so you can take the action you secretly long to take.

WHY WE NEED GUERRILLA DATING TACTICS

Single people are sick and tired of playing games. Everyone wants to feel that the best way to meet others is by being yourself and acting naturally. Yet when someone advises you to "be yourself" it's frustrating because it's not enough to be yourself—you want to be your *best* self. We assume that the route to being your best self means being direct and completely honest with those you meet—saying you're interested if and when you're interested. Oh, if it were that simple. If you could walk over and say, "Hello. You look like someone I'd like to know better," *you'd be doing that instead of reading this.*

When it comes to meeting new people, the direct path is not always possible because the mere thought generates too much anxiety. But the surprise is that it's not always best. You may think your anxiety comes directly from the fear of rejection, but that represents only one piece of the picture. Part of your anxiety comes from something else: Your biology. You are about to take a step that will throw your entire biological world off-balance.

We are the most sophisticated of all organisms, but we share something with all the others in Maslow's hierarchy, from ant to zebra. All organisms seek homeostasis, a sense of internal balance. Any unexpected stimuli represents a disturbance to our sense of balance. That's why you jump when you hear an unfamiliar noise, and why you're jumpy when entering a room filled with unfamiliar champagne-sipping partygoers.

Think about it. What could be more unfamiliar than walking up to a total stranger and expressing attraction? Even considering it rocks the organism.

Because you don't want to scare anyone, least of all yourself, you may want to try indirect Guerrilla Dating Tactics before moving on to advanced Guerrilla Dating Tactics. The indirect approach can actually be experienced as more acceptable, polite, and thoughtful, because it allows someone the opportunity to regain balance before you make it clear that you want to continue to talk.

How to Begin: Your Bag of Tricks

Guerrilla Dating Tactics require action, bravery, coordination, and an appropriate idea. But remember, you don't need to invent the idea at the moment. You can have strategies tucked away in what could be called your bag of tricks.

In every part of your life, whether you are a social worker or a social butterfly, you rely on certain tricks of the trade to carry you through. A salesperson knows to query, "May I stop by Tuesday or would Thursday be better?" rather than, "When may I stop by?" A jazz musician knows that an outburst of dazzling improvisation can cover up the fact that he never actually learned the melody of "Stardust."

Commanding a bag of tricks for your social life does not indicate insincerity or a lack of ability to build a meaningful relationship. It's not about playing games. Instead, it indicates a cultivated ability, when the situation calls for it, to be innovative without being shocking. Your bag of tricks will be divided into four kinds of techniques:

1. Approaches that have proven successful for you in the past.
2. Approaches you are dying to try out—if only you could muster the courage.
3. Approaches you will pick up from this book.
4. Approaches you will invent in the future.

As you ponder ideas to stock your bag, why not start off with close encounters of the indirect kind?

THE INDIRECT APPROACH

The indirect approach requires a little fiction to help you start a conversation with someone new. It isn't lying and has nothing to do with insincerity. It simply means that you devise a little smokescreen in order to protect the illusion that your target has no idea that you are talking to him because you want to meet him. Of course, in truth, you know, they know, you know they know, and they know you know, but remember, this is fiction. We pretend no one knows.

Your smokescreen is a device to help you tolerate your anxiety while maintaining as much as can be maintained of your homeostatic state. It is a form of self-protection so you don't have to feel that you are taking a big risk by talking to someone. As long as you are able to drop it when it no longer serves the purpose of providing comfort and the potential for honest connection, you needn't portray fabricating a story as a negative attribute. If you think they're sneaky, that's okay. What are you trying to do? Sell swamp land in Florida? No, you just want to meet someone whom you would otherwise not get to meet.

INDIRECT GUERRILLA DATING TACTICS

You are: On the street
Guerrilla Dating Tactic: Ask for directions

Al was walking to work down a wide Boston street when he noticed Meg walking toward him. She was about eighty feet from him at this point, but he loved her Indian print dress and her walk, and she had a certain aura that spoke to him (Al has always been prone to romanticizing this "aura" business). By the time she was twenty feet from him, he knew he wanted to meet her. Yet he didn't want to scare her and "shock" was not his style.

As Meg approached, Al said, "Excuse me, I've lost my bearings for a minute. Could you point me in the direction of Arlington Street?" This is a Guerrilla Dating Tactic because Al asked Meg to point him in the same direction that she was *already walking.*

This gave him the opportunity to turn around and walk a few blocks with her. At first he acted lost when he really wasn't. After a few minutes, when he felt more comfortable, he bashfully admitted he worked nearby and wanted to meet her and give her his card (writing his home number on the other side). He invited her to call him after she'd had the chance to think about it.

Why This Could Work

Al demonstrated chutzpah and confidence. Yet he hasn't asked Meg to take a large risk that would make her uncomfortable, like giving him her phone number. She can call him. He's given her his business card so she knows how to reach him at work, and he's written his home number on the back so she knows he isn't married. She's a little intrigued by someone who would go this far to meet her.

Will She Call Him?

She might. Either way, his odds have significantly improved over what would have happened if he'd done nothing. When this scenario was put before hundreds of men and women in the 1987 flirting workshop I conducted, more than 50 percent said they would, at least, be flattered enough to make that first call. By 1991, as people became more comfortable with taking a proactive approach toward their social lives, the percentage had risen to more than 75 percent. Certainly, fewer would actually follow through, but *some* would.

Variation

Here is a story that happened to me on the busy midtown streets of New York City, the last place on earth where it seems appropriate for someone to approach you out of the polluted blue. I was in a phone booth talking when a man in the booth next to mine tapped on the glass. He held up his hand to show he wasn't wearing a ring and gestured to my own ringless hand. I did what any sane New York woman would do: I turned the other way and ignored him. When I emerged from my booth he was standing there. He handed me his card and said, "I couldn't help but notice you. I'd love to meet you, but I don't want to scare you. Please take my card. I'm single, and my name is Michael. I don't know if there's anything between us, but I'd like to at least talk to you on the phone. It's just a phone call. I'm not asking for your number because you'd have to be crazy to give it to me, but maybe you could call me? All I'm asking from you is a ten-minute phone call."

He showed savvy by identifying my fears and offering solutions for them. He showed smarts by stating clearly that all he was asking for was a phone call. I called him later that day.

Remember: If you don't *take* a chance, you don't *stand* a chance.

You are: In a drugstore
Guerrilla Dating Tactic: Drop change

Stacy was buying antiperspirant when she noticed Sam examining toothpaste. Her instincts told her to walk over and recommend Tom's All Natural Fennel Toothpaste, but by the time she had mentally exhausted all the reasons not to trust her instincts, Sam was in line to pay at the counter. The heat was on because Stacy *really* wanted to meet this guy. She got in line behind him, whipped out her purse, and dropped her change, a total of twenty quarters that she was saving for the laundromat, all over the floor.

Needless to say, Stacy dropped her change on purpose, and Sam helped her scoop up her quarters. She managed to get a really good look at him as he dove after the ones that rolled under the counter. Stacy decided she wanted to keep the conversation going, so she said, "Crest? A smile like yours deserves the best. Have you ever tried Tom's All Natural Fennel? Before you pay for that, let me show it to you."

Variation

Wander over to the toothpaste and drop a few tubes (do not use this tactic if the person is examining light bulbs). This same technique can be used in a supermarket, football stadium, or laundromat (not recommended in church unless you plan to put the quarters into the collection box).

Why This Could Work

It just so happens Sam had noticed Stacy too, but he was very shy. Her feigned clumsiness gave him a reason to talk to her.

Remember: Sometimes the one you are secretly eye-ing is secretly eyeing you.

You are: Waiting in line
Guerrilla Dating Tactic: Broken Watch Tap

James was in line to buy concert tickets when Sandra moved in the line behind him. His impulse was to smile, but his body wasn't responding because her deep, blue eyes made him momen-tarily catatonic.

He continued to face the front of the line, trying to think of a way to get another peek at Sandra. Finally he came up with an idea. He was wearing his watch on his left hand. He looked at it quizzically, tapped it twice, and raised it to his right ear, turning his head to face Sandra as he did so. Catching her glance, he smiled and asked for the time, saying that he thought his watch was running slow. When Sandra checked her own watch, James admired it, saying it reminded him of a watch he'd once owned, and began to tell a story about how he'd lost it.

Suppose Sandra was not wearing a watch that reminded James of anything. That doesn't mean the conversation ends. It simply means they talk about something else. Anything else (what hap-pened the last time you waited in line for three hours . . . the story you told your boss about having a doctor's appointment . . . the last time you saw this band in concert). Appreciate the value of small talk and understand that not only does no one expect you to be Albert Einstein or Margaret Mead, no one *wants* to talk about anything major during a close encounter of this kind. The point is to keep talking.

Why This Could Work
James and Sandra are standing in line together. They already have one shared interest to build on—the concert they will both at-tend. Perhaps they share other interests too.

Remember: Occasionally your watch is better suited for making time than telling time.

All these examples use little fictions—made-up reasons to talk. There are a multitude of ways you can enable yourself to speak to someone for a few moments and see if there is any chemistry. One advantage of indirect approaches is that if there is no chemistry, you can move on.

ADVANCED GUERRILLA DATING TACTICS

With Indirect Guerrilla Dating Tactics there is always a way out. Your target may *suspect* you are trying to meet them, they may even *swear* you are trying to meet them, but they can't *prove* you are trying to meet them. You've created a tinge of doubt. Advanced Guerrilla Dating Tactics remove all doubts: You know, they know, you know they know, they know you know, and *there are no illusions about it.*

Amidst the many direct approaches to meeting, only the truly brave belong in this category. Here are four of my favorite stories, as told to me by workshop participants. All four can be adapted for a variety of situations. Can you think of ways they can help you?

You are: In a bar
Guerrilla Dating Tactic: Say it with flowers

Jim sat down at a bar one night with three friends and was entranced by the beautiful bartender. Asking his friends to save his seat, he went to the nearest open shop, purchased a single red rose, tucked it inside his jacket, and returned to the bar. He ordered a beer. She brought it over to him. Then he asked her for a glass of water. She appeared slightly irritated because it meant another trip. She placed the water in front of him and went about her business. Jim put the rose in the water and said, "Excuse me. There's something in my water." She turned around and was surprised to see the rose. She thanked him and explained she was married. Undaunted, Jim replied, "That's okay. I'm just rewarding loveliness wherever I see it."

Jim didn't get a date, but he certainly benefited from his action. He made the bartender smile, he felt a sense of his own power to act fast, and he impressed the living daylights out of his friends.

Variation
You can say it with a flower to almost anyone. Put one on someone's desk. Leave one for your favorite waiter. Tuck one

under the windshield wiper of someone's car. In the sixties giving someone a flower meant love and peace. It means the same thing today, but, hallelujah, you don't have to wear those clunky Birkenstock sandals or eat magic mushrooms.

> Nobody, but nobody craves carnations. Be more interesting. Try a single rose (red, yellow, or white), a bird of paradise, or something with a wonderful scent. Leave the carnations for the floats on the Thanksgiving Day Parade.

You are: Near a place where greeting cards are sold
Guerrilla Dating Tactic: Giving a stranger "your card"

Matt, who lives in a small Minnesota town where the liveliest site is the state prison, often commented that there were very few single women around who weren't doing time. But one night in a local supermarket he noticed a curly-haired brunette with no ring looking at greeting cards. He sauntered over and said a few words, but it didn't go anyplace. He decided to wait outside the door of the supermarket for the woman so he could try and strike up a conversation. On this freezing February night, he stood a full half hour before she appeared. He handed her an envelope, asking her to open it. It contained a birthday card on which he'd added, "Happy Birthday whatever your name is, whenever your birthday is. My name is Matt. Please give me a call at ..."

As in the first story you read in this chapter, Matt has observed the fundamental underpinnings of any Guerrilla Dating Tactic:

He has placed 100 percent of the control in regard to what happens next in her hands.

When you approach a stranger with a Guerrilla Dating Tactic, they experience a range of feelings from being intrigued to being frightened. Having all these feelings at once causes a sense of being off-balance. Give the person back their balance by awarding them the power to decide what will happen next.

Variation
Liz looked up the address of a man she'd danced with once or twice at a club. During the conversation he had mentioned a particular band he loved. She waited until she saw that the band was

appearing at a local club, clipped the ad, placed it in a card, wrote, "Want to join me?" and mailed it to him.

You are: In your car
Guerrilla Dating Tactic: Mobile Phone Mania

Marsha is a sales rep who spends countless hours a day on the highway between calls on her accounts. She brings in a lot of business when she is on the road with her mobile phone. One sunny afternoon as she pulled off the interstate and was delayed at a toll booth, she spotted a nice-looking man talking on his mobile phone. She passed him, got his attention, smiled, and held up her phone. He smiled, and pulled up next to her at a red light. He seemed game, so at the next stoplight she held the wheel with one hand, wrote her mobile phone number on a big piece of paper, and held it up against her window facing him. He called her. It turned out that he was married, but that did not affect how great Marsha felt about taking action. Now she keeps that sheet with her number on it on the dashboard for highway usage so she doesn't have to take her life in her hands by trying to write when she should be concentrating on driving. In fact, this little incident has given a whole new meaning to keeping her eye on the road.

You are: In a restaurant and you're attracted to one person who is there with a group
Guerrilla Dating Tactic: Passing a note

Trevor was having lunch one afternoon when he heard wonderful laughter pealing from a table nearby. His heart stopped when he realized that the adorable, laughing woman was engaged in what he viewed as an impenetrable situation: She was part of a group.

He and his friends always moaned that it's impossible to approach women in a group, but the more he watched her, the greater his desire to meet her became. When he ascertained that she wasn't wearing any rings, he knew he had to make a move, but what move? He ran a couple of scenes through his head. When he found himself considering standing by the Ladies Room in the hope that she might need to use it, he realized how ridiculously remote his chance of meeting her seemed. Then a brainstorm hit him. He took out one of his business cards and wrote on the back, "You have a wonderful laugh. I can see you are busy with your friends, but I wish you'd been alone because I'd love to meet you. Please call."

As he left the restaurant, he passed by her, smiled, handed her the card, and said, "Hello, this is for you. Have a nice day." She called him that night. Part of Trevor's success was handing the card directly to her—establishing brief contact without pushing her into an uncomfortable situation.

I know several women who have written a variation of this note to tackle meeting one man in a group of men. I know many men who wish more women would try it. In fact, overall, men respond with great enthusiasm to these stories. Their only complaint is that these things don't happen to them often enough. (In later chapters there will be more about meeting one person in a group.)

MANAGING THE RISK FACTOR

When you try Guerrilla Dating Tactics, a portion of your targets don't turn into dates. You must be mentally prepared for a numbers game. The greatest baseball players have batting averages that hover around .300. The crowds adore them even though they only hit the ball three times out of every ten turns at bat. A salesperson once told me that he makes sixteen calls before he expects to make one sale—sixteen people say no for each person that says yes. When he applied the same odds to dating, he discovered that he never gets as far as those sixteen no's without making a date. In fact, he actually thanks women who turn him down because he knows that he's one step closer to success. More to the point, we all know couples who met in extraordinary ways because one partner took a risk that they swore was completely out of character *and* totally successful. But only you can decide, when the moment presents itself to you, if it is worth the risk. After you begin taking more risks, you will probably discover what many others have already discovered—that taking the risk, whether it works out or not, makes you feel good about yourself.

When it comes to meeting a stranger, it's hard to seize the moment. Take time, in advance, to build your "bag of tricks" before the moment occurs so you will be prepared to utilize them. Memorizing strategies and talking them through in your head makes it easier to use them when the time comes because, in effect, you've rehearsed. The possibilities are unlimited, and chances are you've only scratched the surface of your creativity.

Remember, no one is asking you to do something that is excruciatingly uncomfortable, but just to take the ceiling off your thinking and stretch yourself. When you've stretched yourself to the point where you are ill at ease, don't stop! You're making progress. Keep in mind that "guerrilla" implies searching for a mate, while "gorilla" implies searching for a primate.

CHAPTER 2

In Search of the Perfect
Pickup Line

Pickup lines have always been with us, and nowhere is this more apparent than on the silver screen:

"I've loved you since the beginning of time."
"But you only met me yesterday."
"And that was when time began."
——Errol Flynn to his first conquest,
The Adventures of Don Juan

"I was bored to death. I hadn't seen one attractive woman on this ship since we left. Now, isn't that terrible? I was alarmed. I said to myself, 'Don't beautiful women travel anymore?' And then I saw you, and I was saved——I hope."
——Cary Grant to Deborah Kerr, *An Affair to Remember*

"My mother taught me never to go to a man's room during any month that ends with the letter 'R.' "
——Deborah Kerr to Cary Grant, same movie, the month was September

"I suppose you know you have a wonderful body. I'd like to do it in clay."
——Lola Albright coming on to Kirk Douglas, *Champion*

"How do you sleep? In pajamas or a nightgown?"
"Neither. I sleep only in two drops of French perfume."
——an exchange between Anita Ekberg and a reporter interviewing her, *La Dolce Vita*

Warning: These examples are pure Hollywood. Use
of such lines without a Screen Actor's Guild card
may prove hazardous to your health!

WHY WE USE LINES

In spite of the fact that Hollywood lines are scripted for Hollywood stars, the rest of us continue to try variations of them, and
it's fascinating when you think about why. The reason is that in
the movies, *lines always work.* Cary Grant snags Deborah Kerr.
Errol Flynn has his way with a bevy of dissembling señoritas.

They tap into our fantasies as well as our doubts. Our doubts
say that lines are unoriginal, and we wonder who else they've
been used on. Our fantasies long to believe that any line used on
us was meant only for us and is born out of someone's intense attraction to us.

Even people who have sworn never to resort to them find that
they open their mouths and lines sneak out. Since this is so, let's
explore what makes them click and what makes them flop—in
other words, how to be discriminating so we can understand the
distinction between words a screenwriter tailored for Robert
Redford or Elizabeth Taylor and words used in real life.

REAL LIFE

A good line can break the ice in three ways: It can charm, disarm, and/or let someone know that their life will be, at the very
least, a little more interesting if you are in it. But it's tricky. After
all, what can you say in twenty-five words or less that will capture
interest, rivet a stranger's positive attention, and not sound like
something out of a movie? If you still don't believe it can be done,
read on.

GUIDELINE TO LINES

The Friendly Line

Friendly lines aren't sexist, and they don't ask for sex. They let
the person being approached know that you want to get to know

him or her. The bearer of the Friendly Line demonstrates a desire to pay attention and to listen, while confirming a sense of the value of the person.

Larry attended a local meeting about environmental issues in his community. During a coffee break, he moved closer to an exuberant woman speaking to some of her neighbors. He decided that he had to get to know her better. He casually joined the group and the conversation. Soon it was the two of them talking about the perils of spray cans on the ozone layer. Larry aimed to draw the conversation a little closer to earth. After thinking and rethinking about how he might refocus the discussion, he finally paused and said, "Do you have room in your life for a new friend?"

Most of us have room for a new friend. In fact, most of us could use several. The nice thing about this line is that the woman, Nina, felt immediately relaxed. Here was a guy who was not putting the moves on her (at least, not for now). Here was a guy saying that if nothing else, there was a potential for friendship. Here was a guy who clearly wanted to *talk* to her.

A line does not necessarily come in the first few words of conversation. Sometimes a well-placed line *during* a first encounter is the clincher that refocuses talk into the here and now, the you and me, and possibly even the us. Larry was wise to develop a little rapport with Nina before "handing her a line."

Eleanor was waiting in a train station. Her train, already twenty minutes late, was announced as being further delayed. With all her heavy baggage, leaving the station was out of the question. There was nothing to do but wait. She began to get cranky when a warm voice said, "Would you like some conversation?" The warm voice belonged to the even warmer Herb. With relief (now, at least, she had someone to watch her bags while she went to the Ladies Room) she replied, "Sure." As it turned out, Herb was waiting for the same Amtrak train, so he was able to watch her bags several more times over the next few hours.

The key to the Friendly Line is in what you ask for. In Herb's case, what he asked for was "talk." You, too, have simple friendly things you can offer, such as conversation, company, friendship, or a handful of Reeses Pieces. In this world of wheelers and dealers, it can be very refreshing.

The Seductive Line

The Seductive Line demonstrates sexual or romantic interest and requires the willingness to take a risk. Actually, any line has an implicit element of risk, but this type of line requires aplomb to carry it off.

Seductive lines are sensual but not seedy, and dramatic but not dirty. They are a little Bette Davis and a little William Powell, and you need to say them with a straight face and a hint of smiling mischief. Because a Seductive Line implies sexual attraction, you'll want to know if this attraction is shared by the other person before you opt to use one. If you're wrong, you run the risk of frightening off someone or having him or her experience your seduction as harassment.

To find out if the object of your affection shares your passion, first spend time engaging in less loaded flirtatious behavior such as mutual eye contact. The key to knowing whether a seductive line is appropriate is that by the time you use it, you should have already received strong positive cues from your target that it will work.

Today's seductive lines are just as frank (and just as corny) as the lines you've read from the old movies. José tells of an evening he spent in his favorite haunt, a good part of which was spent in eye contact with a redhead. Shy, he couldn't come up with anything to say and probably would have left without a word.

After what seemed like forever, she approached him and said, "I've been watching you from across the room and saying to myself, 'Self, you deserve a man like that.' " José, who swears this was the most exciting moment of his life, will probably bore his grandchildren with this story. An unabashed and welcome comment like this can do more for bolstering your esteem than twenty-two self-help books.

Randy used a seductive line at a party to meet Ruth. After making some eye contact with her from across the room, he sauntered over and said, "You are the sexiest woman in this room. I hope you don't mind that I had to come over and tell you that." Ruth boldly met Randy's eyes and said with a mischievous smile, "I was hoping you'd notice."

Randy's line was hardly original. We've all heard something comparable in the movies, but Randy decided to forgo the movie for the main event. Ruth didn't care if the last person to use the line was Charles Boyer or Clark Gable because they didn't use it on her.

Some of the most effective seductive lines occur later in a conversation. Rita went on a blind date with Mark. He seemed pleasant enough, but she was ambivalent about whether or not to see him again because they seemed to have such different backgrounds. He changed her mind with a line. During the double espresso he said, "I've been looking for someone to concentrate all my attention on, and with you it would be easy." Rita was torn between wanting to believe this and thinking it was absurd. The flutter in her heart won, and she decided to see him once more. Now Rita and Mark have two kids and mortgage payments that would make any heart flutter.

Warning: A seductive line should stir, not shock. It should disarm, not disgust. *Think twice* before asking someone you don't know to come up to your apartment and break a few commandments. Never look at a woman's breasts and say, "Hey baby, your headlights are on." *Don't* look at anyone and say, "Surf's up in my water bed." *Don't* make lascivious gestures. *Don't* introduce yourself by telling someone your sexual fantasies of what you'd like to do to him or her. *You'd better be smiling* if you say, "Can I buy you a drink or would you rather just have the money?" *Don't* use disgusting slang and refer to women as wenches or having bodacious tatas. She'd better know you're kidding when you utter the words, "Baby, I could drink your bath water." Take a good, close look at yourself before you tell a woman she "ain't had a man till she's had you." *Think three times* before telling some guy that your body is like an outlaw because it's wanted all over town. And even if you idolize Mae West, *don't* walk up to a man and ask him if that's a gun in his pocket, because these days it just might be.

The Offbeat Line

Offbeat lines command attention by retrieving an icebreaker out of left field. One nice thing about an offbeat line is that you don't have to worry about whether you are making sense. You aren't *supposed* to make sense.

Kathy told a story about the time she and her friend went to a huge outdoor party. They wanted to meet new men, but they were both hesitant about what to say. Kathy got the kooky idea that she and her pal should take a poll. They should walk up to people and say, "Are you a physicist?" Silly? Yes. Did these men want to know more about these women asking strange questions? Yes. I have known others who have used the poll-taking technique by asking a question to a group of people at parties or bars as a way of starting conversation. One man approached a woman he'd had some eye contact with and said, "I'm taking a poll about where Manhattan women really like to go on a first date."

A producer for a popular Boston radio station finds that his favorite offbeat line, "Do you think we'll ever convert to the metric system?" has helped him make quite a few friends. When I put this opening line up for discussion in several workshops, there was a wide range of responses. Some people adored it, while others thought it was too weird. In general, almost any line you use can provoke a wide range of responses. Remember that when you use offbeat lines, they appeal to those who share your quirky vision of the world. Finding a true soulmate with an offbeat line that fell flat on others may well be worth it.

Irv discovered that he can make a woman smile by saying, "I'm looking for an opening line. Do you have any suggestions?"

Of course, the king of creating the offbeat line is Woody Allen. In *Annie Hall*, an actor at a party walks over to Diane Keaton and says, "Touch my heart—with your foot." This line may leave you confused. Does it belong under the heading of offbeat or under the heading of off-color?

The Humorous Line

Some singles take their quest so seriously that they forget to have fun. A funny line requires that you be responsive and on your toes, and for those nights when you are feeling "on," there is no better way to *have fun* than to *give fun*. After all, we could all use a good laugh. This story came in on a call-in radio show in West Palm Beach, Florida, from a woman who swears this happened to her:

An elegant older woman was dining alone in a restaurant. She noticed a man seated at another table looking at her. Every time she glanced in his direction, he was looking at her. After a while he sauntered over and said,

"Excuse me, I believe I know you."

"I don't think so," the woman replied and continued eating.

"But you look very familiar to me."

"I don't know you."

"But you look so familiar. Do you work near here?"

"I don't work," she stated haughtily. "I'm an heiress."

He snapped his fingers and said, "I knew we had something in common. I'm a Sagittarius."

Eddie, a quirky jazz pianist, met a group of women in a restaurant when he walked over to their table and said, "Excuse me. I just dropped my Congressional Medal of Honor. Would you mind if I looked under your table?"

Bob stepped into an elevator with a pretty woman. After a couple of moments of complete silence he broke the quiet by saying, "So what's a nice girl like you doing in an elevator like this?"

Lucy was walking her dog when she passed an attractive man she had noticed on several other evenings walking his own dog. This night she was prepared and said, "Excuse me. My dog wants to meet your dog, but he's too shy."

Jeff and Frank were spending a Saturday night in a local dance club watching the crowd. Soon their attention turned to a pretty woman sitting alone at the bar. They watched as several men walked over, apparently asking her to dance. Jeff mimed an imaginary dagger sticking in his heart as, again and again, her head shook in a silent no. Finally Frank said he knew she would dance with him and sailed off. Jeff, standing on the sidelines, saw Frank ask, and saw the woman turn him down. Undaunted, Frank said something else, and Jeff stared in amazement as the woman smiled and led Frank to the dance floor. Jeff could hardly wait until his friend returned with a full report. "I said, would you like to dance," Frank told him. "She looked me straight in the eye and said no. So I looked right back at her, grinned, and said, 'I'll let you lead.' "

As you can no doubt see from the amount of time I've spent on these, I favor people who can join another with laughter. If you have a humorous line that you might like to try out on someone, remember that there is nothing wrong with rehearsing it in front of your bedroom mirror. Comedians rehearse everything over and over to get the right inflection and perfect timing. Even the ad-libs that you thought were spontaneous are rehearsed endlessly so they will come out the way they were written.

Harry, a workshop participant, tells of a Carol Burnett/Harvey

Korman performance he attended. During the middle of a romantic sketch that placed them eye to eye, Burnett broke character and commented on Korman's bad breath. The audience was on the floor. Two weeks later Harry's parents attended the same show and Burnett again broke character to deliver the same "ad-lib."

If you are concerned that rehearsing will limit your spontaneity, consider that memorizing a few good things to say can make you sound brilliant (even if you aren't always brilliant). Sounding brilliant builds the confidence that will lead you to spontaneously think of other brilliant things to say—the kind of things you will go home that night and try desperately to remember so you can use them again, but won't be able to.

The Altar Line

Altar lines indicated that you are already hopelessly smitten even if you haven't met yet. An Altar Line lets it be known that your instincts tell you that this total stranger could become a serious relationship, even a marriage, in no time at all. They must be spoken with a glint in the eyes or you risk sounding maniacal or, even worse, desperate.

A seventy-three-year-old woman walked up to a man sitting on a park bench and said, "You look just like my third husband." The man on the bench peered up at her and asked tentatively, "How many husbands have you had?" With a twinkle in her eye she gamely replied, "Two."

Iris and Priscilla were at a Jewish singles dance. They noticed Al sitting by himself quietly, seeming very uncomfortable. They decided to have a little fun with him. They walked over and told him that things couldn't be as bad as they looked. He looked up and smiled. Priscilla said out loud to Iris, "What a great smile! A person could marry that smile. What do you think, Iris? Should I call the rabbi?"

Rob, a New York drummer, considered many opening lines to use on a splendid blonde he saw at a bar. He finally settled on, "Let's buy furniture." Once, completely bewitched by a woman he spotted on the street, he walked over and said, "I'd like to take you home to meet my mother."

The Written Line

Not all lines are spoken. Remember in second grade when you passed a note to that cutie in the first row and promised to let him pet your frog at recess? You may have been forced to write "I will not bring my frog to school" one hundred times on the blackboard then, but you probably won't get into that much trouble for writing love notes now.

Carmen was sitting at a bar with a few friends when she received a cocktail napkin folded in half. Opening it, she was surprised to see the words, "Equal parts of love and lust." You might think Carmen didn't like this note, but she did. And so did her friends, who marched over to the note sender and demanded that he join them.

I ran a singles party where I used a series of exercises to help people get acquainted, one of which included paying compliments to different people at the party. At the end of the party a woman approached me to show me a compliment she had received in the form of a note. One of the men gave her his business card. On the front next to his name he wrote, "You have a wonderful smile." On the back he added, "This card may be traded for a cup of coffee or an ice cream cone at the place of your choice. This card is not transferable."

Not all note passing happens without a hitch. Some years ago I had dinner in a restaurant and was knocked out by my charming, blue-eyed waiter. Too shy to pursue him then, I decided to ask the manager to point out his car so I could leave the waiter a note on the windshield with my phone number. When I found his car, I was astonished to see a note (calling the waiter "Blue Eyes") was already tucked under a windshield wiper. I decided I did not need to waste a therapy session on my guilt for ripping up that note and replacing it with mine. Hey, it's a jungle out there.

A LAST WORD ON LINES

Sometimes the brightest and wittiest of lines will be met by, at best, a vacant stare. Your charm will go unacknowledged and unappreciated. It is unrealistic to expect 100 percent of the people you meet to share your ideas about what is funny, fetching, or seductive. When this happens, or when you are doing nothing because you fear it might happen, keep in mind the advice of a very wise man who attended the flirting workshop:

When you are ninety and sitting in your rocking chair reflecting on your life, what do you want to be thinking about? All the opportunities you missed, or all the opportunities you took?

3

Dropping the Camouflage: How to Be Memorable

We use camouflage to blend into the terrain—a way to be someplace while appearing not to be there. It's the ultimate disguise, rendering us invisible and unnoticed. The purpose of camouflage is in direct opposition to the purpose of Guerrilla Dating Tactics, which is to get noticed. Identifying personal camouflage is one way to begin looking at new possibilities for improving our romantic identities because if we know what we're working with, we can initiate change. Like everything else, it's easier said than done. And, like everything else, the only way to do it is to *do it*.

To acquire more information about whether you've fallen into the camouflage mentality trap, respond to these statements:

I present myself in a way that makes people want to find out more.

___Often ___Sometimes ___Rarely

I know how to stand out in a crowd.

___Often ___Sometimes ___Rarely ___Not on your life

I can ask someone for ten minutes of their time.

___Often ___Sometimes ___Rarely ___Never Never

I wear clothes that fit right, reflect my style, and look good on me.

___Often ___Sometimes ___Rarely ___I attend parochial school

I show how interesting it can be to spend time with me.

___Often ___Sometimes ___Rarely

I have not placed an "Always" in these responses because if your answer to any of these questions is "Always," you are lying, placing undue pressure on yourself, fast becoming an emotional basket case, or suffering from delusions.

WHY WE USE CAMOUFLAGE

While our rational thoughts understand that we won't get attention unless we do something to get it, our emotional tone often reflects a fear of drawing attention to ourselves. Attention can mean both positive and negative things. For example, when we were little children we received attention for our accomplishments and our naughtiness. Sometimes, believing we'd accomplished something wonderful by painting the bathroom walls with Mommy's lipstick, we discovered we had done something wrong. It could get so confusing to be our own unique little selves that some of us began choosing neutrality (safety) over attention. It wasn't only our parents who encouraged us to curb our impulses. Our school system favored uniform appearance and behavior. An important part of our development, this served a purpose. After all, if everyone sought simultaneous attention we'd have total chaos.

When we were younger and wanted attention, we weren't sure about acceptable ways to get it, and we made erroneous calls. Moreover, sometimes it was very, very hard to get it, so we acted out in socially frowned upon ways—ways that brought us negative attention. Much of our childhood is imbued with memories of learning about social control—the hard way.

As adults, we can have a much clearer sense of how to draw attention to ourselves without doing damage, wreaking havoc, making people angry, or getting into trouble. Nonetheless, old lessons die hard, and today, when we might choose to stick out in the crowd, we have fears and conflicts about what that might mean.

Such thinking affects behavior. Even if our deep wish is to get attention, we may continue to dress or act in ways that deflect or even avoid it. When we have successfully avoided drawing attention to ourselves, we then see it not as the logical outcome of our camouflage behavior, but as universal agreement that we're not worth the time of day.

CAMOUFLAGE IN DAILY LIFE

Sometimes we know we're in hiding, but other times the urge to camouflage operates on a subconscious level. We remain unaware of disguising things about ourselves that we would really like other people to know. Recently a friend related a story that illustrates camouflage in daily life. Jody, a very pretty flight attendant, was given the responsibility of introducing herself over the intercom when all of the passengers were seated. She promptly used her seniority to get someone to replace her. She continued to do her job while maintaining anonymity by remaining unidentified and impersonal. This went on for years. Her initial reasoning was that she couldn't be bothered, and anyway, what difference could identifying herself on a flight from New York to Denver make in her life?

One day when everyone was tired of covering for her, she was forced to take on the task of introducing herself and pointing out the features of the aircraft. Afterward, as she passed by one passenger, he called to her by her name. It was the first time anyone had done so because it was the first time she had ever bothered to let anyone know she existed. This tiny incident held enormous impact for her as she noticed that offering a bit of herself changed the way people responded to her. People acted friendlier when they knew who she was. Because she had been doing some reflective thinking about her impact on the world, she recognized a key component of this shift. The people were exactly the same as they had always been, but she had done something different. She had reframed the system and the experience had changed, which led her to relate in a warmer way. When she became more generous, people responded with more generosity. In this instance, we are talking about Jody's job performance, but she noted the parallel to her personal life.

Jody automatically camouflaged herself, which left her feeling unnoticed and isolated. She realized that she'd always seen this as something being done to her (the response of the world to her), and not as something she was doing (her response to the world). The power to shift it was only a hello away. If you, like Jody, have spent time believing that the world is unresponsive to you, consider that you may be unresponsive to the world.

BEGINNINGS

When it comes to romance, we often aim to begin someplace besides the beginning. We imagine grand solutions instead of first steps. If our grand solutions don't work on the first try, we want to give up immediately and go back to doing nothing or rush out and try something else. Real beginnings allow time for reflection. We look at what we've done and think about which parts have been helpful, which parts haven't, and what stopped us if we opted to do nothing instead of something. Real beginnings allow new ideas to be tried in small increments, where the risks feel smaller and more manageable.

This is our ultimate goal—to turn something that feels immense and scary into something that is small and manageable, to turn the beginning back into a beginning instead of a last chance.

> "Small and manageable" isn't stress free. Of course you'll feel stressed. GET USED TO IT! There's good stress and bad stress. This stress promises personal growth and the immense pleasure in being yourself.

M.U.S.T.

To spur your thinking, I'm going to tell you how others have approached this terrain and dropped the camouflage by using the acronym MUST. Of course, only you can decide if you MUST do something, but if you feel you MUST, Guerrilla Dating Tactics can be categorized in this way:

M emorable
U nexpected
S omewhat sneaky
T otally sneaky

Distinctions between categories blur, but that's okay. It's meant as a lighthearted guide, not a stone tablet.

Memorable

Twenty years ago Roselle went on a vacation to Spain with a few women friends. Sipping wine at a beautiful outdoor cafe in Barcelona, Roselle noticed a man at a nearby table making eye contact with her. After two more rounds of Barcelona peekaboo, the waitress walked over with a tray upon which sat a single looming orange which she delivered to Roselle, indicating it was from her admirer. Roselle was surprised and charmed. In these past twenty years many men have sent over drinks, but she doesn't remember most of them. The man who sent a single orange has never been forgotten.

The story of the orange reminds me of a Boston workshop participant's Guerrilla Dating Tactic that will always be remembered by his date. He met her by answering her personal ad, which stated that she was a passionate Red Sox fan. When he arrived for their first date, instead of bringing flowers, he offered her one brand-new baseball.

All memorable gestures don't take circular shapes, but these two stories came to mind as turning an ordinary meeting into a memorable one. Certain moments become memorable because somebody does, carries, or says something that is completely out of context with their surroundings. Melina tells of going to the airport with a three-foot pepperoni that she planned to carry on the flight and take home. Melina certainly got noticed, and she does *not* recommend the "pepperoni method" to anyone who can't stomach seedy remarks. Barry Farber, a radio personality, says that a few people are likely to remember him as the character who carried a large metal bird cage on a flight from Sweden to New York.

Unexpected

Cultivating the ability to surprise people is part of cultivating your Guerrilla Dating Tactic bag of tricks. Most people fall into a daily routine that has become automatic and lacks spontaneity. It's easy to land in the land of the blahs. Why not shake things up a bit, keeping in mind that unexpected does not mean scary?

Adam used the same bank every week, and for the past few months he stood in the line of the same cute bank teller. Each week they conducted business, and although he tried to generate a little "interest" of his own, he found that she tended to stick to the numbers. One day, as he was filling out a deposit slip, he tucked in a little note telling her that he thought she was adorable. I learned of this story when I called Adam to ask his help in hosting a singles party I was organizing. He said he couldn't do it because he was engaged to be married to an adorable bank teller with whom he'd finally connected using a Guerrilla Dating Tactic.

Bob's Guerrilla Dating Tactic went into action when he bought a flip chart from a company called Autographics. It is a device to help you flirt from the comfort of your car. Each large page has a different message that can be held up with one hand (via a plastic pole) while you're stopped at a light. Messages vary from "NICE CAR" to "CHECK YOUR REAR DOOR" to "SMILE." Where Bob once dreaded his hour-long commute, he now faces even the worst of traffic jams with anticipatory delight. Though it's not for everyone, Bob considers himself in top flirting form when he is behind the wheel.

No one needed an unexpected jolt more than Kristin, a lovely elementary school principal from Providence, Rhode Island. Fairly new to the dating scene, she found one unerringly common theme: As soon as she told men what she did for a living, they clicked off. Men automatically behaved as if they'd been caught smoking in the boys room. She came in search of a witty comeback that would let them know that her idea of having someone stay after class was nothing like detention. One initial response that workshop members offered was that she should wait before telling a man what she did for a living. But the theme of Guerrilla Dating Tactics is how to use what you have to your advantage, not how to underplay or hide it. One man shared two brilliant suggestions. The next time she said what she did for a living, she should follow it by saying, "It's my job to make sure everybody behaves, but in your case, if you behave, I'll be disappointed." His other suggestion was that she follow up on first dates by sending a report card rating performance—positive feedback only. She loved both of these ideas, and whereas she had viewed her job as a dating liability, she now reframed it as a playful opportunity.

While the principal sought to diminish her impact as an authority figure, Sarah used the idea of an authority figure to have fun. When she was in Wyoming she purchased a child's sheriff badge to wear on her jacket. Some men used it as an opportunity to strike up a conversation by playfully accusing her of impersonating an officer, and sometimes, when she was talking to a man that struck her fancy, she ceremoniously placed him under house arrest. On one evening, feeling particularly sexy, she told her date that she'd remembered her sheriff's badge but left her handcuffs back at her apartment. What do *you* carry that puts people in a playful mood?

Somewhat Sneaky

Sometimes the only way to keep a conversation going is to do something downright sneaky. You aren't being sneaky to *take advantage,* but to *gain advantage.* Manipulation refers to taking something from someone that they don't want to give you or that you don't really want. It's pushing the point to use such words to refer to your desire to meet someone. A few sneaky anecdotes will convey what I mean.

While waiting to see a client, Calvin visited with the client's secretary. He had noticed her in the past and liked her, but had trouble getting past the formalities. Finally, in a moment of desperation to keep talking, he "accidentally" tipped over her pencil holder, spewing pencils in every direction. As they both scuttled the carpet on their hands and knees, he found the icebreaker he was looking for.

A Boston woman tells a story of sitting at a table in a club with a group of her friends when a very tall man approached her and said, "Mind if I sit here?" She said she didn't mind, and he promptly lowered himself onto her lap.

Heather was lunching on a park bench when a very appealing man sat on a bench near hers to eat his own lunch. After rehearsing the words, "Nice day" in her head twenty times and still not being able to get them out of her mouth, she tipped over her soda, asked if he had an extra napkin, and moved next to him to avoid the mess.

Totally Sneaky

A Guerrilla Dating Tactic is categorized as sneaky when you think it up at the moment and immediately act upon it. However, when you put great pains into developing and carrying it off, it's elevated from "Somewhat Sneaky" to "Totally Sneaky."

Ed attended a party and was floored by a dark-haired woman. As usual, a snag arose. She was with a date. Although he tried to steal a few minutes of her time, it seemed inappropriate to push it. Yet he got a clear feeling that she wasn't deeply involved with her date—it seemed like a casual thing. The next day he called the host, Carl, to find out who the mystery woman was, but Carl said it was a mystery to him, too. All he knew was that her first name was Debbie, that she lived in Sudbury, and that she was Greek. Do the odds against Ed seem overwhelming? Then you don't know Ed.

Ed pulled out the phone book and checked the listings for Greek Orthodox churches in Sudbury. He found only one, and he drove over. He entered the office and explained his dilemma. The office manager figured out who Debbie was and gave Ed her parents' phone number. He then called her parents and explained the whole thing over again. Her parents gave him her number. Imagine how flattered she was when she found out what Ed had done to track her down. Although this never turned into a full-blown romance, it represents a memorable moment for Ed and Debbie.

A Boston woman tells of a similar tracking-down process administered by a man she met on a ferry to Martha's Vineyard. After twenty minutes of pleasant talk, the ferry was about to land. Flustered, she told this man she'd enjoyed their conversation and hoped she might run into him again. With a distinct twinkle in his eye he said, "You can put money on that." She never ran into him on the Vineyard, but she returned home to find a message from him on her answering machine. She was shocked, since she never even told him her last name. However, he had used his totally sneaky smarts and memorized her luggage tags. After that, it was a simple matter of calling information or, in the event of an unlisted number, writing to her.

In 1959 Tone took Audrey out for a first date, then didn't call her again. Audrey saw an ad in a magazine for the then-popular gift of purchasing a live turtle through the mail (this was before our current awareness of animal rights). She ordered one. When it came, she wrote her name and phone number on the shell, safely repackaged it, and sent it to Tone. They married soon after. (The turtle lived a long, long time.)

Dick found a totally sneaky way to turn a personal snafu into an engaging opening line. He attended a ski weekend after taking the first half of one of my two-part workshops, and his homework assignment was to approach a few women and talk to them. In great spirits, he went to the ski lodge, walked over, and sat down with two women to make conversation. He was flirting and having a great time when he excused himself for a moment to go to the men's room. Upon returning, the bouncer told him to go home. Dick couldn't believe it. He was not drunk or acting out, but the bouncer repeated that he didn't like Dick's face and he'd be wise to believe it. He took a closer look at the bouncer's nineteen-inch biceps and retreated. The next day Dick discovered from a pal he'd left behind that he had tried to move in on the bouncer's wife. Now when he meets a woman in a bar, the first words out of his mouth are, "You're not the bouncer's wife, are you?" Then he tells his story as the perfect icebreaker.

Michael, a man in his early twenties with the biggest eyes I've ever seen, attended a flirting workshop and told this story of imaginative problem solving. Walking through the local mall, he spotted an adorable security guard. He wanted to talk to her, but he was too shy. He passed by her several times, but because he'd camouflaged himself, she never noticed him. Drastic measures were required. So he walked out to his car, opened the door, and locked his keys in it. Then he returned to the mall to ask for her help.

CONCLUSION

Remember MUST. Drop the camouflage and use the element of surprise to meet people. Demonstrate your willingness to have impact on the world. In the spirit of reframing romance, the element of surprise is not so much about surprising other people as it about surprising yourself. You're not a kid anymore, so ease up on the fear of doing something wrong. Instead, concentrate on the pleasure you get when you follow through on your own ingenious, creative ideas. Use that feeling to your advantage. You are a deep well of untapped resources and creative ingenuity. Dip into that well.

Ammunition 101: Flirting Maneuvers

Induction into Flirting Maneuvers

I was riding across town on the bus at the end of a Tuesday that felt like a day of losses, which included one favorite jade earring. Completely wrapped up in my thoughts, I hardly noticed at first when a toddler, sitting next to his mother in front of me, turned around to brazenly face me. His eyes peered over the top of the seat and he threw me a look that said, "You know I'm adorable. What could be more important than sharing this moment with me?" I smiled back. He quickly averted his gaze and, after a minute, coyly met my eyes once more—this time with slightly more daring attention.

Aren't children wonderful? They flirt happily with no intentions greater than finding a pleasant way to pass the time. If you think this behavior is just for kids, think again.

THE NATURE VERSUS NURTURE OF FLIRTING

Some people think that we are born knowing how to flirt—that flirting acumen is a chromosomal mystery located in the DNA of certain lucky individuals. Others think that the ability to flirt is a series of learned behaviors, a skill that we develop at an early age. It's the age-old nature versus nurture controversy of human development. One camp says we are genetically endowed, while the other cites environment as the source of our gifts.

I have set up most of the pegs in my tent in the nurture camp, and I'm worried about those who talk about "born flirters" because they are almost always talking about someone other than themselves. You may never be as smooth as Cary Grant, but neither is anyone else. In fact, Archie Leach (Cary Grant's real name) wasn't as smooth as Cary Grant because Cary Grant was invented, not born.

Back on the Bus

I turned again to the little boy and broke into a huge smile. He smiled. I cooed. He cooed. We were getting into the spirit when his mother told him to sit down, face front, and stop bothering "the lady." This got me thinking:

1. Children flirt more easily than adults.
2. Children who flirt seem to have a common denominator: A caretaker who tells them to cut it out because it isn't proper.

It was a parent's job to protect us. As children, we lacked experience and this affected our judgment, so we were protected from placing our hands on a hot stove. We were told over and over what we could and could not do. Our lives often felt defined by the limitations imposed upon us.

As we grew older, we internalized our parents' voices into our lives. We no longer needed them to be present to know right from wrong. For example, you learned that stealing was wrong and you don't steal. You learned that turning your string beans into projectile missiles was wrong, and you don't need a mother to tell you not to do that anymore.

At three, you needed to be told not to talk to strangers because you couldn't make informed decisions about strangers for yourself. Today, when you have ample capacity to make decisions for yourself, do you still hear those automatic old voices telling you not to do it? The advice and training that protected you as a child may actually be getting in your way now that you are an adult.

So when you read the following chapters on flirting, read them with the eyes of a child. Ignore all other voices, and open your heart. You may discover that flirting is more like riding a bicycle than it is like hurling yourself into outer space minus a capsule. It's more like an old neighborhood than a new world. It's more like a comfortable pair of shoes than a spinal tap.

The little boy inched slowly around so he was looking at me again. The glint in his eye spelled intrigue—he knew he was slightly naughty and that made it all the more dramatic. He slowly reached out his hand to make a grab for my one remaining earring, which I hadn't bothered to remove from my ear. His mother, with every mother's astonishing peripheral vision, reached out and took his hand in hers. She gently maneuvered his body so that he was again facing front and she told him, once and for all, to stop bothering me.

And that was that.

CHAPTER 4

Cracking the Code

When we call someone a flirt, it is *not* a compliment. Still, part of us remains envious of those who flirt well. The other part views flirting as insincere dalliances executed shamelessly by persons of dubious integrity. Flirting is one of life's little dualities: We criticize it while feeling personally deficient for not knowing how to do it.

You can break the code of contemporary flirting by reframing your thoughts about it. Keep in mind that flirting stirs the element of intrigue, but it shouldn't be shrouded in mystery or feel unattainable.

The first step in reframing flirting challenges years of negative stereotypes, including characters such as these:

Indiscriminate Gigolo—He flirts with you for twenty minutes. Then he excuses himself to flirt with every other single woman, unabashedly moving from one to the other. Soon you notice his jacket pocket overflowing with phone numbers.

Sleazy and Easy—She has the brains of a sand dune. She spends her life making double entendres, dressing in inappropriately seductive clothing, and maintaining a 9.1 on the Richter scale of sexual arousal.

Looking for a Black Eye—His radar is activated by the amount of trauma he can cause, so he only flirts with someone else's date. We aren't talking about harmless bantering, but rather out-and-out passes. He predates the wheel, is a resident on all soap operas, and thinks of relationships in threes instead of in twos.

> If you get nothing else from this book get this:
> ## THIS ISN'T FLIRTING!!

A person who engages in the above behaviors elicits anger, upset, confusion, and disappointment from others—not the respect and pleasures of flirting.

Real flirting

Real flirting is not a superficial ritual that some are meant to observe and others are meant to do. It is not an omen of trouble ahead, nor is it a way to hurt people. And it can fit in neatly with the changing roles of men and women today. The behaviors you choose from the multitude of flirtatious signals will be what distinguishes you as a saint or a sinner.

Some flirting behaviors are easier to master than others—in fact, you've been doing them for years. Others will be a stretch. But all behaviors require the proper flirting mind-set to carry them off. Most important, if you care to learn how, you can.

Dancing through the dictionary

The *Oxford English Dictionary* has at least fifteen different definitions of the word "flirt" for a period covering the past few centuries. Though I'm sure we flirted before this time period, I guess we called it something else. The dictionary states that "flirt" could mean anything from "a smart stroke of wit" to "a pert, young hussy." Definitions take the tone of something that happens briefly, and they are generally unflattering. It makes me long for an entirely new word that isn't loaded with five hundred years' worth of ambivalent baggage. Since that doesn't seem feasible, let's offer a suitable outline for flirting for the nineties.

Contemporary flirting

Here are the five characteristics of the healthy flirt:

1. *Flirting is a form of communication that demonstrates appreciation, attraction, and interest.*
   Make flirting part of your everyday communicative style that tells people how carefully you've noticed:

   - the time they took to put themselves together today
   - the thought they put into something
   - any positive attribute that would please them

2. *Flirting is of the moment and is offered without long-term goals.*
   When you flirt, have only flirting in mind. Don't think about

what it could turn into, because you don't flirt to get somewhere. If you're flirting, you're already there. Flirt for the pure pleasure of putting your good feelings out there. Give yourself full permission to live in and enjoy the moment without having to take it further.

3. *Flirting can be genuine and sincere. Flirting in and of itself is not flighty or irresponsible. It depends on the person doing it, not the act of flirting itself.*
There will always be irresponsible flirts, but those people have always been out there. As you come to understand more about good flirting, your flirtations will be affirmations of your life.

4. *The ability to flirt goes hand in hand with the ability to take control of your life and have impact on the world.*
Flirters make things happen. They are not content to wait passively for others to make them feel good. They know how to make themselves feel good.

5. *Flirting is a gift that you have the power to give.*
In the spirit of reframing romance: You don't flirt to get something from someone. You flirt to *give* something to someone.

It is not appropriate to give a gift and then ask what you will get in return. Give for the pleasure of giving, then let go of what you have put out there.

THE GIFT OF FLIRTING

Richard had been using the same car mechanic, a woman named Bernice, for many years. Every time he saw her, with her mass of auburn hair tucked under a baseball cap, he could not help but reflect on how cute she was—even though he knew her to be happily married. He had a long-standing conversation with her that always ended with, "I'm leaving a quarter on the counter. If that husband of yours ever gets mad at you, if he even looks at you cross-eyed, you walk to the nearest phone, drop in that quarter and call me." Bernice looked forward to Richard's breakdowns and tune-ups because seeing him always gave her a lift. Even if she was feeling lousy that day, and as grubby as ... er ... a car mechanic, Richard gave the gift of making her feel renewed. And, if the truth be known, Richard enjoyed generating a little electricity as much as Bernice liked being the recipient. He felt a notch taller for the rest of the day.

Richard hadn't thought of what he was doing with Bernice as flirting because, since she was married, he felt it didn't count. He didn't comprehend the fact that he could actually make someone feel terrific without being on the prowl. He needs to consider ways to flirt with someone who is actually *available*. There is safety in flirting with the unattainable. For many people, it's all they do. It isn't unproductive if you make someone feel good and you feel good too, but it's a dead end when it comes to dates.

Sarah, a freelance writer, tells a similar story. She's always sending out manuscripts, which means frequent trips to the post office. For two years she has chosen the same line, where a friendly stamp seller always takes a moment to tell her he hopes she gets published this time while she always takes the time to tell him how nice he looks in his uniform. In fact, once in a while, when she hits a spell of writer's block, she'll buy stamps she doesn't need just for the boost.

Can you think of people with whom you have had an ongoing rapport that you can reframe through a flirting lens? It may be someone you run into regularly for brief periods of time, like a UPS deliverer, so there's never enough time to get into trouble. Or it may be someone who is so far out of your age range that a match is unlikely. Or it may be someone whom you know is unavailable and therefore safe. Safe is nice, but chances are you bought this book because you are ready to explore what it might be like to live a life that is less predictable.

Chances are, even if you think you don't know how to flirt, you can scratch the surface and recall situations where you *do* flirt. Don't denigrate your skills by saying that what you already do doesn't count because it's with someone old enough to be your grandfather or with someone in the office whom you would never realistically consider.

> ### STOP HERE AND GIVE YOURSELF CREDIT
> ### FOR THE FLIRTING YOU HAVE
> ### ALREADY DONE

Consider yourself the possessor of some flirting skills that you plan to refine and rechannel. Your next step is to know exactly where the bulk of your future refining lies.

TASK DEFINITION

Define and break down flirting tasks into workable parts so you don't feel overwhelmed and consequently unmotivated. Remember, change doesn't occur overnight. For example:

1. *If you flirt regularly but only with unavailable people or people you don't want to date:*
   Your task is to do what you already do with someone you really long to do it with—in other words, investigate ways to move your skill to a more rewarding arena.

2. *If you are sure you never have flirted, even as a child, and you don't know how to proceed:*
   Your task is to read the chapters on flirting and get started.

3. *If you're stuck with an echo from yesteryear that blares, "NICE GIRLS DON'T FLIRT":*
   Your task is to challenge this thinking. You've been misled because a) "nice" is overrated, b) girls are females who haven't reached puberty, and c) nice women flirt all the time.

4. *If you experience unmanageable anxiety at the thought of flirting:*
   Your task is to probe the source of the anxiety so you can start to work on your issues. (If you're getting nowhere with this on your own, you can still do something positive by seeking counseling to explore what is stopping you.) Unspecified anxiety weighs more. Define it and it won't disappear, but you'll possess a better understanding of why you feel the way you do. With understanding comes action.

In the following chapter, we'll examine specific flirting behaviors. But keep this in mind: As you start spreading your charm around town, don't be surprised that opportunities to use your new skill multiply at an ever-increasing rate. They've been there all along . . . just waiting for you. When you flirt from the heart, you build bridges instead of walls.

The Five Phases of Eye Contact and Other Nonverbal, Front-Line Techniques

---

JOAN: Good God. Pat's going in for the kill. Oh, now that's a nice turn ... coy.
DEBBIE: With just a hint of giddiness.
JOAN: Her big move should be coming up at any moment. The combination hair flip with a giggle.
DEBBIE: (In the voice of a television sports announcer) There's a 3.2 degree of difficulty, Joan. Let's see if she can pull it off.
  —Two women sitting at a bar observing a third woman caught in the act of flirting, *About Last Night*

Flirting has more movements than a symphony. Some movements are aggressive and action-packed, while others are mysterious phrases repeated in a variety of tempi and with changing emphasis. All movements recapitulate the main theme of flirting, which is, "I appreciate you. Please know that."

Upon hearing a symphony, you may prefer one movement over another. Perhaps the tempo matches your personal tempo or reminds you of someone special. Perhaps one movement feels as if it were written with you in mind. As you consider how to flirt, you will also have personal preferences. What feels natural to you may throw your friend into a tailspin, while the way in which she flirts may feel way out of your grasp. It is quite a big mistake to lump all flirting behaviors into one category and then decide you can't flirt. By the same token, it's sad to limit your repertoire to only what you already know how to do, because the more flirting gifts you can offer, the more opportunities you will create to use them.

Good flirting requires finding truth in the behavior. It's much like the key to good acting. When you watch a bad actor, you are all too aware that he or she is stiffly reciting lines. When you watch good actors, you believe the material. Even though reality dictates that the silver screen Gandhi is Ben Kingsley and the silver screen Jake LaMotta is Robert De Niro, even though you know the lines were rehearsed over and over again, the feeling is that you are seeing events unfold for the first time. Good actors capture the authenticity of their experience. Good flirters do the same.

FLIRTING GROUNDWORK

Frequently, flirting groundwork occurs before a single word is uttered. Nonverbal gesturing and movements can signify everything from friendly interest to out-and-out passion. As we approach nonverbal flirting, two little words jump out:

> ### EYE CONTACT!!

Eye contact, the deluxe battery recharger, lets you know that you are alive, reminds you that unisex is a Madison Avenue creation, and puts the "p" back in *pulse*. While it often lasts for evanescent seconds—the amount of time you are stopped in your car at a red light and notice someone dazzling in the next lane, or the amount of time it takes the bus to pull away from your stop as you feel the spellbinding pull of someone's pointed glance from the departing bus window—you will remember it when you are ninety.

> Eye contact involves two people:
> The eye contact activator and the eye contact target.
> If you're peeking at someone but they aren't aware of it, you can't call it eye contact.

A Word for When You Are the Target—Responses fluctuate from boldly returning the gaze to quickly averting your eyes. Both responses are completely normal, although more people avert their eyes (even when interest is greatest) than immediately return the eye contact.

A Word for When You Are the Activator—Initiating eye contact condenses megawatts of personal electricity into one intense wallop. Not everyone is ready to absorb such a direct hit. Handled improperly, you can make someone feel awfully uncomfortable when you meant to make them feel awfully good.

Bad Eye Contact—Leslie wanted to let her cooking class instructor know that she thought he was adorable, so she asked her roommate, Amanda, for advice. Amanda suggested that the first step was to make serious eye contact during the next class. Surely, by the end of the two hours, he would surmise that her interest was in more than Bernaise sauce. Leslie, not quite attuned to the principle of discretion, stared at him for the entire class without once looking away. After ten minutes he appeared damp at the collar. After two hours, his shirt was drenched. His discomfort took on a palpable life of its own as Leslie reduced this cordon bleu graduate to a glandular earthquake.

Remember: Making eye contact is not the same as staring. If you have ever been the receiver of someone's unrelenting ogle, you can attest to this.

Tom was struck by the beauty of a woman seated across from him on the bus. He locked his eyes on her, hoping she'd get the message. She caught his glance and looked away. Tom continued to stare even when she began to shift uncomfortably in her seat. Tom thought that this was a sign that he was getting to her. He was. She rose and moved to another part of the bus.

Paquito was told by his Uncle Ernie that eye contact worked vertically. Thus advised, he foisted the old elevator eyes on women he found sexy, slowly looking them up and down. To his surprise, he met with hostility and irritation. Uncle Ernie told him that the irritation was disguised lust. Luckily, Paquito pursued the subject, asking Uncle Ernie exactly how many women he had met using the elevator eyes routine. For once, Uncle Ernie had nothing to say.

REFLECT ON YOUR OWN EXPERIENCES

The best way to think about inaugurating eye contact is to reflect on your own past experiences as the receiver of eye contact, those times when you were the target. Consider how you responded to the overpowering awareness of someone's glance directed at you. Were you surprised? Worried? Confused? Shy? Perhaps you felt all of these feelings at the same time. That would not be surprising because most of us experience the five phases of eye contact indiscretely. Stages can occur simultaneously or spill over into each other.

Here is a guide for using eye contact to go beyond briefly flirting to the point where you meet someone. It also represents the social norms of eye contact—although, in keeping with the spirit of Guerrilla Dating Tactics, norms are inchoate and you can invent your own.

THE FIVE PHASES OF EYE CONTACT

Phase 1: Connection

The first step, after choosing your target, is capturing her or his attention. Gaze in brief increments of time until she or he gets the message. Offer your gaze for slightly longer than you would when scanning a room (about three seconds). If she or he doesn't pick up on you, wait a few minutes and gently try again.

For Men: Many women are appropriately concerned with safety issues, and eye contact can be experienced by them as exciting *or* scary, sometimes exciting *and* scary. Wait between attempts to see if she peeks back. Using your good judgment will avoid having your eye contact perceived as harassment. Spacing attempts is also a way to gauge interest, using the barometer of her body language as an indicator of her physical comfort. She may just give you the go-ahead. Don't get so nervous about making the effort that you forget to pay attention to her response.

In the Connection phase, keep two important things in mind: First, the person you choose may be thinking about something else and, consequently, a lack of immediate response may have nothing to do with a lack of interest. Second, we all have peripheral vision that allows us to pick up on things that would appear to be out of our range of sight. She may see more than you think she sees. She may need to collect her thoughts before responding, because she has moved to Phase 2. Don't rush her.

Phase 2: Confusion

If you're anything like the rest of us, many thoughts jump into your mind when you first sense that someone is making eye contact with you:

- Is he looking at me or someone near me?
- Were we scanning the room at the same time so it isn't really eye contact but mutual scanning?
- Do I have spinach between my teeth?
- Is my fly unzipped? (although that isn't *eye* contact)
- Does she think she knows me? Do I know her?
- Oh God! He's making eye contact.

Because of our psychological makeup, our first thoughts are anything but the most flattering explanation—he finds me attractive, and he'd like to know me better.

When you take the role of eye contact activator, your target's initial reaction will be much like yours when you think someone is looking at you. He will need to be certain your look was meant for him. And he may not be direct about finding out, because, above all, he, like you, would not want to run the risk of making a mistake and looking foolish. The confusion stage of eye contact can last anywhere from three seconds to the rest of your life. If you consistently feel like your confusion will last for the rest of your life, you may want to consider seeking professional help.

Phase 3: Corroboration

She has processed the varied explanations for your gaze and settled on a possible conclusion: you are interested. Build her confidence by letting her know she guessed right. Repeat your look in a clear and friendly manner.

Now the delicate and titillating maneuvers of demonstrating and reciprocating interest take place. The Corroboration phase can also be called the "Now What?" phase because that's exactly what your target will be thinking—Now what?

Do you appear to be someone she'd like to meet? Should she send over a drink? Should the two of you continue trading glances for a while? Should she walk over to you and say hello, or wait till you head to the men's room and accidentally bump into you? Since walking over and saying hello is the response of the truly brave, chances are that the two of you will continue sneaking peeks for a while longer. A properly handled Corroboration phase builds confidence, interest, and excitement.

Phase 4: Candor and Charisma

The time has come to combine your candor with your charisma and let your target know you'd like to pursue this further. So smile, smile, smile—the universal expression of happy and positive feelings. Lift your glass and silently toast him. Women increase their nonverbal repertoire by twirling hair, drink straws or anything else they've gotten their hands on. Men can be turning a drink glass, playing with change on the table, or straightening a tie. Establish yourself as friendly or sultry, but *never* easy.

Phase 5: Conclusion

Time to venture into the intriguing world of post–eye contact. You may not have to do anything because there is every chance your target will respond to your hint by striking up a conversation with you. However, some people are quite shy, and even the choicest of come-hither looks may require you to go thither. Some who have happily participated in the eye contact balk at following through.

Having already gone through the first four phases successfully, the most direct approach is usually the best. Drum up the surge of power that will propel you off your bar stool. Push yourself.

RISING FROM YOUR BAR STOOL:
AN OPERATOR'S MANUAL

- Make sure adjacent bar stools aren't touching yours, or you may push one over as you rise.
- Make sure your empty drink glasses are pushed away from edge of bar so you don't tip one when you rise.
- Check that your raincoat isn't stuck in your bar stool leg.
- If in a tight space, face front and place both hands on the bar for balance lest you land in your neighbor's lap.
- **Don't appear to be doing any of this.**
- If still unconvinced that you can rise gracefully, don't sit in the first place or buy a bar stool and practice at home.

Remember, eye contact is a reminder that you're alive. It can be as fleeting as a single shared moment with someone you will never see again, or it can be the precursor to something more.

UNRETURNED EYE CONTACT

If around this time you are saying to yourself, "I've tried that and it never works," my response is, "Of course." Of course it won't *always* work, of course you'll fancy a few people in your life who will not want to meet you. This is a very different thing from saying it *never* works. If your successes have been minimal, are you giving yourself enough time to allow for the five stages of eye contact?

Peter didn't. His chief complaint was that he couldn't meet women, and although he went out frequently, he wasn't getting anywhere. I asked him why he thought this was so, and he explained that he was too shy. I asked him, as a shy person, how he approached people. He said that he would wait until a small group formed, sidle over to the periphery, show interest in their talk, make a little eye contact with the women who appealed to him, and hope that someone would include him into the group.

I thought this was a resourceful technique for a shy person, but he said it never worked. I couldn't quite get a handle on what was going wrong. Finally, I asked him how long, from the moment he entered the place, this tactic took. He said that he never stayed at any one place for more than a half hour.

A half hour isn't enough time. It would take most people close to a half hour to realize he was in the room. Peter needed to build his tolerance for anxiety long enough to get through the five stages of eye contact and start a conversation. What Peter lacked was endurance.

Although the five stages of eye contact can happen in a split second, they can also happen slowly, over a period of time, especially when your target is with friends. So if it isn't working for you, run through this list:

- Take time to get settled before doing anything.
- Follow it up with time to go through the five stages.
- Choose people whose body language says they are receptive to meeting someone new (see Chapter 12).
- Expect that it won't work on occasion, and that it's a mistake to characterize all eye contact on the basis of a few flubs.
- If you meet with repeated disappointment, nix eye contact from your list and develop the rest of your flirting repertoire. Not all techniques work for all people. Seek out your strengths.

ADDITIONAL NONVERBAL FLIRTING

Here are other nonverbal behaviors from my "72 Ways to Flirt" workshop. Some require more explanation than others, but all, when used properly, can enhance your magnetic properties.

A Smile—Randy, a Connecticut workshop participant, said that a smile is like opening a door. It saves a lot of guessing because you don't have to wonder if someone is feeling friendly. Keep in mind the vast difference between a smile that is used as a minimal polite gesture and one that lights up the world.

You give a Minimal Polite Gesture Smile when you:
- Greet the auditor from the IRS
- Attend your high school reunion and get asked by a loud-mouthed former classmate what's wrong with you because no one has scooped you up yet
- Deliver your urine sample to the lab

- Are asked by someone who's boring you to tears if he's boring you

You give a Heartfelt Smile when you:
- Attend your daughter's first piano recital
- Are told by your best friend how special you are
- Receive flowers from a secret admirer who's no secret
- See someone walking a new puppy

A Wink—Winking must be done with good spirit. It is more of a pleasant jolt than an "I want to meet you" behavior. The three rules of winking are:

Wink only in public places.
Smile, don't drool, when you do it.
W.O.O.: Wink only once.

Karen, a shy Bostonian with a yen to master winking, decided to practice with her sunglasses on. She figured that by winter she'd have the winking down but wouldn't need the sunglasses.

Body Positioning—Ask yourself if your body tone reflects your emotional tone. Make sure that when your brain is saying, "Come on over," your body isn't saying, "Get lost, I'm not feeling friendly." Tensely crossed arms and legs aren't invitations. Splayed arms and legs don't need invitations. Find a middle ground that frames you as approachable.

Shoulder Orientation—I thought that the phrase *giving the cold shoulder* derived from two people seated side by side in a bar, with one purposefully avoiding contact. In a Boston workshop, Amy told me that the phrase really developed in the Old West. Back then, when you went to visit your relatives, you packed everyone up in the wagon train, stocked it with vittles, set out on the open plain, and planned to stay at least a month before making the rigorous trip home. When you verged on overstaying your welcome, your host would let you know by serving a cold shoulder of beef for dinner.

What a perfect contemporary ice breaker! Next time you are seated next to someone shoulder to shoulder, why not strike up a conversation that begins, "You know, I always thought the phrase *cold shoulder* came from two people sitting just as we are now ..."

Execute the Brush-By—A popular technique from my book *50 Ways to Find a Lover,* this involves passing by someone at least once before approaching him or her. In keeping with the homeostasis theory of off-balance organisms, brushing by gives a psychological sense that you are familiar. When you walk over to someone who has not even been aware that you are in the room, you reduce your chances of a positive outcome.

Share the Moment—Your aim is to build on the idea that you are doing more than occupying the same space, you are sharing it. Draw your mark closer by building a mini-intimacy that binds you together. For example, if the two of you are in a jazz club and the bass player executes a phenomenal riff, catch her eye, indicating that this is a shared moment between you. The same technique can be used if someone enters the club dressed outrageously or does the tango on a table.

Twirl Some Object—This may be more sexual than you'd care to get and involves manipulation of drink straws or the lascivious fingering of bar peanuts. Minor fumbling and twirling gives the impression that you are genuine, yet slightly nervous. Since the person you are eyeing is as nervous as you are, it's nice for him or her to believe that you don't do this every day either.

Touch—Feathery touches and minimal grooming gestures such as pulling a fleck of dust off her collar have long been part of our flirting repertoire, but before you engage in these, I'd recommend that you read Chapter 22, "Growing Bold Together," so you can get a picture of what to consider when you want to reach out and touch someone.

These are just some of the twirling, winking machinations of an elaborate drama called Nonverbal Flirting that unfolds like a silent movie. You can be Cecil B. DeMille and stage your own drama, or Georgia O'Keeffe exploring intricate variations on a theme. Your theme is "I'd like to get to know you."

One thing is sure—as long as we have bodies, we'll invent ways to communicate feelings and thoughts with them. So dig out of the trenches, dust off your come-hither looks, and begin to practice. Think of all the ways you can say hello without uttering a word.

Social Events

> "There was no Cary Grant until I invented him and then became him."
>
> —CARY GRANT

ENGAGING

Sal was flipping through the paper looking for something to do on the weekend when he noticed an advertisement for a gala Tri-State Singles dance benefitting a popular charity. His favorite band, NRBQ, was playing, and as Saturday night approached he found himself muttering under his breath about the futility of such events (while getting dressed to go anyway). When he walked through the door, he realized that there were close to a thousand people there. The old claw in the throat gripped him as his excitement turned into terror, and he squeezed into the nearest corner of the room to nurse his orange juice. From there, he surveyed the throng while envisioning that he had swallowed the "Drink me" potion in *Alice in Wonderland* that said "smaller."

Andrea opened the mail to find an invitation to attend the third wedding of an old college roommate with whom she'd shared many an all-nighter. Although she and her friend had vowed to attend each other's weddings, Andrea hadn't counted on this many marriages when the promise was made. The invitation was for Andrea only (not that she had anyone to take), and it didn't look like she would know many people. Those she knew would probably be sitting at the happy couple's table, while she envisioned herself placed near the rest rooms with the rose-water aunts and cigar-toting uncles. The RSVP was overdue and still sitting on her kitchen counter next to her ticket for an upcoming singles cruise. She figured if she could get herself to the wedding, she could practice being friendly for the cruise.

Every year Lisa, a bubbly manufacturer's sales rep, looks forward to her company's annual convention. She networks, meets people in the hotel bar for cocktails, and writes more than her share of business. In each crowded room, on every name tag, she sees golden opportunities. She tells coworkers she lives for the challenge—it is where she feels closest to her peak experience. Put this same Lisa in a setting where she is representing herself instead of XYZ Manufacturing and watch Lisa shudder. Put Lisa at a singles dance and she can hide in the corner with the best.

In the nineties, along with all the recognizable traumatic events where you will be asked to work a crowd, there is a burgeoning social phenomena called singles events or singles programming. These activities range from volleyball games to dinner dances to Club Med, and, because this industry is growing faster than the national debt, you may at some point consider attending an event. I'm not recommending that you do things you can't stand to do. What I want is for you to turn down a specific event because you don't want to go to it, not because you can't face a crowd.

The fear of a crowd is pervasive. In 1990 I led a shyness support group at Lehman College in New York. All of the participants said they were very shy, but it turned out that they weren't talking about one-on-one interaction. They were talking about freezing in crowds or groups. In fact, they saw discomfort in crowds as a factor that ruled their lives. One woman, a straight-A student, was failing an overcrowded English class because part of her grade was based on class participation. When the professor asked her to explain, during class, how she could write top-notch papers, yet was unable to orally answer a single question, she got so flustered she began hyperventilating.

Job Hunting

Part of the discomfort at a crowded singles event is that we fear being judged at a time when we have no idea of what is expected of us. This contributes to the out-of-control sensations. Other self-presentation situations make us just as tense, yet we understand them much better, so this allows us to maintain control.

For example, job hunting has much in common with mate hunting. It generates anxiety and rates high on the scale of emotional stressors. Yet we can predict many qualities of job hunting because we know the formal schemata of looking for a new job. We've identified the common framework, otherwise known as a "mental map" of the task.

If you've ever hunted for a job, you know where to concentrate your attention:

Appearance—You make certain that your grooming is immaculate and that you not only wear your good clothes, but clothes that are appropriate for the company with which you are interviewing.

Intellectual Preparation—You learn in advance about the company.

Anticipation—You anticipate normal interview questions. You will not be at all surprised if you are asked what your contribution to the company will be or where you hope to be in ten years.

Tolerating Anxiety—You worry that the interviewer won't like you or you won't like her. However, you understand that anxiety is part of the job-hunting experience.

Follow-up—Even if things don't go as smoothly as you hoped, you write thank-you's. After all, the person they've hired may not work out.

Your framework provides the tools for successful job hunting. You need a framework for successful date hunting too—especially when the hunt takes place at a crowded singles event.

Working a Singles Event

The way to work a singles event can even be memorized by an oaf as long as said oaf brings his OAF MAP. OAF MAP is an acronym for a set of strategies that are repeatable at every party or gathering and also repeatable over and over within any party or gathering. OAF MAP stands for:

O observation
A assessment
F friendship
M mood
A anticipation
P positioning

Think of the event as your Theater of Operations and your OAF MAP as your game plan—an explanation of what to do and what order to do it in. If you looked at the party as a circle and the OAF MAP as your guide within the circle, it might look like this:

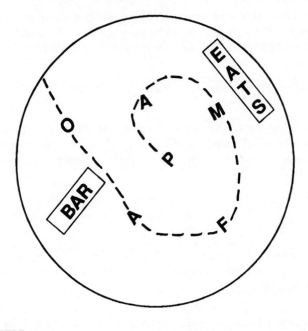

OAF MAP

Observation

It's nuts to think your goal is to enter a roomful of strangers and be at ease. All that spells is P-R-E-S-S-U-R-E. In such circumstances, the first thing to do is take ten to twenty minutes to observe and absorb. Don't worry about who to talk with, and don't make plans for what you'll do next.

Calvin, a Washington, D.C. accountant, always begins with a room survey when he attends any function. He looks for the rest rooms and fire exits first—in other words, a way out. Once he knows he can get out, he concentrates on how to get in. He observes whether people seem to be having fun or not. He imagines himself as an outgoing person and a welcome addition to everyone's evening. He visualizes himself handing out five of his cards before the night is through. He does all this before he says his first hello.

Observation lets you reachieve a homeostatic state with the least amount of pressure to act. Avoid making judgments, since early judgments are often a function of projecting your own discomfort onto the room. Use observation as an exercise to see what information you can pick up about appearance, room format, ratio of men to women, age range, and location of the refreshments.

Take stock of your thoughts and mental responses to different people. Notice everything while doing nothing. You may pick up on interesting opportunities that you might have otherwise missed. You may even develop a third eye that sees beyond the surface.

Assessment

Make an assessment of what you've observed in an empirical or scientific way by forming ideas based on the data you have collected. Be wary of allowing anxiety to reduce your ideas to flat black-and-white statements such as:

This looks awful
No one looks friendly
Everyone decent is in couples

Right now, relying on "just the facts," move from the concrete data of the Observation stage (things you see) into the interpersonal relational date of the Assessment stage (what are people doing):

Who is talking to whom
Who is circulating
Who looks as uncomfortable as you are
Who looks like they could use a friend
Who looks friendly
Are there groups or one-on-ones

If you aren't a "Dragnet" fan, choose your favorite detective instead and, since Chapter Twelve will round out your knowledge of the principles of body language, use those principles to make your appraisal. Don't rush yourself. Perhaps you will get a canape because you spot someone approachable in that area, perhaps you will give yourself more time to observe by moving to a new part of the room—whatever you end up doing will be because that is what you've decided.

The purpose of an assessment is to formulate a "thinking-based" plan of action rather than a "feeling-based" one. Feelings based on irrational fears can spiral out of control, and small steps like saying "hello" are experienced as catastrophic.

Assessment draws on cognitive, rational thoughts. You shouldn't ignore the anxious feelings; just don't concentrate on them and let them take over.

Friendship

The question to ask when you attend a singles function is never the high-expectation, low-return question such as, "Will I meet the love of my life?" Concentrate on more liberating personal missions, such as the question from Chapter 2: Do you have room in your life for a new friend?

Even if you think you already have more friends than you can handle, consider nurturing acquaintances with folks who have completely different social circles than yours. Each new person you meet knows at least one hundred people you have never met. Such possibilities!

Another Reason to Make New Friends: As we grow older, friends pair off and there are fewer and fewer with whom to attend singles-oriented events. At any singles event, there will be people in the same position as you. Some would love to find a buddy to attend the next party with—someone who could help them make the most of the event.

Besides making friends, you can always BYOF (bring your own friend). Consider working out a mutually beneficial system to help each other connect. You could agree to introduce each other to five new people or that you will have a signal between you so that you can rescue each other if necessary.

Janet told a story that illustrates this point. She attended a party with her friend Lillian, and they both had a decent time. As they walked to Lillian's car, Lillian asked about a nice-looking man she saw Janet talking with by the bar. She wanted to know if Janet had gotten his phone number. When Janet said no, Lillian made her get out of the car and refused to give her a ride home until she did so. Janet sheepishly went back into the party and told the man what happened. Delighted, he gave her his number, and they made a date for the following week. Left to her own devices Janet would have let this SNAG (Sensitive New Age Guy) slip by.

Mei Ching recommends that you attend singles events with a friend of the opposite sex. She takes her friend Paul and says, "Okay, which women do you want to meet?" And she asks Paul to introduce her to the men she fancies.

On a personal note, when I go to a party, I take my friend Jody. She has no qualms about talking to anyone. Within ten minutes of her arrival, she has spoken to everyone at least once and is making her second go-round. She's a magnet. Even though I feel shy in such a setting, I only need to follow her trail and I get to meet everyone too. There's nothing wrong with knowing your own limitations and tackling them by choosing the right friends.

Mood

Your mood is not a chronological step. It's something you work on before you attend the party and over and over again until you start feeling relaxed. Cognitive therapists believe that mood is controlled by the thoughts, or messages, you relay to your brain—messages that signal pleasure or messages that signal that your ego is a Ping-Pong ball and dozens have signed up to play slam dunk in the tournament. They believe that these negative messages are as automatic as the impulse that makes a smoker reach for a butt. In fact, the negative thoughts can be just as addictive, hovering over and clouding your potential good time. Cognitive therapists have claimed success in lifting deep long-term depression in clients by reprogramming negative thoughts onto a more rational course.

We are very complex creatures and many, many factors enter into how we feel about ourselves, but reframing your Mood can help you feel comfortable for the evening. Here's an example of setting a Mood through Rational Thinking:

What are some of the worst things you can tell yourself about being at a crowded singles party?

- If no one talks to me, I feel terrible.
- If I say something stupid, I'll be marked by everyone as an idiot.
- I always wear the wrong thing.
- No one will like me.

Weigh these unadaptive thoughts against the messages gleaned from a rational mind-set.

- It's quite unlikely that no one will talk to me unless I'm unfriendly and uptight.
- I'm not always Shakespeare or Maya Angelou, but my friends find me entertaining so why shouldn't others?
- In the nineties there is no wrong thing to wear.
- Some people will like me and some people won't like me, but I am taking control of my life when I get out there and try. Besides, I don't like everyone, so why should I expect everyone to like me?

How rational are these expectations?

- I can't be happy when I meet a new person unless something romantic comes of it.
- If every conversation I attempt doesn't lead to a lasting relationship, it is a failure.

Can you substitute the following more realistic expectations?

- If I talk to three people, I am improving my social skills. I have to play the odds.
- The more people I approach, the more people I meet. The more times I go out, the better my chances.
- Some parties are more fun than others. I must be patient and find satisfaction in making the attempt.

As I said earlier, don't just work on your mood *before* you attend the party. Set aside a few minutes every hour at the party to *give yourself credit* for attending and for the people you've talked to. Focus intentionally on positive thoughts. We tend to be quick with the self-criticism and short on self-praise. When a nervous panicky thought comes into your mind, identify it as such and talk back to it. Actively argue for your homeostasis. Take three deep breaths and tell the worried part of you to stifle itself. Your goal isn't to stop panic reactions forever—that's too big a goal. All you want to do is take it ten minutes at a time. Is that too much to ask?

Consciously changing the message you send to your brain from a negative helpless one to a positive realistic one affects your feelings. Keep in mind that it takes practice—so start practicing for a few minutes every day. That way you'll be prepared in advance for the big event.

Anticipation

Anticipation is a dress rehearsal which, like mood, is something you work on before you get to the party as well as at the party. You mentally walk through the event—contemplating what, when, where, and how things might happen. Every pleasurable moment and every cog in the wheel are thought through, so that no matter what actually happens, you have never been in better shape to handle it.

Anticipating gives you a sense of the makeup and personality of the party itself and can help you to enjoy yourself in a variety of circumstances. For example:

- If you are a woman who is attending the party to meet new men, how can you enjoy the evening if you show up and there are only three men?
- If you are expecting to meet four of your friends and they all bag out, what will you do?
- If you are attending this party because a woman you fancy told you about it and she shows up with six friends from whom she is inseparable all night, what will you do? And what will you do if she shows up with a date?

Anticipation of circumstances should lead you to form contingency strategies that will protect you from being led around the room by your disappointment for the rest of the evening. Sometimes the best surprises are no surprises.

Another Effective Use of Anticipation: Take the spotlight off yourself by anticipating the needs of others. By placing yourself in a helping position, you can reduce your own self-consciousness. Walk around the room and observe who looks like they could use help to join the party. Does the woman staring repeatedly at the ceiling look excruciatingly uncomfortable? Instead of worrying about yourself, go over and help her out. Coax her down from the chandelier. Try to find out something about her. For example, did she tell you she loves video games? Take her and introduce her to a computer-literate guest. Make sure to give them a little information about each other. Say something like, "Hi, Frank, I wanted you to meet Marie because she is a video game champ and you are a software genius. Maybe the two of you can invent the next Pac Man." Then let the chips fall. Your mission is to help people connect, not to babysit them.

When your glass is empty, look for someone else who could use a refill and offer to get her one. Or invite her to walk to the bar with you. If you are feeling "hot" tonight and have the true Guerrilla Dating Tactics spirit, grab a tray of canapes or a pitcher of ice water and walk around offering them to guests. Several people have told me that this is exactly what they have done to liven up a dull gathering.

Instead of looking at your anxiety as one impervious force, consider that it may be your personal drama, born from expectations of what the party can be to you and how you will be at the party. Anticipation offers alternatives. You aren't stuck with one mental scene to play out, and, therefore, if the real party doesn't meet your fantasy of the party, you can still have fun.

Positioning

You can't meet many people if you stand in a corner.

You can't meet many people if you sit in a chair.

You can't meet many people if you latch on to one person all night.

You can't meet many people if you wear headphones.

You can't meet many people if you avert your eyes every time someone looks over at you.

Circulate. Place yourself in the midst of the action. Talk, laugh, visit, listen, and move on. If you have to push to do this, THEN PUSH. Once you get going, it gets easier. Let yourself be seen so people know you are there. Repeat to yourself, "I can be noticed at this party without ever having to put a lampshade on my head."

Carol was complaining about a host of holiday parties she attended. They were big parties, but she ended up sitting around with the same old people she knew before she got there. I had only one word to say: Why?

After one flirting workshop, Lucy told this story. She attended a party with the same three friends she attends all parties with— but this time she excused herself from them and circulated. In the past, when she had been introduced to someone she said a cursory hello and returned to her friends. This time she made a decision that when she was introduced she would prolong each conversation for at least ten minutes. She spent time with her friends, but each hour she forced herself to leave them and reframe her position at the party as someone who was available and amenable to being approached. The difference amazed and delighted her.

DISENGAGING

Reframing your thoughts on Positioning also helps because knowing that you will be moving on in just a few minutes can make it easier to approach someone. Yet this requires further discussion because many people find that disengaging from someone is just as hard on them as engaging someone. Saying no is no simple matter.

No sooner had Rita walked into a party than Werner approached and started a conversation. Rita could see from the get-go that he wasn't for her. Though her eyes darted around the room and her body tone shifted, Werner did not pick up on her nonverbal cues. Rita found herself feeling sorry for him, so she talked with him for hours. She should have felt sorry for herself. Because she tried to be "nice," she let the entire evening slip through her fingers. In addition to losing an opportunity, Rita stole Werner's opportunity to meet a woman who actually liked him.

You won't want to pursue every connection that you make or date everyone who wants to date you, and there is nothing nice about sacrificing your good time for someone you don't want to be with. This brings us to a quick lesson in gracious ways to move on at any social event.

THE ART OF DISENGAGING

Politely speak with anyone who approaches you for ten minutes. If nothing clicks, end it by saying:
Because I:

- haven't attended a party in months
- haven't left my desk since 1987
- haven't had a date since Elvis died
- have found myself addressing men in the same tone of voice I use with my three-year-old daughter

I promised myself that tonight I would circulate.
It was so nice to meet you.
Maybe we'll bump into each other later.

Five Further Considerations in Parting

1. *Say Thank You:* When you don't want to dance, say, "No, but thanks for asking." That can go a long way toward letting someone feel okay about themselves.

   Alan, a thoughtful man from one of my workshops, says that he can tell a lot about a woman by how she says no to him. Some, he claims, don't even think about how they say no. If he asks someone to dance, she may shake her head and never utter a single word. He states that it is important to be polite on a dance floor.

   In some cases, you may want to say "not right now" instead of no:

   "Thanks for asking, but I'll sit this one out. But can I come and ask you later if I decide to dance?"

In this way, you have time to decide, and he won't be asking again in five minutes. Remember, the person you turned down has to walk back across the dance floor and ask someone else. Many men describe this as feeling like having a huge spotlight that captures everyone's attention following them across the room.

> If you turn down a dance because dancing with someone else is on your mind, that someone else may be watching very closely as you say no. He may decide not to take the risk. Maybe he'll ask someone he's already seen say yes. It's almost always better to be the person who says yes.

2. *Say You Have Some Unfinished Business:* If someone asks for your number and you can't be forthright (many, many people have trouble with this), you still have options that don't include weird excuses. At a singles event, your usual line about being involved with someone else is useless. Why not say, "Thanks for asking, but right now I have some unfinished business." They can attribute whatever they want to a statement like that, whether it conjures up someone lurking from the past or a general lack of readiness on your part.

3. *Hunger or Relief:* Excuses older than Adam: You can always go to the rest room or refill your cranberry juice. However, general rules of politeness would dictate that you refill their drink as well. If you're cornered by a nonstop gabber and you can't seem to get in a word, excuse yourself for a refill and get him or her one too. Upon returning, hand them their glass, as you thank him or her for the conversation and move on.

4. *Offer Clarity with Empathy:* After polling many singles about how they want to be turned down, I know that most prefer the truth:
   You're really nice to ask, but no.
   Thank you for asking, but no.
   No means no. Any way you look at it, it's spelled the same way. Say no in the way you'd like to hear it if your roles were reversed. Remember—it's a small world and word travels fast.

5. *Master the Short Talk:* You find someone physically attractive but don't know in advance if the person matches the appearance. The Short Talk lets you connect briefly and check out your instincts by letting the person know, in advance, that there is a time limit on the meeting that doesn't have anything to do with him. Here are a few examples:

- Can I talk to you a few minutes?
- I'm supposed to meet a friend who is notoriously late. I hate waiting. If he's not here in ten minutes, I'm going after him.
- I'm leaving soon, but I wanted to meet you before I did.

With the Short Talk, you don't have to reject someone at all. You could actually turn disengaging into a *good deed.* And who knows, after ten minutes you might just decide to stay longer because putting a time limit doesn't just free the other person from expectations about what this encounter could hold. It also frees you. And when you aren't expecting *anything,* it's easier for *something* to happen.

FURTHER TIPS

What If No One Likes Me?

As I said earlier, there is a common fear that we will be judged unfavorably by others. Unfortunately, some people, because of their own problems, will judge you no matter what you do. And if they judge you as good one moment, they can just as easily judge you as bad the next. You will make yourself more neurotic if you rely on the opinion of others to determine your self-worth.

The judge you need to concern yourself with is the judge inside of you. Will you forgive yourself if it was too difficult tonight, or will you turn a rough night into a weapon to use against yourself? Will you accept progress, or do you heartlessly demand perfection? Will you give yourself another chance, or will you sequester yourself in your room for six months? Will you offer yourself the same kind words you would offer another? Are you intent on proving to yourself that your worst suspicions about your essence are true?

In keeping with the spirit of Guerrilla Dating Tactics:

- Congratulate yourself for making the effort.
- Forgive yourself if you couldn't make the effort tonight.

- Ask not what the party can do for you, ask what you can do for the party.
- Lighten up! Your life is not a test.

In Addition:

- Watch the booze! Ruth felt that wine helped her relax. One night she felt particularly nervous and drank three glasses. Shortly thereafter, she met someone she really hit it off with. However, after talking to him for ten minutes, she was forced to excuse herself to go to the Ladies Room, where she spent the rest of the evening pressing her head to the cool tiled floor in an effort to stop the planet from spinning.
- Even if you are given a huge plate for your food, only take a tiny portion. That way you can return to the table when the person you are sneaking peeks at goes to get his food.
- Don't be so intent on your OAF MAP that you fail to notice someone else's.
- If the whole idea of parties is not for you, that's fine. Don't go! Try an activity instead. Play volleyball. Hike with the Sierra Club. Take an Adult Ed class and learn to channel. You may find out that in a past incarnation you were Fanny Brice. *Now, she knew how to work a room.*

Mobilization
of Forces
and Resources

7

Borrowing from the Best: Closely Guarded Secrets

In a tiny cave in Sicily, a wall painting depicts a cavewoman from one clan mulling over her dilemma regarding a caveman from another clan. She thinks that the bump on his head means he's married, but she isn't sure. On a piece of parchment dating back to Roman times, a certain Marcus Attilius bemoans the futility of approaching one woman in a group of women at the baths. A notebook found in Paris in the late seventeenth century describes a minor member of the court who, in spite of extensive minuet lessons, had no luck in getting women to dance with him. I jest, of course. Yet archetypal problems of meeting seem initially hopeless no matter what era they appear in, returning us over and over to our initial question: What's a well-bred Neanderthal to do?

It doesn't make sense to reinvent the wheel. Because men and woman have muddled through similar predicaments since we've stood on two legs, solutions already exist, and some have worked better than others. This chapter takes a contemporary look at how to come up with aggressive solutions by revealing the best-kept secrets of others for approaching classic dilemmas. These Guerrilla Dating Tactics are a win/win proposition. Either your own creative genius will get you moving, or someone else's tactic will act as your springboard to a more rewarding social life.

Here are the top contenders for sticky situations and unmanageable thoughts, followed by ideas on reframing them into manageable tasks:

How to Draw Positive Attention to Yourself at a Gathering
How to Approach One Person in a Group and Ask for a Dance
How to Find Out If He or She Is Married
How To Mobilize Your Kids as a Plus
How to Leap Out of a Slump

How to Use Conversation Pieces to Get Noticed
How to Feel Romantic Again (with Foreign Films).

How to Draw Positive Attention to Yourself at a Gathering

Once upon a time a guy named Joe lived in a big condominium inhabited by sensuous singles who congregated in scanty Jantzens around a built-in pool. The same women and men appeared every weekend afternoon, and though he'd memorized their tan lines, he'd never met any of them. One night as he was eating a taco TV dinner, he had a vision. Not a vision of God, like Moses, or even a vision of love, like Mariah Carey. He had a vision of how to meet people at the pool. The next day, instead of the usual paperback, he brought a pitcher of ice-cold margaritas, a container of salt, and sixteen recycled paper cups. By six that evening, his brainstorm had become a tradition.

One of the women at the pool, Deborah, adapted Joe's strategy for her own use. She and her friend, Evelyn, had noticed a softball tournament scheduled in a local park. Deborah and Evelyn (who was not sure whether softball had innings or quarters) showed up with a packed cooler of soda and beer. They met every guy on both teams and couldn't remember a time when they'd had so much fun. Deborah worked smart. Instead of racking her own brains for good ideas, she borrowed Joe's good idea.

One way to draw positive attention to yourself at an informal gathering is to bring something unexpected that others can enjoy with you. Joe would have done just as well if he'd brought a batch of homemade cookies—and Deborah could have lugged something lighter, like a pizza. Choose something that makes you memorable. If you're going to a party and everyone always brings wine: DON'T BRING WINE! Instead, bring:

- Tarot cards and tell futures
- Fortune cookies (slip your phone number into the one you give to that cute guy)
- Glow-in-the-dark strings that people make into necklaces
- Aunt Minnie's eggnog
- Scruples (the game)
- A banjo
- Your ventriloquist skills and your dummy (If you forget your dummy, ask a friend to stand in.)

Remember: Whether or not you stand out in the crowd needn't be left up to fate. Stop looking to *find* the right person and start looking to *be* the right person.

HOW TO APPROACH ONE PERSON IN A GROUP AND ASK FOR A DANCE

What do wolves, monkeys, hyenas, and humans all do? Of the many answers to this question, I refer to the fact that all hunt in groups. The difference is that hyenas, wolves, and monkeys don't complain about it. Men and women, on the other hand, heartily complain that the opposite sex is generally detected in packs, hordes, and impervious tribes. How do you separate one out— especially when your goal, unlike the animals in PBS wildlife specials, is *not* to catch the weakest member?

Lester went to ask Teena, who was with four friends, to dance with him. She turned him down, so he asked her friend Valerie. Valerie turned him down too. Then he asked June who also said no. Teena said that she and her friends call this a Down-the-Liner . . . this poor guy was going down the line and he'd never get a yes. Since Teena was asked first, each friend felt like second, third, or fourth choice. Their openness to Lester decreased accordingly. He's lucky that the last woman in the group didn't slap him when he asked.

It can be hard to get one of the women in a group to separate. Within the first half hour of arrival, they may act responsible for each other's good time as a self-protection device. A woman may not want to dance with you, or she may simply be worried that her friends won't get asked. Or she may not be ready to dance *yet*. However, there is a sensible way to approach. Walk up to *all* of them at once, smile in a friendly (meaning not seductive) way, and ask if *any* of them would like to dance. Chances are that one will be eager to dance and say yes. If you are approved by one, the others will probably dance with you too. By making it an open invitation to all of them, you have not chosen one of them over the others. You may be able to dance with all of them and see which one you hit it off with.

Some men have said that this idea sets them up for Group Rejection, or a Mass Putdown. However, they think it may be preferable to hear it all at once and move to the other side of the room than to have it doled out four times in one spot, like Chinese water torture, taking longer to happen and longer to forget. Also, after you ask, count on shared glances and ten awkward seconds until someone responds.

Variation

When Lyle sees a group of women and he wants to dance, he starts looking over at them, smiling, and bopping to the music. Usually, after a few minutes one of them comes over and asks him to dance.

Karen said that she and her friends have been tackling the task of asking men in groups to dance. They discovered that while men are generally compassionate toward a woman who asks, because they know what it feels like to be turned down, women can experience a few Down-the-Liners too. Karen came up with an idea to get men off their duffs. She approaches a group of men with a group of women. She and two friends walk over to three men, take their hands simultaneously, and lead them to the dance floor. It almost always works.

> Men travel in groups for the same reason women do: protection, insulation, and the assurance of not being alone. There is also the primitive instinct of the hunt, the sociological idea of the team, and the hope that with the support of friends, you may act braver.

Vera's Closely Guarded Secret

Mike asks another group question: Why is it that when he's taken twenty minutes to get his courage together to approach one woman in a group that they always, as if they know he is coming, rise simultaneously and head for the Ladies Room?

Vera says she used to do that, but she learned a secret that has changed her life. When all her friends go together, she stays behind and waits for them—alone. Normally shy, Vera feels safe because she knows they will come back in ten minutes. She has found, and she didn't want to part with this secret at all, that men approach her the moment her friends leave. Often their opening lines reflect the fact that they know they only have ten minutes until her pals come back, and they give it their wittiest and best shot. This has worked out so well for Vera that she actually tells her friends that their hair is a mess when it isn't so that she can have a few precious minutes alone.

Final Group Tip

Don't approach one person in a group without observing the group first. Are they in a deep discussion, or are they just hanging out? Are they seated at a back table avoiding the crowd, or are they simply keeping each other company? Is someone making eye contact with you or looking distracted and bored? Rely on visual cues to tell you if, how, and when to approach.

HOW TO FIND OUT IF HE OR SHE IS MARRIED

A prevalent fantasy of singles shame is based on mistakenly flirting with a married person. While we all know intellectually that people make such errors, we cringe at the thought of making them ourselves.

Ilene brought up her fear of accidentally flirting with a married man in a singles support group. Ruth, a social worker who was also a group member, asked Ilene to role-play her worst fantasy of what might happen. Ilene chose a restaurant filled with people. She imagined that when she flirted with this man whom she did not know was married, every person in the restaurant stopped eating and looked over at her, making fun of her and laughing at her. She imagined that her ineptness and stupidity were no longer her secret—now everyone knew. As the support group probed her grand personal drama, it hit her: She had seen herself as the center of the universe, with everyone intensely interested in her failure.

Two questions were raised. Did the world care as deeply as she thought about her mistakes? Was her flirtation a failure? Ilene agreed with other group members that when she observed someone boldly flirting, she was in awe of her, even if it turned out that she'd chosen a married target. Why would Ilene be so impressed with someone else's overture and so critical of her own? These are questions worth probing, but the upshot was that Ilene began to reevaluate and gain perspective on the difference between her self-flagellating fantasies and what might really happen.

The world has no shortage of married slimeballs who will purposely try to deceive you into believing they are single. They may not always be immediately apparent, but if you have your antennae adjusted properly, clues accumulate. For example, I particularly wonder about a man who doesn't give you a home phone number but does give reasons why it's easier to reach him at the office. Most of us have answering machines today, so even if his point is well taken, a message can be left. I wouldn't automatically assume that a person who doesn't give a home phone after a date is married or, at the very least, entangled, but I'd think about it. Conversely, a person who *does* give a home phone is saying, I'm not married, I'm not entangled, you can call me at home and that's fine.

Certainly, some women rightfully withhold their home numbers as a safety precaution, but if you're walking down the wedding aisle in two weeks, you still don't have her home phone number, and she tells you that the best place to reach her is at her personal trainer's steam bath, this would be a definite red flag.

The Sneaky Approach

Bernie, a saxophone player, swears by his corny technique to immediately establish marital status. After he's talked to a woman for a few minutes, he compliments her in some way and follows that up with, "I hope your husband appreciates you."

Variation: Patty says, "Great tie. Did your wife pick it out?"

Gail uses humor to find out. One night she walked up to a stud in a bar and said, "We were talking about you in the Ladies Room. Are you married? We wanted to know because if you are we'll take your name off the Ladies Room wall."

These may appear theatrical. Alan, a workshop participant, points out that there is a certain amount of theater in all social interactions, and we are all social actors to some degree. Therefore, you always have the option to rewrite the script in a way that you prefer.

Certain wedding bands are indistinguishable from other kinds of rings and some people, mostly men, don't wear rings at all. When you are the one approaching, you can't always know up front if the person you want to get to know better is single—what

you *can* know is that they are human. Humans like being appreciated and admired, so stop your self-recriminations when you find
that the person is not available. If he or she is healthy-minded, and
you don't exceed the boundaries of decency, he or she will enjoy
your subtle attention. After a long, hard day or a long, hard life,
you forget that other people find you appealing and it's lovely to
be reminded.

In addition to how you consider other people's rings or
lack of them, consider your own. Don't wear rings on your
third finger. If there are two attractive people and one has
something that from fifty feet away could be a wedding
band, which one would you approach?

The Direct Approach

The sneaky approach is more transparent than it is sneaky.
You both know exactly why you're asking. Another option is making the simple, pleasant query: Are you married?

If the response is yes, you can express your disappointment,
but with a smiling face. Don't immediately dismiss this person.
You may make a new friend, or he may have a single friend who's
a lot like him.

Don't turn your worry about marital status into one more way
to avoid meeting others. It doesn't hold up as a defense for doing
nothing.

How to Mobilize Your Kids as a Plus

At one time we thought that children could never be a dating
plus. Today, we don't even assume that someone with kids is married. It can be easier to be friendly to someone with kids because
the kids can allow you to warm up in ways you ordinarily
wouldn't. I find myself smiling at men and women with children,
but who would have thought it would turn into a best-kept secret
for meeting someone?

Kenny takes his adorable nephew out every week. Last week
he took him to the park for the day, and he saw a very pretty
woman sunning herself on a bench. Kenny asked his nephew if he
wanted an ice cream cone. He told him all he had to do to get one
was to bump into the lady sitting in the sun. Kenny took it from
there.

Cleo takes her daughter to the beach and together they build sand castles. Cleo swears they have never finished a castle together without some male insisting that he design the moat. Cleo also finds that it's easier for her to strike up a conversation with her daughter at her side.

Darlene has five adult children ranging from twenty to thirty-three who still live at home with her. When she dates a man, she tells him that she lives in a commune with five other people who also happen to be related to her. She treats the subject with such humor that she reframes it for the men she dates as something about her that is appealing rather than alarming.

The Down Side of Kids: Barbara, a thirty-eight-year-old accountant, asked a six-year-old boy in her building if he knew any single guys he could introduce her to. The six-year-old said he did and maybe she could come by later and meet his cousin who was grown up. When she stopped by, she found that the cousin was fifteen. The moral here is that everyone looks grown up when you are only six.

Men and women who have children—even large families—marry and remarry every day. Stepfamilies are a social norm. Books to help stepfamilies adjust line the shelves of the bookstores. If you're concerned as to what joining an already-made family might be like or about bringing someone new into your family, buy one of these books and start finding out. It's easy to accept the myth that states that men don't wish to marry women with young kids or women don't want to take on a man, his children, and his ex-wife. In keeping with our previous discussion of rational thinking, certainly *some* men aren't prepared to take on young kids and *some* women aren't either. But it is absurd, untrue, and nastily self-defeating to decide that 100 percent of all men and women share this feeling. Some men and women would be thrilled to join an already existing family. In fact, that's precisely what some men and women are looking for. Maybe yours.

How to Leap Out of a Slump

Laura shimmies out of a dating slump by updating her address book to reconnect with old friends and make new ones. She's so busy that she often finds that friendships simply slide away. There are other people whose cards she took yet never managed to get to know. She takes a weekend, starts at A, and keeps calling till she reaches Z. If it's around the holidays, she may tell people that the time of year inspired her to catch up on old friends. If it isn't, she may say that she bought a new address book, was transferring names, and realized she hadn't spoken to this friend in a while.

Laura's benefits include making social plans and getting out of the house, party and lunch (and wedding) invitations, and a feeling of being more friendly all over. For her, it's a comfortable and comforting beginning.

Hi Jerry, Yes I Know It's Been a Long Time

If you meant to contact someone ages ago, can you call after all this time? What excuse do you give for not having done it yet? First off, even if you think you need an excuse, you don't. We tend to worry that we will bother people, interrupting their lives—that they have moved on and that we haven't crossed their minds in years. In reality, when *we* receive a call from old acquaintances, we are almost always glad to hear from them. When they tell us that they've thought of calling for a while, we wish they'd done it sooner—and we are rarely annoyed that they waited. The way you feel when you hear from an old friend is the barometer to use when thinking about how that friend is going to feel when she hears from you. We tend to put such calls off. Starting to date is a good reason not to put them off any longer.

At some point mention lightly that you are dating, because:

- It puts you in a dating frame of mind, identifying you *to yourself* as someone who is dating. Verbally owning up to it can translate into a new way of carrying yourself.
- It reframes you as an active dater for your friend.
- Your friend gives you support—something we can all use.
- And maybe your friend knows someone . . .

HOW TO USE CONVERSATION PIECES TO GET NOTICED

What you wear, carry, or hand out says a great deal about who you are and can act as a creative icebreaker. Jackie, a firefighter, had cards printed up. On one side they say, "You light 'em, we fight 'em." The other side reads, "And we still make house calls." Diane carries heat-sensitive business cards; when you touch them, they change color. Ernie has a gorgeous collection of antique fountain pens, and he never leaves home without putting one or two in the pen pocket of his shirt. Leslie wears a beret that is completely covered with pins, buttons, tiny flags, and tie tacks from all over the world. She's a walking UN poster. I noticed several people asking a man in a recent workshop about a beautifully designed button he wore on his coat. He explained that it was a logo for an organization he supported called "Artists Fighting Against AIDS." Marilyn meets men by carrying her art canvases. Bob wears his softball team's jacket.

Jack wears a hat that he tips to women, a gesture that leaves them smiling. He says that response to him is different than the response sans hat. Michael wears a T-shirt that says, "This is what a nice guy really looks like." Carla wears a T-shirt with the name of a local tractor-pull event. Gary copied lines from Italian love sonnets onto his tattered jeans. Kim Hong sports a wild tie designed by Nicole Miller that is covered with personal ads.

Of course, you can always walk your dog—but be careful to avoid what happened to Rodney Dangerfield. He said that he bought a dog and planned to use the dog to meet women. However, he discovered that the dog was using him to meet other dogs.

Gum, Anyone?

When my friends travel to foreign countries, I never ask them to bring me a silk scarf. I always ask for unusual chewing gums. They are cheap, easy to carry, and an intriguing way to pique interest. I have one gum from Japan called "Kiss Mint." On the wrapper it says that it is "perfect for dates." I also have Kiss Cool, Flavono, Black Black, gum in Hebrew, Spanish, and other languages. It's an adventure to offer a piece to a person. In addition, I wear a necklace that conceals a tiny bottle of bubbles with its own bubble wand. You may think it wouldn't be appropriate to walk up to someone and blow bubbles in their face and you would be right. Nonetheless, I have found innumerable occasions to use it. For example, it's a big hit with kids.

One day, I took a very slow elevator to the third floor. I entertained myself by blowing bubbles furiously on the way up. When the elevator stopped, the bubbles were put away. When the door opened, several people were waiting to get on. There I stood, arms at my side, in a cloud of bubbles. One thing I've learned from my childlike antics is that the day passes much more quickly when you find ways to entertain yourself rather than relying on others to entertain you.

Why not think of your clothing, accessories, and other props as the outerwear manifestation of the opening line? What's hanging in your closet or tucked in the back of a drawer that could work for you? If your answer is nothing, then go buy:

A book with a provocative title
A windup toy
A package of chocolate cigarettes
A long loaf of Italian bread
A copy of *Rod and Reel* or *Motor Trend* if you're female
A big bag of penny candy
A tuba

or anything else that will keep you from melting into the crowd. Think of your conversation pieces as a personal signature that you display for the world to see.

> Don't forget to notice other people's conversation pieces. Peter, a Broadway actor, found the perfect opening when a striking blonde rolled through the Manhattan supermarket aisles on a pair of roller skates. He sauntered over as she inspected the tomatoes and, in a completely serious voice, queried, "Skate here often?"

HOW TO FEEL ROMANTIC AGAIN (WITH FOREIGN FILMS)

A sexy foreign film can be a petite rebirth. Put aside realism, politics, rules, and roles, and use one to turn your ordinary Sunday afternoon of avoiding life into a Rabelaisian milestone. If the most exotic thing in your life is the jar of Spanish olives in the refrigerator, then you need an imported refresher.

Every foreign film you rent must be subtitled, not dubbed. The whole point is to use the seductive music of the Romance languages to tickle and delight your romantic nerve endings out of hibernation.

Hit the foreign film section of the video stores and look for romantic films that have won the grand prize at Cannes or other foreign film festivals, and even Academy Awards. Next, go to the liquor store and purchase a bottle of wine from the same country: A light Italian table wine, a deep garnet Spanish wine, or a lusty French vintage. If you do not drink alcoholic beverages, I recommend purchasing castanets, a fine French Brie, or preparing a zesty pasta with hot sausage. Each of these is at least as sensual as the fruit of the vine.

Please don't write me letters complaining that everyone in foreign movies is cheating on their spouses. That's a given.

8

Mobilization of Forces and Resources: How to Get Others to Help You

Ask a Fortune 500 CEO his secret, and he may tell you that he knows how to delegate tasks and responsibilities. Not only does he not do everything himself, he would never try to do everything himself. He knows his limits and possesses a knack for finding the right person to get the job done.

Ask a revered Hollywood director how she keeps getting those award nominations, and she may tell you that she knows how to put the right person on her team. Perhaps when you see her accepting her trophy and thanking so many others, you think she is just being kind. Don't kid yourself. She wouldn't be tottering in those cruel dyed-to-match-and-never-to-be-suffered-again heels in front of the camera, instead of behind it, without the diligent efforts of others.

Successful people are the first to tell you that part of their expertise lies in their ability to mobilize the right people for help. And how do they get the best person for the job to come on board? They pay money.

Obviously, you can't do that. Or can you? People pay for dating services and personal ads which, when used wisely, can supply good dates. In addition to costly ways, you can get help for less than the price of a cup of iced decaf cappuccino ... if you know how to ask.

REFRAMING HELP

Smart people, whether scientists or sailors, actively recruit help. A fellow scientist does not join a project because she sees the one who is asking for help as *helpless*. She joins because it is a grand adventure, because she is interested in the topic, because something exciting could happen, because she's interested in being part of the outcome, and because she knows the person asking is a *winner*.

FIXUPS: HOW TO ASK

These same principles apply when you ask someone if they know someone with whom you could be fixed up:

- You don't get fixed up by acting like you're dependent on being fixed up in order to have a social life.
- You don't get fixed up by appearing helpless at getting your own dates.
- You don't get fixed up by bad-mouthing previous dates.
- You don't get fixed up by gender-bashing (all men are . . . , all women are . . .).
- You don't get fixed up by dwelling on elaborate fantasies of what this date could be.

Mobilizing forces and resources is achieved by presenting yourself as someone whom it would be fun to help. In fact, you don't want help from people who pity you—you don't want to be presented to a potential fixup as poor sweet Lisa or that poor old Charlie, such a nice person having such a hard time.

Remember: Nobody you will want to meet responds to an acquaintance who tells them, "I know this fabulous needy woman."

It's not *what* you ask, it's *how* you ask that matters. Ask with realism, pleasure, interest, enjoyment, and playfulness. If you don't feel this way:

- Wait until you do, because maybe you're not ready.
- Borrow the wonderful Alcoholics Anonymous affirmation and "act as if" you feel better. See if that doesn't help you to actually feel better soon. If it works, ask then.

When you ask people to fix you up, expect a little friendly fire. The key to successfully defusing it is to have some preplanned responses so that you don't get diverted from your mission by comments such as:

Grenade 1: I can't believe you're having trouble.

Defuse it by saying: It's an adventure, and I'm having fun.

Don't start thinking: You're right, I'm having trouble. Oh God, what's wrong with me. *And don't get defensive.*

Grenade 2: I know a few nice women, but none of them seem like your type. They aren't good enough for you.

Defuse it by saying: Thanks for trying to figure out my type, but I'd love the pleasure of deciding for myself, even if you're not sure I'd like her.

Don't start thinking: Well, I guess you know best about my needs, and, if you think I wouldn't like her, I'll take your word for it.

Grenade 3: I don't know anyone.

Defuse it by saying: Thanks for trying. Maybe when you least expect it, someone will pop into your head ... so keep me in mind.

Don't start thinking: She doesn't know anyone. Cross her off as a possible resource.

Grenade 4: What if things don't work out? What if she likes you and you don't like her, or the reverse? It could affect our friendship.

Defuse it by saying: We may not be destined to live happily ever after, but then, I had only planned to invite her for coffee. If you consider her to be a great friend, we could all end up friends. Even if we don't, we'll both appreciate your effort on our behalf.

Don't start thinking: You're right—one bad date could ruin everything.

Grenade 5: Are you kidding? I can't find my own dates.

Defuse it by saying: Maybe we can help each other. Tell me a little about the people you'd like to meet.

Don't start thinking: It's hopeless. No one can find anyone.

Self-Imploding Grenades

Some grenades get set off internally by the anxiety aroused when you consider asking for help. You can actually transform yourself into a psychological minefield. Men and women have both shared and gender-specific difficulties. Although both sexes share anxiety about fixups, men tend to find it very hard to ask to be fixed up. Consider how men have been socialized. It's hard enough to ask for a tiny bit of help, like driving directions. Imagine how much harder it is to ask a friend to find you a date.

The difficulty stems from the fact that it's been drummed into a man's head that he was expelled from the womb a self-sufficient problem solver. Asking for help feels like an admission of weakness or ineffectiveness and threatens the whole "man as an island" myth. John Donne wrote "no man is an island" precisely because men can feel like islands—not because they don't. If they didn't, no one would have to write a poem about why they aren't. For men, the idea of seeking help can make them feel less vital, less independent, and framed in a one-down position.

If men tend to feel in the one-down position for asking at all, women tend to construct a set of rules about who it's okay to ask. They might feel comfortable asking a certain few people over and over again, but shrink at the idea of putting the word out—something that makes many women feel like they are drawing attention to themselves by shouting "me, me, me." Women often seek a sense of permission to go public with their needs.

Men and women need to follow through with the credo of Guerrilla Dating Tactics by throwing self-proscribed rules and Hollywood roles out the window. Perhaps the lone-man methodology made sense for the Cro-Magnon male or Schwarzenegger flicks. Perhaps telling the same women the same things makes sense in a Cynthia Heimel parody, but in the nineties real world, it makes more sense to pick up a few tips from the biz whiz of the eighties, Lee Iacocca. I doubt Lee Iacocca felt that he had to hide his face when he sought government funds to keep Chrysler afloat. Instead of being excluded from the best parties, he probably started getting invited to them. He was viewed as a marketing genius as he directed attention toward himself and his company. He went out looking for help, and he got it because *he knew who and how to ask.*

Ask from a position of strength, not weakness.

Don't overwhelm anyone with your search by giving them a blow-by-blow description of how tough it is or frequent reminders of how long it's been since your last date, but make sure that you tell people you are available. Throw a party, send birthday cards (remember and be remembered), take a friend to lunch, and do whatever else you can think of to let the public know just how much fun it can be to spend time in your company.

I know a lovely woman, Clarisse, who has been widowed for many years. She has a wonderful job, a beautiful home, and adoring grandchildren. One night she was talking to her sister on the phone and her sister mentioned a couple she'd recently fixed up—a man and woman right in Clarisse's age range. Clarisse asked, clearly hurt, why she hadn't been considered as a candidate to meet this man. Her sister was shocked—Clarisse seemed so happy and had never once mentioned that she might be interested in meeting a man. Clarisse got angry, and snapped that her own sister should have been able to figure that out for herself. Her sister countered that while there was blood between them, she was unaware of crystal balls running through the bloodstream. Blood didn't quality her as a mind reader.

No one can read your mind either. Don't expect people to assume that you are open to fixups . . . not even the people closest to you . . . not even the people most interested in your happiness.

Scientists have puzzled for years as to why yawns are contagious. They aren't sure why, but they know for a fact that they are more contagious than the common cold. So is *enthusiasm*.

WHAT TO DO IF YOU'VE TRIED THIS AND NO ONE WANTS TO FIX YOU UP

Occasionally, people have told me that, in spite of an awareness that their acquaintances have single friends, no one has been willing to make introductions for them. If this is a feeling you've shared, see if any of the following reasons pertain to you:

- For years, Alice has dated several times a week—always different men. She's had difficulty sustaining a relationship with any of them, although she swears it's a simple matter of lousy luck. No one wants to fix up Alice because she's never hidden the fact that every fixup in the past has disappointed her.

If you are Alice, then you need to demonstrate that you are ready for a relationship by having one. This is no easy task, but asking for fixups won't work for you. Look to other parts of this book for help instead.

- Andrew has strict requirements for women he'll date. They must have an advanced degree, be in a required age range that spans four years, have never been married before, and take an AIDS test. Since he fits this description, he simply won't settle for less from her.

  If you are Andrew, people are going to feel limited in the face of your demands. Maybe she's out there, but you are going to have to find her yourself.

- Maya, a brilliant college professor, is at the top of her field. She's been so busy doing research for her next paper that she hasn't bothered to notice that her clothing is ten years out of date, her body has changed in that time so nothing fits her right, and her hair, which she cuts herself, looks it. No one is suggesting Maya put down her books. But she does need to put energy into her physical appearance, which, in her case, acts as a wall instead of a bridge. After all, that's what people see first.

  If you are Maya, update your appearance by shopping for flattering clothing, springing for a good haircut, and integrating a sense of your physical appearance into your full life. When you've done this, ask your friends again.

POST-FIXUP ETIQUETTE

After you've been fixed up and gone out on the date, call and thank the person responsible. Say, "I went out with Lucy. I wanted to call and thank you for thinking of me. I really appreciated your efforts." If, in reality, Lucy was not your cup of tea, look to the positive aspects of the date:

We had dinner in a nice restaurant.
She has quite a sense of humor.
She's nice.

Don't talk like you'll see her again if you won't. The point is to give positive reinforcement to the person who made the effort on your behalf.

I CAN'T BELIEVE YOU FIXED ME UP WITH HIM!

A friend may fix you up with someone whom you believe is completely inappropriate for you. Your impulse may be to feel angry with your friend and to wonder how your friend ever thought the two of you might hit it off. Don't hold a grudge, and don't blow it up. Who can ever understand what one person sees in another? Mismatches are inevitable, but the fact that you're willing to take risks in the first place puts you two steps ahead of where you were.

The point of mobilizing forces and resources is to start building options for finding dates and to take you beyond your current thinking of how to do it. The more scouts on the lookout for you on a regular basis, the more dates you'll have on a regular basis. Yet it's not enough just to make your wishes known. You must make them known in a constructive way that increases your options.

When we talk about poverty we speak of limited access, opportunities, and options that people live with every day. You can be dating poor, too. You can have limited access, missed opportunities, and narrow options when it comes to dates. If you're inclined to fluff it off, saying it's just your social life, remember that feeling lonely and without choices is a tragedy of its own.

Scanning Your Future

M aybe you thought you could get all the way through this book without me asking you to participate. Oh, sure, I threw in a few fill-in quizzes you probably didn't fill in, but maybe you thought that would be it. Wrong. I am going to ask you to do something that requires thought, self-exploration, time, and planning. I want you to paint a picture of how you spend your time every day by recording what you do. You may be in for a surprise, like the one my friend Ross got when he went on a diet. He took a week and looked up the calorie count for every morsel of food that passed his lips, and discovered he'd had no idea of his calorie consumption. I got a shock just last month when I recorded the number of hours I spend in front of the television set. Ross's big surprise was that lentil soup was so fattening. Mine was that I tell people that I hardly watch any TV and my experiment proved that just the opposite was true. Your surprise may be that your time doesn't go where you think it goes.

Believe me, I understand those of you who are reluctant to go along. No one likes to feel reduced to one slot in a bell curve. No one even likes to get up and look for a pencil, generally prey to the same gremlin who steals one sock from the dryer. Bear with me anyway.

The charts I want you to work on are bar graphs. They look a little like those bar codes that get scanned by the checkout computer in a supermarket, but these bar graphs are going to illuminate your social life rather than tell you the price of a box of cereal. A computer gets important information from scanning a bar code, and you'll get important information from scanning your bar graphs.

Here is a blank bar graph so you can begin to get familiar with it.

Bar Graph for How You Spent Time
Week of _____

	1	2	3	4	5	6	7	8	9	10
Routine Errands										
Bars										
Religious Group										
Sports										
Volunteer Work										
Committees										
Health Club										
Conferences										
Travel										
Way to Work										
Way Home										
Hang Out w/ Friends										
At Work										
Lunch										
Restaurants										
Movies										
TV										
Outdoors										
Fixups/Blind dates										
Children										
Classes										
School										
Dating Services										
Personal Ads										
Singles Events										

_____

_____

_____

The left column represents your daily activities. There are blank spaces on the bottom that you can fill in if you have regular activities that aren't reflected in this list. Depending on which type of bar graph you are doing (there are two), the horizontal column reading 1 . . . 2 . . . 3 . . . represents either the amount of time you think you are engaged in each activity—from 1, which is very little time, to 10, which is a lot of your time—*or* the exact number of people you talk to, approach, or have dated in the past—1 equals one person. So the horizontal line can change meaning depending on the purpose of your bar graph—you'll find out more about that later.

When Carl came into the workshop, it was with the intention of making his social life a priority. Owning his own business had kept him in the office more than he felt was comfortable and less than he felt he needed. He realized that he had trouble slowing down long enough to start a relationship. But, he pointed out, that was changing. He had answered personal ads, and believed he was making a real effort to get out. I asked him to think back to the week previous to attending the workshop and write down every person he remembered starting a conversation with, even people he already knew, even if he'd just said hello . . . so long as he'd said hello first.

When he finished I asked him to count the number by completing the Bar Graph of Where You Met People, noting in what capacity of his life these conversations had taken place. Here is his graph:

Carl's Conversations, Week of 12/15

	1	2	3	4	5	6	7	8	9	10
Routine Errands	████									
Religious Group										
Sports										
Volunteer Work										
Committees										
Health Club										
Conferences										
Travel										
Way To Work	███████									
Way Home	████									
Hang w/ Friends										
At Work	██████████									
Lunch										
Restaurants										
Movies										
TV										
Outdoors										
Fix-ups/Blind dates										
Children										
School										
Avoiding Life										
Dating Services										
Singles Bars										
Personal Ads	█████████									
Singles Events										

When he completed the bar graph, even counting a few people he may have forgotten to add in, he saw, in black and white, that he barely spoke to people outside of work at all. He thought he had been talking to many more people, but the graph pointed out that it had been business as usual.

Carl filled out the second graph one month down the road, and it measured the number of introductions he'd made for himself during the last week of that month—since he actively decided that he wanted to reach out and touch someone. Now he had a way to measure whether he was doing what he thought he'd been doing.

Carl's Conversations, Week of 1/13

	1	2	3	4	5	6	7	8	9	10
Routine Errands	████████████████████									
Religious Group										
Sports										
Volunteer Work										
Committees										
Health Club										
Conferences										
Travel										
Way To Work	████████████████									
Way Home	████████████████									
Hang w/ Friends	██████████									
At Work	██████████████████████									
Lunch										
Restaurants	█████████████									
Movies										
TV										
Outdoors										
Fix-ups/Blind dates	████████									
Children										
School										
Avoiding Life										
Dating Services										
Singles Bars										
Personal Ads	████████████									
Singles Events										

For your first bar graph, you will estimate where you spend your time at present and how much of your time you spend in each place. The purpose is not to get an exact measurement of anything. It is to scan your impressions of your life.

Bar Graph of Where You Spend Time
Week of _____

Purpose: To offer a visual picture of what your life looks and feels like to you.

	1	2	3	4	5	6	7	8	9	10
Routine Errands										
Bars										
Religious Group										
Sports										
Volunteer Work										
Work Related										
Health Club										
Travel										
Way to Work										
Way Home										
Hang Out w/ Friends										
At Work										
Lunch										
Restaurants										
Movies										
TV										
Outdoors										
Fixups/Blind dates										
Children										
Classes										
School										
Dating Services										
Personal Ads										
Singles Events										

_____

_____

_____

Reflections

In this overview of what you do and how long it takes you to do it, does your life appear balanced, or do you get the sense you are in a rut? Is your longest line next to watching television? This bar graph isn't meant to suggest that you should spend as much time in the health club as you spend at work, but simply that you should observe your life in a different way.

The next bar graph requests that you paint a picture of where you think those dates of yours, the ones you don't have yet, are hiding.

Bar Graph of Where You Think You Will Meet
Potential Dates

Purpose: To assess and identify your thoughts about where romance waits and where you think you could target your efforts.

	1	2	3	4	5	6	7	8	9	10

Routine Errands
Bars
Religious Group
Sports
Volunteer Work
Work Related
Health Club
Travel
Way to Work
Way Home
Hang Out w/ Friends
At Work
Lunch
Restaurants
Movies
TV
Outdoors
Fixups/Blind dates
Children
Classes
School
Dating Services
Personal Ads
Singles Events

_____

_____

_____

Ask Yourself

Is the amount of time on the bar graph of where you spend time compatible with the bar graph of where you think you can meet people? Do you see a logical overlap? Or does it seem that the places where you spend time aren't places where you would meet new people?

TESTING YOUR HYPOTHESIS

Are you right? Let's test your impression by completing a bar graph of where you have met people you've gone out with in the past to see if it matches where you think you'll meet people.

Make a list of your last ten dates. If you haven't had ten dates yet, use ten people whom you might have dated.

Bar Graph of Where You Met Your Last Ten Dates, Even If You Have to Retrace Thirty Years

Purpose: To see if where you actually meet people coincides with where you think you'll meet them. Give yourself one point per person.

	1	2	3	4	5	6	7	8	9	10
Routine Errands										
Bars										
Religious Group										
Sports										
Volunteer Work										
Work Related										
Health Club										
Travel										
Way to Work										
Way Home										
Hang Out w/ Friends										
At Work										
Lunch										
Restaurants										
Movies										
TV										
Outdoors										
Fixups/Blind dates										
Children										
Classes										
School										
Dating Services										
Personal Ads										
Singles Events										
_____										
_____										
_____										

Any Surprises?

Did the exercise of scanning where you *have met* people coincide neatly with the bar graph of where you *think you would meet* people? Perhaps you'd wish to reframe your thoughts about good places to meet. Often, we make assumptions about where people meet people that have not proven true in our own lives. Did you actually meet a quality person in the place you swore you'd never be seen, such as a singles bar? I'm not suggesting that singles bars are the place to be, but maybe you are more comfortable approaching people (or more approachable in certain environments than you are in others). There may be things to learn about yourself.

Note: I completed one of these myself and experienced surprise at my meeting patterns. Here's my ten-man tally:

Hang out w/ friends	2
Travel	1
Blind dates	1
Personal Ads	1
Bars (gulp)	4
Work	1

HOMEWORK: SCANNING YOUR FUTURE

Over the next weeks and months you will be putting Guerrilla Dating Tactics into practice in your life as methods of meeting and engaging the world. Bar graphs measure advancement in your basic skills. From here on in, you will be measuring, to the best of your recollection, the actual numbers of people you converse with and/or meet. The idea is to keep a record, not of your dates, but of talking to new people. Fill one out once a month, or in any time period you see fit, to appraise your past, present, and future people-meeting trends. We tend to underestimate our progress, and here is a concrete way to stop underestimating yours and start believing in it. Remember, magical transformations only happen in fairy tales.

Use a different color marker for new activities you try. Think of it as giving yourself a gold star.

Remember: As you start out, do not merely count people you would date. Count people you initiate conversations with or respond to, without regard for gender or age. Increased comfort in engaging new people may not be completely separate from increased comfort in engaging new dates.

Variation

After you try bar graphs for one month by tracking how many people you talk to, begin tracing your progress in how many people you talk to for *longer than five minutes.* Each increment on the scale can be for every five minutes of conversation. Watch as you work your way up in terms of how long you can sustain conversations with new people.

Bar Graph of Where I Met People
Month: _____

	1	2	3	4	5	6	7	8	9	10

Routine Errands

Bars

Religious Group

Sports

Volunteer Work

Work Related

Health Club

Travel

Way to Work

Way Home

Hang Out w/ Friends

At Work

Lunch

Restaurants

Movies

TV

Outdoors

Fixups/Blind dates

Children

Classes

School

Dating Services

Personal Ads

Singles Events

_____

_____

_____

Bar Graph of How Long I Sustained Conversations
Month: _____

	1	2	3	4	5	6	7	8	9	10
Routine Errands										
Bars										
Religious Group										
Sports										
Volunteer Work										
Work Related										
Health Club										
Travel										
Way to Work										
Way Home										
Hang Out w/ Friends										
At Work										
Lunch										
Restaurants										
Movies										
TV										
Outdoors										
Fixups/Blind dates										
Children										
Classes										
School										
Dating Services										
Personal Ads										
Singles Events										

_____

_____

_____

As you fill out these charts, an interesting change is taking place. You aren't just scanning your future, you're taking charge of it.

CHAPTER 10

Personal Ads: The Good, the Bad, and the Ugly

Christian Singles—$34.95 immediately brings you
"hundreds" of Southern California profiles, photos, phones.
Your profile published free. God is the Matchmaker.
Nondenominational. Free Samples.
                    —an advertisement in *Los Angeles* magazine

In major cities, we find more magazine and newspaper space devoted to personal ads than to local political issues. Everyone from the desktop publisher who markets ad-filled booklets to the esteemed *New York Review of Books*, which promotes a section for the single literati, has discovered that the meet market has merely changed form to keep up with changing times.

When used correctly, personal ads can bring fun and adventure into your life. Used incorrectly, they can be an exercise in frustration and confusion. In *50 Ways to Find a Lover*, I delineated the basics of the personals, from which I can extract simple truths:

For answering one:—Make it brief. No one wants to read ten pages on the story of your life. Unless he's in prison.

For writing one:—Show, don't tell, who you are, because we're all so suspicious that if you tell us, we won't believe you anyway.

One day, as an experiment, I took an orange highlighter, planning to highlight one page of *New York* magazine's personals every time I saw the words "attractive," "pretty," or "handsome." My arm was sore after two columns—the page was largely orange. These generic adjectives have lost all meaning.

The bottom line of the personal ad biz is that someone healthy will want to meet you because they believe their life will be richer and more interesting with you in it. That's why. That's the reason. That's what you need to figure out how to show in a few lines of print.

For the past eight years I've been reading and clipping personals on a regular basis. My fiancé has watched my growing file with a mixture of amusement and irritation. My friends have asked me over and over why I've asked them to save all periodicals across the country that have a personals section. Although I waved my arm in dismissal and muttered things like "longitudinal sociological studies," I never was sure why I was saving them. Finally, I have an answer. I've been saving them all these years so that I could share them with you.

HOOKS

With the personals section growing by leaps and bounds, I can't read them all anymore. If I, who take a special interest in them, get exhausted, I bet that many people only scan them. That's why grabbing someone's attention immediately matters so much. Here are some eye-catching "hooks" (otherwise known as the first few words of the ad) from my files:

Nora and Asta replacing Nick . . .
Sipping prune juice by candlelight . . .
Gentle Tigress . . .
Part-Time Grownup . . .
I want to slow dance . . .
Attention: Mature Egghead . . .
I know where the best ice cream is . . .
A date with destiny . . .
Slightly over the hill major beauty . . .
A Mermaid Sheds Tail . . .
Ready to trade briefcase for diaper bag . . .
Mahogany Woman . . .
Dark Chocolate Eyes . . .
Tin Man . . .
You were a tomboy . . .
In his vigorous 60s . . .
Spread sheets to satin sheets . . .
Renegade redhead . . .
Adventures of Dadman . . .

Hooks like these make your eyes move to the next line. SBF, SWF, DBM, and DWM tend to have the effect of making your eyes close.

THE GOOD

Good ads have pieces of the same three qualities in them—heart, soul, and wit. When you read them, you know that there's a real person there—a person with passion, compassion, empathy, and a hint of mischief.

Your ad will be placed with hundreds of others, so after you come up with your hook, you'd better find a way to keep distinguishing yourself like the following folks did.

Women's Ads

... looking for a man with the creativity and brilliance of Malcolm Forbes (but doesn't have to be that rich) and the warmth and sensitivity of Kermit the Frog (bald is ok but needs deeper voice) ...

Emotional luggage must fit under seat ... looking for a man with a silly streak wide enough to land a 747 on ...

Great gams, love yams, part ham, mostly baloney. Tomboyish, affectionate ... seeks man who can hammer a nail & whistle a tune ...

Divorced woman seeks man ... children have flown the coop, large ill-mannered dog remains ...

... seek a man aged 40 to breathing ...

... At age 56, age has added patina but not wrinkles or blubber ...

Marilyn Chambers, Gloria Steinem, Shirley
MacLaine, Eleanor Roosevelt, Gwen Verdon,
Gilda Radner, Joy Adams, Edith Piaf
                    seeks
Harrison Ford, Steve Jobs, Adam Smith,
Carl Sagan, Yoda, James Beard, Jacques
Cousteau y d'Amboise, Henry VIII, Moondoggie

... Rock 'n' Roll and all the barbecue you can handle ...

... Seeks man above 50 and up to (but not quite) 100 years old. I am widowed and ... tired of talking to my dog.

... Man Ray, Ray Charles, Ray Carver—For full list and photo send your list and photo ...

... I'm 5'10" (50% legs) ...

... Papagena seeks Papageno ...

... looks like Betty Boop and sings like Patsy Cline ... seeks white single male who looks like Superman and sings like Randy Travis. Let's be crazy and fall to pieces ...

... I'm pretty and fun and I wish I were French ...

... I'm no trophy but can be gorgeous with subdued back lighting ...

Men's Ads

... I survived Catholic schools ... I do not kill whales, build nuclear bombs or start forest fires. If this also describes you ...

... looking for a woman who must be willing to lie about how we met ...

... Podmate wanted ... Couch Pea ok.

Mr. Excitement ... handsome (once the wrinkle cream works). I've bored women on three continents. Please hurry. You could be saving some other poor woman's life ...

... I ain't Pretty, I can't Sing ... WM seeks a female who is optimistic, ... even-tempered ... and who can stand a little cat hair in her food ...

... 007 ... Blonde Bond, licensed to exaggerate ... Diamonds may be forever, but I could be a girl's best friend ...

Legal beagle seeks fertile Myrtle ...

Just Visiting Earth ... Friendly alien with expense account ...

I'm a one-woman man looking for someone to serenade with my guitar ...

She saw the ad ... Her heart began to pound ...

... man with a passion for Delta blues and travel ... seeks woman with a sparkle and passion all her own ...

It's perfectly fine to list your quirks, likes, dislikes, and so forth—and what you want in someone—BUT, somewhere in that ad, along with your "list," show your nature. For example, it's more appealing to have one of the writers mentioned state that the woman who responds to his ad must be able to stand a little cat hair in her food than it would be to have him say she must love cats. He gets the same point across, but he does it with spirit.

THE BAD

Truly nice people write bad ads. Bad isn't evil or hostile—it's simply boring, unrealistic, or misleading. These ads leave us feeling suspicious because they rely on too much that is open to individual subjective interpretation. In so doing, they are vague.

Hooks to snore by:

Women
Beautiful Lawyer
Beautiful Feminine lawyer
Beautiful Petite Feminine Lawyer
Beautiful Petite Feminine Successful Lawyer
                    and
Beautiful Petite Feminine Successful Lawyer (I really mean it)

Men
Handsome Man
Handsome Successful Man
Handsome Affluent Successful Man
Handsome Articulate Affluent Successful Man
Handsome Artistic Articulate Affluent Successful Man
                    and
Handsome Artistic Articulate Affluent Successful Man who is tired of clichés

You can meet nice people writing and answering ads such as these, but it's harder to do because someone else's Beautiful Petite Feminine Successful Lawyer may only be your Not Remotely Interesting J.D.

More Boring

It's one thing to type your looks and say that you are an Ed Norton type or an Alice Kramden type. It's quite another to say what these people have said:

Women

Jackie Kennedy looks
Jackie Collins look-alike
Looks like Faye Dunaway
Natalie Wood's double
Joan Collins's double

Men

De Niro Type Guy
Tom Selleck looks (Boston Man, 5'6")
Redford/Baryshnikov look-alike
Robert Redford looks
Burt Reynolds looks
Sean Connery look-alike
... looking for Connie Selleca look-alike
... favor Jaqueline Bisset looks

What exactly does a Redford/Baryshnikov "look-alike" look like? And saying that you look like Tom Selleck, who is 6'4", when you are 5'6" is an oxymoron.

Initialitis

I implore you not to try and save twenty dollars by loading your ad with initials and abbreviations that serve only to confuse and camouflage the man behind the DWCMNRINK. This is an actual lead-in I copied from a personal placed in a New York periodical. Two others I spied began SWCMNRNM and SWJMNMNRNS. I think these guys are nonreligious, never-married nonsmokers, but I will have to get an expert decoder just in case SWCMNRNM means Sadistic Weird Cruel Man, Not Real Nice Man.

HELPFUL HINTS

Think carefully before stating: Looking for clean, honest, caring, sincere, warm person. Who, I ask you, is looking for a dirty, dishonest, heartless, insincere, coldhearted person? Listing your needs in this way does not distinguish you from every other decent, breathing human. Search your mind for a detail that would describe a good potential match for you, and try using that instead of the same old adjectives. For example, the woman above who sought a man who can hammer a nail and whistle a tune has actually described much of what she seeks in temperament. She's picked details that help us visualize the man rather than asking for a friendly, even-tempered, hand/eye-coordinated guy.

Again, it's okay to ask for what you want—to say you love tennis and moonlight and brunch—but be careful of ending up with an ad that looks like every other ad. Your mission is to stand out of the crowd and get noticed. In addition, instead of concentrating on what you wish for from someone, place some of your focus on what you have to offer. Why should that great woman answer your ad when all you've written about is what you want to get, without a single phrase addressed to what you have to give?

Don't act bummed out

I find it sad to read the personals of people who are "tired of the singles scene," but I wouldn't answer an ad with a distinctly sour, negative tone. Avoid using these phrases:

I can't believe it's come to this!
I'd be surprised if there are any good men left.
I hate bars.
Abashed at having to place a personal ad.
I promised I'd never do this.

The truly ugly

You don't need to be a Rhodes scholar to get the translation:

What he said—"Looking for relationship with the proud possessor of a Dolly Parton figure . . ."
What he means—Don't expect to walk down the street with your arm in my arm unless your arm is connected to a 42″ chest.

What she said—"If you are in the 50% tax bracket but have figured out how not to pay . . ."
What she means—Please be a crook because I am.

What he said—". . . Considerate, intelligent, attractive, affluent, successful man . . ."
What he means—Substitute an evening with me for a sleeping pill. As Roxanne said on "L.A. Law" after her first date with

Dave, "I'd marry him if I only had three months to live because he'd make every day seem like a year."

In a class of its own—"Seeks non-assertive size 8 maximum for sure, non-busy gal. Please be sure to state dress size . . . since . . . some 'slender' women turn out to have a 35" waistline."
No comment!

I think it's supposed to be a joke—"Daryl Hannah Look-Alike—Fabulously wealthy, 5'6", natural blond hair, bonded and beautiful teeth, body by professional trainer, and I look this way first thing in the morning. Interests include shopping, doing lunch . . . personal pampering . . . If you are an established doctor with a thriving practice and would like to share in the life style to which I'm accustomed, please submit 35mm color photo and we'll do lunch. Will not sign a prenuptial agreement."

COMPUTER PERSONALS

There is a huge personals scene among the techies that consists of personal ads placed with "on line" bulletin boards. You can log on, read them, and leave messages for a person you wish to meet. I know couples who met each other this way. It allows the opportunity to write back and forth, anonymously and at your own pace. You can find out what you want to know without the usual awkwardness.

Using her computer on an international line, Regina spoke at length with a single man from Gstaad named Paul. It turned out Paul had attended college in a town about fifty miles from her. He asked Regina to call an old roommate, Jack, who had remained in the area, and she did. Regina and Jack talked on the phone and made plans to meet briefly for a beer. Although they never dated, the excitement of doing this paid off. Regina felt so daring that later that night she placed a personal in a local paper and started dating a man she met soon after.

> Being proactive has a snowball effect. It shouldn't matter if the situation you focused on momentarily doesn't pan out. You did it this time, so it's easier the next time. Every avenue you explore increases your chances of meeting someone nice.

FOR THE TRULY ADVENTUROUS TRAVELER

In addition to all the local places where you can read or place ads, there are personals in foreign periodicals and in the *International Herald Tribune*. Granted, it's hard to consider flying to Paris for a cup of coffee—but if you are about to be relocated to Paris, if you are filthy rich, if you are going to spend the summer there, or if you could use an exotic daydream, you might want to take the leap. Remember that Europeans list their weight in kilograms, so that 58 kg woman weighs 127 pounds! What I also found of great interest is that many French people place their first names in their ads—the personal touch. In these foreign periodicals, you will also find international partnership agencies, or, in plain English, dating services for the well-heeled traveler. *C'est magnifique.*

TO ANSWER OR TO PLACE— THAT IS THE QUESTION

You have more options and more control when you place your own ad, but answering other people's ads is a good, cheap way to start off. Many people do both. When you see an ad that catches your eye, understand that other eyes are on it, too. Good ads can get up to 150 response in a single week. Discouraged? Don't be! Dazzle him with your response. Choose a funny greeting card or a brightly colored piece of paper. Imbue your response with fun and mystery. Write from your heart.

Barry saw an ad written by a woman who loved trekking in Nepal. In his response he enclosed a photo of himself atop one of Nepal's highest peaks.

Carol saw an ad by a man who asked to meet a mysterious woman. She started off by sending him a clue for a forthcoming letter that would also hold her photo. With the photo she sent a clue for a cryptic note she'd be writing. By the time Carol sent this guy her phone number, he was wild to meet her.

FIVE DO'S AND DON'TS FOR ANSWERING ANY AD:

Don't recycle generic computer printouts or xeroxes where all you've done is change the box number and your age.

Don't clip your ad from the paper and send it in lieu of a response.

Do let someone know why his or her ad intrigued you and why you chose to answer.

Do be conscientious about grammar and spelling.

Don't try and sell yourself as if you were your own used car.

EXCEPTION: WHEN YOU CAN GET AWAY WITH A COMPUTER PRINTOUT

One smart, funny, and indisputably quirky Washingtonian named Greg sends computer printouts. Although he began responding to ads by hand, he discovered that his hand was tired before he could convey his true personality. He states, "I realize that by sending a form letter, I am eliminating that percentage of people who categorically don't respond to form letters, but I believe the rest of them are far more likely to be the kind of person I attract (and am attracted to) anyway. And I do try to put some kind of personalization into each one. For instance, if her ad says she likes science fiction, I will put a drawing of a flying saucer, etc. I try to be cute."

I thought you might like to see Greg's "form letter" in its entirety.

Hi!

Of Course this is a form letter—I'd wreck my wrist writing all this by hand!

I sold my computer store 9 years ago; since then I've been a consultant, primarily for small non-profit firms (you meet a better class of people). I work when and for whom I feel like, and I can't see how anyone can stand a 9 to 5 job—it's a waste of life!

I don't care how things look—it's much more important to know how they are. *Your looks or education count far less to me than your personality and attitudes. I go for the steak rather than the sizzle. I wore a suit every day for years and finally got fed up with wearing a uniform; now I wear a suit one day a year: Halloween.*

I have traditional values, while still being a social liberal and an economic conservative.

It's never too late to have a happy childhood.

My car is a bright red Chevy van. I think of it as a Corvette with a glandular problem (I drive that way, too).

Bach is better than rock because there've been 300 years to weed out the crap; nevertheless, I like both.

I've been described as a man with one foot in the next century, and the other firmly on a banana peel.

Never ask me a question unless you want an honest answer. My worst character flaw is that I always tell the truth.

"Be vewwy, vewwy quiet; I'm hunting wabbits."

Anything that is not growing is dead. A closed mind is one that has stopped growing.

Is the glass half-full, or half-empty?
Hah! Gotcha. Neither: It's twice as big as it needs to be!

What do I want? I'm interested in friendship first and foremost, with the ultimate goal of perhaps a permanent relationship. My best friend in the world is a happily married lady; I'm not going to say what kind of person interests me, since that might discourage you.

—Of course I'm different; by definition, if you are above the norm you must have deviated from it. I know you're special too, because you placed an ad . . . so surprise me!

Answers to infrequently asked questions:
   Quiet and introverted, but not pathologically so
   Shy and occasionally naive
   Avoider of crowds and loud noises
   Non-druggie, non-smokie, non-drinkie, except socially
   Wish I was a vegetarian (but I'm definitely not)
   No contractable diseases (is weirdness contagious?)
   Weirdness magnet (ummm . . . probably)
   Voracious reader
   Intellectual omnivore
   Insatiably curious
   Sushi/sashimi lover (I make my own at least once a week)

Computer and tech-know phreaque
Invertebrate punster (so slug me)
Speak poor French; need someone to learn sign with
Not rich, not poor, not athletic, not a couch spud
Not Quasimodo, not Mel Gibson (but I have Hamlet's beard)
Music lover (everything)
(Lousy) piano and chess player
Science fiction fanatic
Fact-finder ("Quick Watson, the encyclopedia!")
Trivia pursuer
Night owl
Strictly monogamous
Favorite radio stations: WCXR, WHFS, WJFK
Favorite TV stations: the Discovery Channel, any PBS
Favorite musical groups: Renaissance, Buggles
Favorite book: The Moon Is a Harsh Mistress (Heinlein)
Favorite cartoonists: Chuck Jones, Gary Larson
Feline-person (meet my teenage mutant paranoid cat)
Occasional cook
Politically astute and aware
Movie-goer (I get paid to go to movies!)
Bicyclist, skier, walker
Avid swimmer, beach buff
Watcher of sunsets, waterfalls, rain, fires, & especially thundersnows
Eager to try anything at least once
Extremely open minded about everything

The world is our oyster, and I love seafood!—Let's go!

Physical: SWM, 31, 5'9" 185 lbs, Teddy Bear
Intellectual: Techno-whiz, walking encyclopedia
Emotional: Yup (Myers-Briggs INTP)
Planet of Origin: Good question

BEFORE YOU PLACE YOUR AD

Now that you have a picture of what constitutes personal ads that will leap off the page, you can begin to write your own, keeping these tips in mind:

Read one hundred ads written by both genders before you start writing. Figure out what appeals to you and try to capture that spirit.

Purchase a few major magazines with ads (*Boston* magazine, *New York* magazine, *The Washingtonian*, *The New York Review of Books*, and *Los Angeles* magazine). See if you can't scoop a few good ideas from someone who lives two thousand miles from you. After all, you aren't competing with him.

To know where to place your ad, read all local periodicals that carry ads. Put yours where most of the people you'd like to meet are placing theirs.

Don't write your ad when you feel dateless and desperate. IT WILL SHOW!! Wait until you feel tickled and adventurous.

Hold on to your ad for one week after you've written it so that you can make changes.

Be as flexible in terms of your requirements as you can.

Don't forget to indicate the gender you are and the gender you seek.

Get feedback by showing your ad to friends of the gender you hope to attract—before you place it.

If you get stuck writing, don't give up. Ask your friends to help you.

Recognize that it may take you more than one try to write the ad you're meant to write. If it doesn't work out as you'd hoped the first time, refine it, hone it, and try it again.

If writing your ad is hard work and you find yourself rewriting it twenty times, then you are doing it right. Don't expect to shrink your essential self into a one-inch space without a little sweat.

ASKING FOR PHOTOS

There are nice ways and less nice ways to ask for a photo in your ad. In fact, an ad that reads, "no response without photo" or "photo a must" can actually antagonize people. Why not ask nicely, as these people did:

Photo appreciated.
Thanks for your photo.
Photo?
Total picture.
Let's exchange photos.

Photo appreciated. Stick figure ok.
Photo please.
Photo preferred.

SENDING YOUR OWN PHOTO

Invite your friend over to take *an entire thirty-six-shot roll of pictures* of you. With luck, you'll be able to live with one. Print up twenty copies. If you decide not to send a photo ever, that's fine. At least you'll have a decent one if you should change your mind. And if you meet someone wonderful on your first try, I'm certain all your relatives would like one of the nineteen pictures you have left.

Through the years, I've seen or heard of people receiving everything, from a photo that's thirty years old, to photos in the buff, to photos with a deceased spouse, to photos with an ex slashed out. One man actually sent a photo of himself lying in a hospital bed recovering after major surgery. A current, simple photo of you and you alone is perfect.

AFTER YOU'VE PLACED YOUR AD

Sit back and wait. Read the responses carefully, including between the lines. Not all great guys write like Dave Barry. Look for warmth, wit, a friendly quality, a personalized response, and realistic expectations. Then start making your calls, using these tips:

If no one is home, you may leave a message on a machine:
Hi, this is Jim. Sorry I missed you. I'll try you again or perhaps you can call me at 555-5555. I'll be there after seven tonight.
Never leave a message referring to the ads (Hi, this is Jim. You answered my ad). You don't know who will be with her when she takes her messages off the machine. You risk embarrassing her.

People who answer ads often answer a few at a time. When you reach her, identify yourself clearly:
Hi, this is Jim. I placed the personal you answered ... the one that read that I know where the best ice cream is ...

If you are nervous about making the call, write down a few key words to prompt your memory—including your name, in case you forget it.

Keep the first conversation light. Tell what you liked about his or her response to your ad. Make pleasant queries. Don't ask probing questions such as, "Where do you see yourself in ten years?"

If you don't get a sense of someone from one conversation, you can always talk more than once before making plans to meet. Say, "It's nice talking to you. I'd like to talk again before we meet. I'm sort of new to this and still a bit anxious." If someone is in such a big rush that they can't talk to you twice, I might wonder about that.

Once in a while you will be floored by a photo, call her, and know right away that this is a bad match. You may have caught her in a vile mood, so you can talk again if you want to, but, if the first conversation stinks, DON'T MAKE A DATE YET. Kevin talked to a woman and within the first five minutes she asked him if he had AIDS or herpes, told him she expected to be taken to a fancy restaurant, and told him she didn't have time to waste with bozos. In every part of your life, from your workplace to your volunteer work to the personal ads, you are bound to find a few people who are slightly "off."

IF YOU DECIDE TO MEET

Set up "The Short Date" as described in Chapter 26.

Always meet in a busy, public place during peak hours. Always supply your own transportation. Do not have a stranger pick you up at your home or office—even if he is the minister of a neighboring parish. If you are questioned about this policy or he insists that he is a nice guy, simply state that you do it this way because it allows you to be most comfortable. Don't defend it and don't dwell on it.

Carry a book, flower, or red hat that will identify you. If you tell him what you are wearing in advance you won't be able to change your mind one minute before you are supposed to walk out the door.

When you are paying to place a personal, there is a natural urge to know you got your money's worth, but here again, let's redefine it so it makes more sense for our lives. No matter how much you pay or how deeply you want to find love, remember: A personal ad can increase your odds, but it can't promise romance. Instead of moping about your half-full glass, appreciate it.

Frame: It's a waste of time if I don't fall in love.
Reframe: It's a bigger waste to sit home feeling lonely waiting for something to happen.

Frame: It's a waste of time and money if I don't concentrate on finding the right person.
Reframe: It's a waste of time if I don't concentrate on being the right person.

Frame: Do I have room in my life for a mediocre date?
Reframe: Do I have room in my life for a new friend?

Frame: Another wasted evening.
Reframe: Another step closer.

If you do decide to try placing a personal ad, keep these last considerations in mind:

It can be a wonderful way to find dates, but *continue* to look on your own. You'll have more options than ever.

Be willing to date G.U.'s (geographically undesirables). Don't limit yourself.

The week your ad is scheduled to appear, you'll probably bump into someone on the street corner and fall in love because life is just that way.

Guerrilla Dating Technology

| ARE YOU EXPERIENCED? |

Once this question was asked by Jimi Hendrix. Today it refers to whether or not you are taking advantage of Guerrilla Dating Technology, the most recent scientific advances that can be harnessed to upgrade your dating profile. Yes, you can go high-tech to develop relationships and lasso dates.

GUERRILLA DATING TECHNOLOGY BY FAX

Why not woo someone by leaving great messages for him or her on the office fax? Ross said that he used to arrive at work on his night shift and find kooky notes from a woman friend who evolved into a romantic interest when he found himself utterly charmed by her creativity. Remember, faxes are rarely private. Your message can and probably will be read by everyone with access to the machine. If you aren't quite brave enough yet to call her and ask for a date:

Fax a valentine

Fax a "Cathy" comic strip that reminds you of her.

Fax a riddle and tell him he has to call you to get the answer.

Fax a coupon entitling her to a shoulder rub.

Fax a newspaper article you thought might be useful to her.

Fax a photo of your finest feature.

Fax a formal invitation for dinner.

Fax anything that will make him laugh.

Fax a coupon entitling him to one free car wash.

GUERRILLA DATING TECHNOLOGY
BY ANSWERING MACHINE

Sometimes you purposefully call to talk to someone, and the best advice is to hang up if you get a machine. If it's someone whom you aren't sure about, this may be wiser because if he doesn't call back, you spend the next week wondering if:

- he is out of town
- you forgot to leave your number
- his machine is broken
- he's got a woman you didn't know about
- she's not interested in you
- he was interested until you left that In-case-you-didn't-know-yet-I'm-a-Bozo message

This kind of wondering can ruin your week.

However, if you *know* she likes you, the machine can be a tantalizing flirting tool. You can purposely call when you know she's not home. Leave her a playful message once in a while:

I want you to know that if you continue to insist on looking so good, I will not be responsible for being unable to fight the urge to kiss you.

Tell her the jig's up (in your best Edward G. Robinson voice), and you want a date.

When was the last time she watched the sunset? Invite her on an after-work picnic where you promise to share your secret recipe for tuna fish.

Always identify yourself, because you don't want to scare someone, but be creative about how you do it.

Make sure you don't use technological connections to *avoid* making real ones. It can be easy to avoid life with faxes and answering machines by communicating through them to the exclusion of actually talking to someone.

COMPUTER DATING SERVICES

You can always take advantage of the high technology that's been around awhile by joining a computer dating service, but keep certain facts in mind. Computers don't have human characteristics. They accept and organize raw data without the human touch, so be careful about how you describe yourself on a computer dating form. If you say on your form that you like Indian food, the computer will spit out everyone in your age range who likes Indian food too. Do you really think you can form a relationship on the basis of a shared love for lamb vindaloo? Spend time filling in that application to present as much of who you are as can be done. Computers match by fact, not intuition.

Buyer Beware

Some computer dating services are national chains looking to pump out volume. They claim thousands of members. Ask how many live in your zip code area before you fork over the dough. If two-thirds of their members live in Los Angeles, that won't help you if you live in Washington, D.C. In addition, over the years I've heard complaints about them being quite impersonal. Call the Better Business Bureau before joining. Do your homework in checking them out. You may prefer a video service where you match yourself, or an introduction service where a trained consultant, preferably with a human services background, matches you on the basis of fact *and* intuition.

1-900-DUPED

The one high-tech dating machine that I do not recommend is any telephone chat line that charges you by the minute. By this, I do not mean telephone personals where you read an ad and respond by leaving a message on a phone line, but the ads that promise instantaneous results because other single adults will be on conference calls with you. Many of these services "invent" their own "single people" to keep you talking on the phone at length. They actually hire people who pretend to be available. Unless you are just plain looking to get off, expect to be ripped off.

PULLING OUT ALL THE STOPS

In the nineties, people dare to use all kinds of ways to tell each other they're out there. One San Francisco woman in her late forties rented a billboard. She put her name, color photo, and phone on it. She received calls from as far away as Australia, when a soldier who was visiting California waited until he got home so his entire platoon could call her. The enthusiasm and support for her zaniness were unanimous.

Are you wondering how many good men she met? *Tons.*

A lonely Long Island widower used his souped-up van to find a wife. He put a sign in the back window stating that he was looking for love. The secondary benefit was that he stopped speeding so women would have time to write down his phone number. Yet another man put a sign on his lawn, much like your traditional FOR SALE sign, stating he was seeking a wife. He found one.

What could you try that's somewhere between leaving a friendly hello on an answering machine and putting your kisser on a Frisco freeway? How can you martial technology to playfully send the message that you are available and fun to be with?

Tick tock.
Tick tock.
Tick Tock.
Are You Experienced?

IV.

Countermoves: Maneuvers for When the Tables Are Turned

12

How to Spot When Someone's Making a Move on You

It was pouring rain when Leon pulled his car into the department store parking lot. He was thinking about work. Things were shaky since they brought in that image consultant who hated Leon's colorful, wide ties. Leon was shopping to find something more "corporate"—a word that filled him with nightmares of having turned into his father. Next they'd be telling him to shave off his beard and lose twenty pounds. He emerged from his dented Subaru, opened his big black umbrella, and walked to the front door. As he entered the store he passed a woman with no umbrella who was huddled in the corner holding several packages. She looked straight at him and said in a soft, even voice, "Excuse me. I believe you're going the wrong way." He looked at her, not quite understanding. She went on, "I was looking for a handsome man with an umbrella who was leaving the store." Leon nodded politely and walked upstairs to pick out a tie. Five minutes later, it hit him:

He had an umbrella.
She didn't.
She was asking him to walk her to her car.

He hadn't picked up on her request until it was too late. To make matters worse, she was adorable. Leon, who considered himself chronically depressed to begin with, really felt depressed now.

Priscilla attended a big party given by an ex-roommate. The ex-roommate had also invited Priscilla's ex-boyfriend's ex-girlfriend, and, although Priscilla didn't want to care about this, she couldn't help but notice everyone the ex-girlfriend spoke to and every hors d'oeuvre she ate. When Tom walked over to Priscilla and started a conversation about whitewater rafting, Priscilla was half listening and half peeking at her ex-rival. When Tom told Priscilla he was going whitewater rafting that weekend and wondered if she'd ever thought about trying it, she mumbled vaguely. Eventually, Tom gave up and walked off. Ten minutes later Priscilla hit her forehead, finally realizing that Tom was leading up to asking her to join him, and she was too preoccupied to get it. She felt too embarrassed to approach him again. Anyway, he had already moved on to guess who.

Part of brushing up your skills of engagement means devoting thought to more effective methods of picking up on other people's pickups. You won't always be the one to make the first move, and if you feel that you've gone home and kicked yourself one time too many, like Leon and Priscilla, read on.

Pay Attention

Years ago, I read an interview with the late great short-story writer Raymond Carver. Asked what advice he could offer young writers, he said he would give the same advice that his idol, Anton Chekov, had offered young writers many years ago. The Russian playwright said that the best thing he could tell young writers to do was to "Pay Attention."

Sometimes simple advice is the hardest to follow. What, exactly, should you be paying attention to? There are billions of fragments of sensory input and stimulation being thrown your way every nanosecond, not to mention uncountable memories and associations stirred by everything you see, taste, smell, and hear.

For example, suppose as Leon enters this shopping mall, he passes a bakery and smells fresh bread. The bread reminds him of the bread his grandmother used to bake. When he was twelve his grandmother died. He misses her and the unconditional love she gave him. No one is giving him unconditional love lately and so the smell of freshly baked bread is bittersweet for him. Suddenly he's sad. All this in a fraction of a second, and without his even being aware of it.

Noticing how the sudden sadness is connected to the bread is one way of paying attention by directing your focus inward. This consists of recognizing your thoughts, feelings, sensations, associations, wishes, and fears. Directing your focus inward is a goal of an aware life, *but* you can overdo it:

> You're overdoing it when you are so focused on your internal experience that you repeatedly miss the actual concrete events that are taking place around you.

As Leon directs his attention inward, he fails to notice an adorable woman asking for his help in keeping dry as she makes her way through the drizzling parking lot. As Priscilla devotes her attention to a relationship in her past, she misses out on the guy in front of her face.

Paying attention means achieving a balance that includes an active focus on events as well as an investigation of feelings. Preoccupation with thoughts and feelings can blind you to events and actually end up as a defense against meeting people. The simple and seemingly simplistic advice to pay attention can have and has had a positive and resounding effect on many people.

Many of us walk around preoccupied with thoughts that have nothing to do with our present environment. Like Leon, we worry, rethink, obsess, plan, strategize, imagine, conjure, devise, invent, formulate, design, and modify as we walk. Sometimes we also chew gum.

As you start paying attention, you will notice things that you didn't notice before, including friendliness on the part of others. The world hasn't changed, but you've displayed your receptivity. This, in and of itself, can bring out the best in others by giving them courage to talk to you.

Here is the model of how it usually works:

Paying Attention leads to
↓
Increased Awareness leads to
↓
Increased Receptivity leads to
↓
Increased Possibilities leads to
↓
Increased Connections

Here's an example. Nancy came in for the fourth session of a small group workshop and gleefully told a story. She was waiting for the elevator when a man walked in with a large bag. Normally, if Nancy were feeling really good, she might have said, "Nice day" and hoped he had the interest to turn that into more. On this day, she saw the name of a popular electronics store on the bag. So she asked him what was in it. When he told her, they entered into a discussion about the contents. They spoke because, out of all the stimuli Nancy could have paid attention to, from the anxiety of being in the presence of a nice-looking guy to the fact she hadn't bothered to eat lunch and was starving, she chose to focus on the concrete detail of a shopping bag—a path to engaging him.

PAYING ATTENTION TO NONVERBAL ATTITUDE

The following is designed to offer you a general picture of nonverbal communication. This model is adapted from a Peer Counselor Training Manual developed at New York City's John Jay College of Criminal Justice. As you pay attention to the body language of others, you aren't sitting on a grand jury trying to ascertain fact. You're merely looking at a guide for what different gestures can mean. It isn't written in stone. For example, when people are nervous about meeting someone new, body parts can tense defensively. Also, one feeling does not exclude another. In the course of five minutes, many attitudes may be conveyed by clustering gestures together.

Attitudes Communicated Nonverbally

Anxiety: Not looking at you
Throat-clearing
Fidgeting
Hands covering mouth
Tugging at clothes
Jingling things in pockets
Ear-tugging
Hand-wringing
Sweating
Glances at exit door
Taking a step back

Anxious behavior signals discomfort. This we know. What's harder to know is whether the discomfort means that the anxious person wants to leave or whether it means that he or she wants to get closer. People fidget for both reasons. Here are key points to look for with an initially anxious person:

Does he try to keep the conversation going?
Are his glances repeated?
Is he smiling in spite of the anxious movements?

If these things are true, keep the conversation going and see if he doesn't calm down. He may be making an unskilled move on you, but a move nonetheless. Try and break the ice.

Open to you: Open body posture
Smiling
Repeated glances

These are signals of receptivity that could suggest she wants to know you better. Pursue the conversation by seeking out common ground. Warmly smile back.

Interested in you: Leaning forward
Facing you directly
Tilting head
Sitting on edge of chair
Hand-to-face gestures
Smiling
Grooming behavior
Moistening lips
Playing with hair or clothes
Picking lint off your jacket
Touching you briefly
Tapping foot to music as you pass

Do something! It doesn't get any clearer than this.

Defensive: Arms crossed at chest
Hands in fists
Pointing

Defensive body posture is a protective device, an emotional armor of sorts. When someone does these things, keep your voice low and soothing, using a tone that tells her you won't bite.

Evaluating: Hand-to-face gestures
Stroking chin
Head tilted
Holding glasses' earpiece in mouth
Pacing
Hand to bridge of nose
Squinting

This person appears to be hanging on your every word. Mix talking and active listening. He wants to hear more. Chances are, he'll be asking you the questions.

Frustrated: Running hands through hair
Rubbing back of neck
Wringing hands
Clenching hands
Kicking imaginary objects on ground

Something's definitely bugging him. You have four choices:

1. Offer him two Tylenol
2. Make a disclosure such as, "You seem distracted."
3. Ask a question: "Is everything okay?"
4. Move on.

**Territorially
Dominant:** Feet up
Leaning against object
Moving things around on table
Standing or leaning over you
Hands behind head, leaning back

He feels more comfortable when he's in control. He may be interested, but has difficulty letting go of his guard. Talk for fifteen minutes and see if he loosens up.

> Try a little Holmesian detective work. Wherever you may be, observe duos and try to figure out their attitudes about each other based on this list, your general instincts, and a little observation. Note what you see. Continue to observe for another few minutes as a way of checking out your accuracy. Was your initial guess correct? Did subsequent behavior substantiate your guess?

TRUST YOUR INSTINCTS

Once you start paying attention, critical self-doubts may rear their ugly heads. You'll worry if you see and hear what you *think* you see and hear. A new question will be raised:

How do I know if someone is just being friendly or really flirting?

This is the question people ask, but the real question is this:

What would happen if I trusted my instincts when I thought someone liked me, did something about it, and then found out I was wrong?

We have elaborate fantasies about this that parallel our fears of discovering we've approached a married person:

- I'd feel ashamed.
- The ground would open up and I would be sucked in.
- Everyone would see and I'd be marked for life.
- I could not recover.
- It would probably appear in a pilot newspaper column, "Loser of the Week."

You can't ignore such fantasies by pretending they aren't there, but you can replace them with more realistic, appropriate, and rational thinking:

- I may momentarily wish the ground would open up, but I don't recall that ever happening. Short of flirting over the San Andreas Fault, it won't happen now either.
- People have their own concerns and marking me for life is unlikely to be a top priority for them.
- Sure, it stings, but I'm being a little dramatic when I state that I couldn't recover.
- It was even worse when I let my chances pass me by.
- Life is full of little losses and big losses. On a scale of one to ten this is small.

If your imaginings are more than moodiness, current upset, or the result of a bad day, it might be wise to seek professional help to clarify why unreturned interest feels so damaging. Help is there for you, but sometimes it cannot be found in a book.

IT'S NOT WORTH IT

Another response to the question "What would happen?" is that it's not worth it to find out. Frequently, to avoid mistakes, people play it safe. Not only does playing it safe fail to protect you, but you pay the additional price of never knowing the truth—always wondering "what if," and kicking yourself . . . again. *It is the chronic wondering "what if" that chips away at you.*

Sometimes disappointment comes from not having the courage to act, rather than from guessing wrong. There are many ways to make a good guess. All of the Guerrilla Dating Tactics you are learning can be performed by others on you. Eye contact, smiling, asking personal questions, hanging around, complimenting, etc. . . . these are all ways to show interest, but none of them guarantee that someone wants to date you. Unless you are willing to take a risk and go with your instincts that someone is making a move on you, you may never find out. As one workshop participant stated, "If I have to have regrets in my life, let them be for things I've done instead of for things I haven't done."

PATIENCE AND TOLERATING UNCERTAINTY

Sometimes, the most accurate indicator of interest is time. If you give an exchange time to blossom, you may find something wonderful. Many people want to go from seed to rose in ten seconds and end up stepping on their own toes. After nine years of exploring how relationships begin, whether you pick up on someone's interest or initiate, I return over and over to what all beginnings have in common:

Starting something depends on the ability to tolerate uncertainty.

If you need immediate answers to spare yourself discomfort, you may stunt the exchange. If you think this means putting yourself on the line, you're right. So look at it this way: You've already put yourself on the line and had success with things that brought you to this point. Every time you started a new job, registered for a class, asked someone out on a date, or gave your friend advice, you were putting yourself on the line. Turning around and flashing a smile at someone you already think is flashing the hairy eyeball at you is just one more gesture in a long lifetime of successfully being on the line.

RECAP

To recap, here's how to spot if someone is making a move on you:

- Pay Attention
- Observe
- Trust Your Instincts
- Have Patience
- Tolerate Uncertainty

This will help you know when someone makes a first move. But remember, that move may swallow all his or her courage. The *next move* will be all yours.

Terminal Buddyhood: How to Get Past Being Pals

DIANE: I just don't want it to get too heavy. I feel really overloaded.... I just can't have a social life right now.
LLOYD: Don't worry about it. We're just having coffee. We'll be anti-social.
DIANE: We'll be friends?
LLOYD: Yeah, with potential.
   —From the movie *Say Anything*

If you end up buddy-buddy when you really want to be more, you're not alone. For a variety of reasons, many people cultivate friendship when that's not really what is in their hearts. Here are the five most common reasons:

- You only wanted to be friends, but after you got to know him, you changed your mind. You just haven't figured out how to change *his* mind.

- You knew you wanted more than a friendship, but sensing she wanted to be buddies, you decided it was better than nothing.

- He was in a relationship. It's over, but you don't know when, if, or how to let him know you want to change course.

- You were in a relationship. It's over. Maybe she'll think you're a creep for coming on.

- Offering friendship is a pattern for you. You're chronically certain that someone who will accept you as a friend will reject you as a lover.

In everything we read about solid time-tested coupledom, the resounding cry is that they are best friends. Couples don't appear to be disheartened by this shift from a sexual love to what in Latin is called "philia," or friendly love. It is a natural progression over time. How this happens can be observed at the moment when a couple who is getting married stands at the altar. When they first connect, the entire world revolves around them as they symbolically stand and face each other. At some point the ceremony ends. They turn out hand in hand and face the world. Though they will continue to face each other in private moments, more and more of their time will be spent facing the world.

Most of the time we face the world on our own. What we seem to need most to survive the rigors of our lives is ongoing support from our most intimate and best friend. Paul Newman and Joanne Woodward are among the many couples who state that their friendship is the glue that has held them together through the years.

Have hope

We used to assume that the sexual part of a romance came first. Often it does. Still, if you've seen *When Harry Met Sally . . . ,* you recognize that friendship can undergo a metamorphosis and turn sexy. In the nineties, with everyone claiming that it's getting harder to find an only slightly neurotic suitable significant other, people are more open to reevaluating existing relationships. Every day, every single day in this world, friends take the leap into lovers. Songs are composed about it. Books are written about it. Best of all, it really happens.

In addition to hope, you need patience. If you've spent time becoming friends, trusting each other, and feeling safe with each other, you'll also need time to figure ways to maintain what you already have while adding a new dimension. Often people don't think through how to choose the right opportunity to broach the subject. They get impatient or anxious and jump into action without clarifying for themselves what they are doing and how to do it best. Let's review how other people have set the stage the Guerrilla-Dating-Tactic way.

Reframing friendship the direct way

Howard dreamed about Nadine. They'd been close friends for months, and he wasn't certain exactly when the shift in feelings came, but he knew he had to at least try and do something about it. He decided to take her to dinner and find a way to tell her without making a heavy scene about it. As they were speaking about something else entirely, he stopped her and said, "My feelings for you are changing. I value our friendship, and I can remain a good friend to you if that's all you want. You don't have to say anything now, but I wanted to tell you how I feel."

Howard has not asked Nadine to respond immediately. He's giving her time to think. He's told her how he feels, and that no matter what, he wants to be her friend. In this way, he is doing his best to protect the friendship while gently making his feelings known.

REFRAMING FRIENDSHIP THE SNEAKY WAY

Carol met Bobby at work. He was a manufacturer's rep who lived out of town and attended monthly sales meetings in her company's conference room. He didn't work with her, but she had some uncomfortable feelings that if she approached him, people might talk.

Carol's reason for choosing to have Bobby as a friend rather than pursuing a romance was situational. She was unclear about how it could affect her job. Nonetheless, she was friendly, and Bobby responded in kind.

One night she invited him to join her regular office crew at a nearby Happy Hour. They began to make this a tradition when he was in town, often with several other people from the office, and occasionally she invited the group to her home for dinner.

On one or two occasions when everyone else was tied up, Bobby came to her home for dinner alone. They began to share many stories with each other. They discovered that they had both gotten braces put on their teeth as adults. The ordeal of having a metal mouth in their mid-thirties gave them lots in common and cemented their bond.

One night Carol learned that a friend from the office had been injured in a car accident. Upset, she automatically lifted the phone to call Bobby. When she hung up, she knew her feelings for him had changed. Over the next few times she saw him, she remained uncertain as to how he felt about her. Did he see her as just a friend? In all their time together, he'd never made a move.

Carol realized that she needed to do something different, but first she had to figure out what she had set up in the first place. She saw a few elements of the relationship clearly: She was *always* available when Bobby came to town, even when she had no notice.

She never discussed the men in her life with Bobby, and, as far as she knew, he assumed there weren't any. She had gone out of her way to frame herself for Bobby as a pal.

Carol decided to shake up his image of her through the use of friendly competition for her time and affection. The only problem was that, at present, there wasn't any. Resolutely, she invented some.

She figured that if her idea didn't work, she could always just come right out and tell Bobby how she felt, but first she wanted to reduce the risk factor by giving him the chance to meet her halfway. She would show him that she was in demand, thus reframing herself in Bobby's eyes from "gal-pal Carol" to "act-now-or-miss-your-chance Carol."

The next time Bobby came to town, Carol invited him for dinner, but instead of wearing what she'd worn all day at work as she had always done in the past, she changed into jeans and a thin white tee shirt. Doesn't sound sexy, but that's not the point. More than trying to be sexy, Carol was trying to change from the business-Carol whom Bobby had come to know to the leisure-Carol with life beyond the job.

There's just one other little thing. When Bobby arrived, there were one dozen long-stemmed red roses on Carol's table with a card that read, "Love, Tony." Bobby looked at Carol, looked at the roses, looked at Carol again.

He asked about the flowers. She smiled mischievously and said little. Bobby tilted his head and said, "Carol, I guess there's a side of you I don't know." When he left that evening, he was still wondering. And he couldn't stop thinking about her. What Bobby never knew until much later was that Carol sent the flowers to herself.

Are you tempted to say she tricked him? And that if she tricked him here, she'll trick him again? All she wanted was for him to notice her as a woman. She *is* a woman—a good, strong, healthy woman with ample capacity to be his loving partner and a hefty set of nerves about coming right out and saying so.

Sneaky Variation

Nicky is a quiet accountant who had a crush on Georgia, a big rock 'n' roll fan who worked in his office building. They seemed to be exact opposites. She was slightly outrageous while he was the accountant's accountant. But there was another side of Nicky dying to bust out—a side that secretly longed for the kind of spontaneous fun Georgia seemed to have wherever she went. He was much too shy to show his real feelings. He had lunch with her once in a while—she always made him laugh. Often she spoke of how her relationships with men were more like death by elevator Muzak than anything else she could think of. One day, when he was reading the paper, he saw an ad that said that one of her favorite bands was coming to town. A few days before the concert he invited her to join him as his guest. He told her that he had a date who cancelled on him. He knew how much Georgia loved the band, so he thought she might like to accompany him.

Of course, this wasn't true. He bought those tickets with *Georgia on his mind.*

Georgia said yes. When he picked her up, he wore bright red suspenders and a dashing hat. He was funny. He was charming. He invited her out for champagne and strawberries after the concert, and he never once brought up the subject of spreadsheets. Georgia had to check her bright blue contact lenses twice. Was this the same old Nicky who obsessed about debits and credits? Was this the same old Nicky whose eyes took on that hypnotic glaze at the mention of balancing his checkbook? Maybe she had misjudged him after all.

Carol and Nicky were sneaky. They used fiction to get noticed in new ways and get a little of the sexy attention they wanted. They didn't mope, and they didn't wait and hope someone would do it for them. Instead they pulled out all the stops. Applaud them for it, because all they wanted was a chance.

DOWNSIDE

Like any other relationship, sometimes a friendship-turned-romance turns sour. Helen and Rob, two longtime friends, became lovers and found that things didn't gel for them in this new format like they had when they were just friends attending Celtics games together. They sat down and painfully talked it through. They talked about resuming their friendship, but Helen felt unable to pick up where they had left off. She told Rob she needed time out, and that she would call him when she felt ready. Two months later, she called with two tickets to a game. She was ready to accept what had happened, and she missed her dearest friend.

The other downside is that you can make your feelings clear and be told that they are not reciprocated. This hurts, and you'll need to make decisions about how you want to handle it.

David had a friend like that named Lila. Lila told David that he was the nicest guy she knew, much nicer than her ratty boyfriend. She and David talked frequently—especially when her love life was rockiest. Finally David asked her if she might not dump the mook and date him. Lila explained that she didn't think of David in that way. At some point, although David continued to care for Lila, he decided that he needed to talk to her less—at least until he got his own social life going. He explained his reasons for backing off temporarily, hoping Lila would understand.

REFRAMING FRIENDSHIP THE DIRECTLY SNEAKY WAY

Nellie and Hector had been friends for over a year. When they met, Hector was dating Rosa, but all reports were that it was a rocky relationship destined to dissolve. So Nellie did the only thing that made sense. She waited . . . and waited. At some point after Hector and Rosa broke up, friends were giving a Christmas party. Nellie was invited, and she knew Hector would be there. She spent the afternoon trying to think up a way to intrigue him. She spent the first half of the evening dawdling near the mistletoe, waiting for Hector to walk by.

When he did, she grabbed him and kissed him. Her next step was to act as if it was his idea in the first place.

She looked down at him (he was two inches shorter than she) and said, "Er . . . did you kiss me to kiss me, or did you *kiss* me?"

Hector, without missing a beat, replied, "I'm not sure. Maybe we better try it again and find out."

After several more attempts at trying to figure it out, they still weren't sure and made plans to further investigate on Saturday night.

Sneaky but Direct Variation

In Chapter One, I talked about Guerrilla Dating Tactic Flower Power. In addition to flirtatious flower talk, flowers have been used by many workshop participants as a way to let a pal know that you want to do more than pal around. Eric had a crush on his pal Violet. He transformed their relationship by tucking a sprig of violets under her automobile windshield after midnight. When she came out to her car in the morning, she found them, along with a note that said, "To my best friend and most special person—Love, Eric." Violet stood flabbergasted in her driveway. Some time after that, the romance bloomed.

Since you are unlikely to find yourself with a woman named Violet, you may wish to consider other types of flowers. Remember that red roses signify love and yellow roses signify friendship. You may wish to give him one of each. If you keep with the spirit of Guerrilla Dating Tactics you will find ways to get those flowers into the most *unlikely* places for the greatest surprise effect and the greatest fun.

For example:

Stick some in his gym bag.
Send a spring bouquet to her office.
Drop a dahlia in her mailbox.
Train your schnauzer to offer them.

Another Sneaky but Direct Variation

Renee, a divorced, fortyish Montreal resident, had a male friend, Thomas, she had known since she was eighteen. They both liked each other and got together on and off over the years, but had never, ever thought of each other as more than that. Approximately three years earlier, the friendship sort of fizzled out, and they hadn't seen each other since then. One week, Renee placed a personal ad in a local paper. When she called one of the men to talk and set up a first date, she realized from the conversation that it was Thomas, but he did not know it was Renee. She only gave her first name, and, apparently because they hadn't spoken in a while, he didn't recognize her voice. Renee decided not to tell him, but to surprise him. She showed up at the restaurant dressed to the nines. He was surprised to see her and told her that he wished he could have a drink with her, but he was waiting for a date. Renee asked him how he'd met the woman. It hit him and he burst out laughing. Renee and Thomas had a fabulous evening together.

REFRAMING FRIENDSHIP THE SEXY WAY

In one Washington, D.C. workshop a very likeable man named Lloyd introduced himself to the group. He told us that he was a musician who played the upright bass in a band. He worked in various nightclubs, a job that prevented him from ever being able to connect with a nice woman. I had to laugh because that is exactly how I met my fiancé, a jazz bassist with the unlikely name of Boots. I met him in the place they tell you that you can never meet someone nice . . . a bar.

I was with a woman friend who was admiring Boots. She kept saying, "Isn't he cute?" I kept saying, "Where . . . where . . . show me . . . I don't see it."

After I requested the Duke Ellington song "Prelude to a Kiss," he came over to our table and sat down. He invited both of us to lunch. On the day he called, my friend was unavailable so I went alone. We had a pleasant meal, split the bill as friends do, and that was about it. I lived in Boston at that time, and he lived in Manhattan. Several times a year, he appeared in Boston, and he called me—usually when he was waiting for the train to go home. Once in a great while I stopped in to visit and hear him play. One night when he finished playing, I noticed he ordered a Remy Martin from the bar. I asked him about it, and he said it was his favorite drink.

Life passed without sparks. But over the year, as I got to know him better, he got cuter. I began not just to like him, but to *like* him. One day I saw an advertisement that a band he played with would be appearing nearby. I went to the liquor store and bought a bottle of Remy. On the given night I put on a semi-obvious, but not too obvious, outfit and went to hear him. I stayed to the very end. He had a few friends there, but I hung out until they all left. It reminds me of the old saying about success: Success belongs to those who keep plugging away after everyone else has quit.

It was 1:00 A.M. when I took a deep breath and invited him out for a nightcap. He said, "It's after hours. Every place is already closed." I moved in a little closer and said, "That's okay. I've got a bottle of Remy Martin in my apartment with your name on it."

At my apartment, I waited close to an hour for him to kiss me. Finally I kissed him. He couldn't get *out* of my apartment fast enough.

The relationship got off to a shaky start. I'd been terrified of making a play for him, and more than once I was almost sorry I'd done it. He told me a few times that he just wasn't sure he wanted to get involved with me.

Years later, he reversed his story, saying he had planned the whole thing. He knew I wasn't attracted to him so he spent a year working on me to get me interested. Then he spent six months acting ambivalent about being with me to cement my falling in love with him. He could be making it all up, but either way, it worked.

RISKS

You don't need anyone to tell you that these things don't always work out. You know that. You do need someone to remind you that sometimes these things *do* work out. In order for them to do so, one person must take a risk. If you choose to take the kind of risk I took, by showing your direct interest in someone who has only been a friend, you need to anticipate the possible outcomes. For me, it was easier because Boots lived in another state. I knew

I wouldn't run into him everywhere I went. If you are considering making a move on a friend you work with or must see regularly, you may prefer to be a little more indirect . . . but at some point you will need to take a risk. Be gentle, truthful, and subtle. If things don't work out the way you hoped, it may be awkward for a while, but it doesn't need to end the friendship. Simply anticipate the awkward time and give your friend space to regroup. You may say you are sorry that things didn't work out the way you hoped, but as long as you didn't do something malevolent, *never, never be sorry* that you took the chance.

A DIFFERENT KIND OF STORY

In the above examples, the main reason that these people became friends was *situational*.

Because of the circumstances under which they met, they opted to be friends before anything else. Certainly, there came a point where feelings changed, and there was some agonizing over whether or not to do something about it. Certainly there were the normal fears about taking a new step. But, in the beginning, these people became friends first because that is what made sense at the time.

Sometimes the problem in getting together is different. It is based on character. This occurs when, because of your personal temperament, you are afraid to show your true feelings. Really, you knew right away that you wanted more than friendship, and that the other person could be available for that—but you couldn't let on how you felt. You acted like you were looking for a buddy and you got a buddy. Every moment of this terminal buddyhood eats away at you like a school of piranhas. Nonetheless, you feel paralyzed at the thought of doing something about it, and it continues this way over an excruciating period of time that could exceed months in length.

MOURNFUL HEARTBEATS

When Courtney first met Mary in the elevator of his apartment building, he was floored. She was funny and flamboyant with a wide Reubens figure, just the way he loved. Instead of asking her on a date, which is what he wanted to do, he treated her as a pal, and he got a pal. They did their laundry together. She asked his opinion on men she wanted to date, she told him when she was feeling premenstrual, and once she even called him to ask his help in choosing an outfit to wear on a first date with a new guy she'd met. As Courtney watched Mary sweep into the middle of the living room floor singing "Ta da" in her new black chemise, he felt as if his heart would break.

This was not an isolated story for Courtney. He could count many times in the past when he had played out this identical drama. In fact, he hadn't had a date with a woman in over four years.

It's easy to make wild guesses about why, but that would be a mistake. Courtney's story caused him ongoing pain, and it seemed to be greater than what most people experience. Clearly, to present himself as a suitor stirred great fears for him. A friend of his in whom he confided recommended group psychotherapy. Courtney definitely wasn't crazy, but he needed help that probably couldn't be found in a self-help book. After working with his group, Courtney slowly began to experience more confidence, until he felt more like the captain of the ship than like a passenger who forgot his Dramamine. Although Mary continued seeing her new beau, Courtney began dating and met someone through a personal ad who became his wife six months later.

If you find yourself stuck in a pattern like Courtney's, it makes sense to stop and take a closer look at it. Taking a look means exploring your patterns, and it can be initially wrenching. Not taking a look can mean going on as you have—it can hurt more in the long run.

ESTABLISH INTRIGUE

Jack was friends with Jill and told her that they might have a future together if she changed her name, because he couldn't take the ribbing. Jill responded to his wit like a cat responds to a bath. But deep inside, he believed he could change her mind. He knew Jill was an avid mystery fan. She could always be found with a whodunit tucked under her arm. He decided to bait her by creating a little mystery of his own. He mailed her a single theater ticket for a local production of *Ten Little Indians*—anonymously. His intuition told him she wouldn't be able to resist. When she arrived at the theater, guess who was sitting next to her? When she called him on the ruse, he claimed someone had sent *him* an anonymous ticket and *he* was sure that Jill had done it.

Jill softened. Jack had injected drama into the situation by making a grandstand gesture. Suddenly he wasn't ordinary old Jack anymore. Lucky for Jack that Jill didn't have the equipment at home to dust her ticket for fingerprints.

CHANGE

To reframe pure amity into something which, in the future, takes on a sexier glow, you must change something. Chances are that if you continue on your current course, the best you can hope for is a seat in the church at her wedding. If you always see him on a Tuesday, make plans to see him on a Sunday afternoon. If you're always dressed in jeans, put on your best suit. If there is always loud music, go someplace quiet. If you always meet in the library, take her to a disco.

CHANGE. DO SOMETHING DIFFERENT. Something that:
- causes him to see you in a different light
- gets him thinking about you in a different way
- lights a fire under her
- makes her stop short
- lets him know you mean business
  OR
- makes her wonder why *she* didn't think of it first

V.

Survival Strategies: How to Protect Yourself While Working Up to the First Date

Besieged by the Perpetual Turn-On: Why We Get Discouraged

You're bound to get discouraged. Part of that disappointment comes from the rigors of day-to-day life. Someone turned you down for a date, someone wasn't who you thought they were . . . these things happen. Another often overlooked part of why we get discouraged is built deeply into the fabric of our culture. Just take a look at what we're told about romance every time we flip on the television or go to a movie.

Ninety-nine percent of television romance is doomed—all the way back to "Bonanza." For years, the members of the Cartwright family fell in love over and over again, but did we ever believe that one of them would marry, leave the Ponderosa, and live it up on his honeymoon? In each episode, the bride-to-be developed a fatal disease, a criminal record, a "presumed dead" husband who suddenly reappeared, or any jaded plot device causing the wedding to be canceled. Commitment had the life span of one episode. How did four straight, desirable guys stay single so long?

If older television shows lacked romantic reality, they had even less reality to thrust at us when it came to sex. Rob and Laura Petrie slept in separate beds. Sitcoms such as "That Girl" presented women as sexual Peter Pans, prim Madonnas playing to a studio audience of irascible censors. Even Mary Richards, in the groundbreaking "Mary Tyler Moore Show," appeared to be perennially celibate.

This isn't because Hoss, Little Joe, Mary, or Marlo were any more neurotic than the rest of us. It's because all a series wants is to survive nine seasons. To accomplish that, they give us what polls show we want. We don't *want* too much change because we're counting on main characters who won't join a cult or move to Tulsa in the middle of the season. And we don't *want* too much reality because we're watching TV to escape it. And we don't want much character growth and development . . . we sure don't want Bart Simpson to see the error of his ways.

BIG-SCREEN BLITZ

TV titillates, and movies blitz. Critics may blast a movie as unrealistic because of how it ends, but frequently the entire premise of the romance is fantasy. Suppose your friend told you that s/he had a close friend who was a:

- Tycoon who bought a hooker's time and then married her.
- Detective who launches an affair with a woman whom he believes is a homicidal maniac.
- Sculptor who maintains a romance with her dead boyfriend's spirit through a fake clairvoyant who ultimately discovers her mental powers are real.

How Romance Movies Work

Watch *Raiders of the Lost Ark* or *Alien*, and it's easy to be sucked into the excitement. No one need tell you that Nazi spirits and space monsters appear courtesy of the special effects department. You enjoy the adventure, but you don't kick yourself for not having similar adventures in your own life. Oh, sure, you might decide to take up a new risk because the movie reawakened your adventurous spirit, but at the bottom of it all, you know your life won't resemble this movie.

We know romance movies are made up too, but they work on us in a different way. There are no monsters or explosions to constantly remind us that this is a fantasy. And for most of us, our hope of finding true love is greater than our hope of finding alien forms of life. Romance movies depict love like a cliffhanger; at any moment things could fall apart as two people experience rapturous sex marked by chronic ambivalence, overcoming the obstacles, fighting for the relationship, and beating gargantuan odds to be together.

Movie romances offer dramatic premises, which we find ourselves accepting in spite of and sometimes because of a standard formula of preposterous plots:

- Two grossly mismatched people, completely unlikely to end up together, end up together.
- Two people who do cruel things to each other find out that they are torturing each other because they are in love.
- One person defends, protects, or saves the other from murder, kidnapping, monsters, or one of an array of foes or mishaps.
- One person discovers that his or her true love is:

  1. dying of an incurable disease
  2. a psychopathic killer on whose list he or she is next
  3. leading a double life that may include multiple relationships with persons of either gender

- One person relentlessly pursues another's mate, as in:
  Drama—*Gone With the Wind*
  Comedy—*The Graduate*
  Tragedy—*Fatal Attraction*
- Two people maintain their romance even though one of them is dead.

or

- Two ordinary people meet and fall in love, like *Stanley and Iris*, but the public doesn't care.

What Movies Reinforce

Movies tap longing. We long to believe in beating the odds. We long to believe that love won at such cost is destined to endure . . . but is it? What happens to the relationship five years down the road, long after the last little cameraperson has packed up her camcorder and gone on to the next shoot?

Movies reinforce the fadeout as the end, but, of course, the relationship is just beginning—it is not frozen in time. We never learn how these characters fare in daily life, and that allows us to glorify their relationship without ever applying the real test of time.

The love in romance movies is more familiar to us than the aliens in alien movies, but in most cases no more real. Sure, prostitutes resembling Julia Roberts run off every day with millionaires, but for most of us, love begins tentatively and in someplace other than a five-star hotel.

In fact, the enormity of the mismatch between Richard Gere's and Julia Roberts's characters is a barometer for the largesse of our affection for them. The more unlikely the match, the harder we root . . . sort of a romantic David and Goliath where, from a group of possible outcomes, we most value the least likely.

In the sexual arena, movies compound their fantasyland. Everywhere, naked bodies are on the rise, with characters talking about sex, obsessed with sex, and enthusiastically simulating sex. You can witness nearly all of your favorite star's moist-lipped longing as he or she writhes and groans in bed to camouflage real writhing and groaning over bad scripts. For variety, you can return home, go to sleep, wake up in the morning, and turn on one of ten talk shows and listen to real people bare their sexual dysfunctions as early as 9:00 A.M., a time when most of us *are* sexually dysfunctional.

Movie sex looks grittier than it used to, but, with few exceptions, it's no more of a replica of life. Stars with more perfect faces, bodies, and diction than ours frolic on more perfect bedding, couches, and kitchen tables than ours. One comedian recommended that we do a study of the sexual act among people who have never seen movie stars have sex. His worry was: What if we learned the sounds we make *from* watching? What if those who never watch don't know what in the world we are doing?

Movie sex is airbrushed, choreographed, rehearsed, reedited, and rewritten, and most matinee idols will tell you they needed to be photographed with a wide-angle lens. Plus, nobody sweats. In real life, even with sweat, the *last* thing we'd want during sex is for a body double to jump in and take over at the climax (unless you're truly kinky).

I love the movies. The best of them, like great literature or art, enhance our lives. I love to be transported into mind-boggling personal drama. I love to chuck the daily drudgery and borrow the David Letterman credo, which states, "Accept the premise and you'll enjoy the bit." Sometimes movies make me cry, not because of the story, but because I crave the intensity displayed in them. I want to love so deeply that I'd jump into a pit of snakes for him, or risk losing my farm so he could put up a baseball field, or become a double agent in a war zone to rescue him. I get sad that my own life will never measure up. I will never find sexual fulfillment in a gondola. I will never be redeemed from the grind. I will never live a movie.

MAINTAINING BOUNDARIES BETWEEN FILM AND LIFE

If you experience a mental blurring between what you can expect to experience from watching romance in the movies and what you can expect to experience from romance in your life, it can screw you up and leave you disappointed. The expectation of living a story worthy of a Coen brothers flick can get in the way of finding a partner.

You risk disappointment when, based on life in the movies:

- You employ unrealistic criteria for what constitutes romance and are continually disappointed in others.
- You employ unrealistic criteria for what constitutes romance and are continually disappointed in yourself.
- You're mystified when real people don't have the same responses as scripted people.
- You're disappointed when your life events aren't dramatic enough, but you miss the difference between healthy drama and a celluloid emotional roller coaster.

Enjoy the larger-than-life characters as you watch their sagas unfold, but remember:

- Reel love is not real love.
- Life is filled with lulls, awkward moments, hours of indecision, rent, office hours, leaky toilets, mixed feelings, breath mints, children from a previous marriage ... all the things that movies tend to glamorize or skip altogether.
- You don't use a double for the tough parts.
- There are no rewrites if you don't like how things turn out.

Television and the movies, as seductive as they are, don't tell the truth about love. When you're let down about how you feel with someone, when the sparks are more like blips, when you find yourself thinking, "Is that all there is?" make sure you haven't fallen victim to the long, bony arm of media magic—and mistaken it for real life.

It is only fitting that I close this chapter with a movie quote because, in addition to reminding you to live your life, I want to remind you that the life you live will be filled with paradox. In the words of Auntie Mame:

"Life is a banquet and most poor suckers are starving to death."

So turn off your TV and make plans with a friend. For tonight, anyway, don't go to the movies.

Reentering the Ranks Safely: Building a Support System

Caroline and her two best college pals (class of '83) called themselves the Three Musketeers. They traveled together, dined together, and poured their hearts out to each other. However, each of her friends has gotten married in the past two years and Caroline is still single and unattached. As recent conversations turn into debates about La Leche, Caroline has begun to feel like the only single, nonpregnant woman left in the world.

Harvey was widowed a year ago. He's not ready to date again, but he doesn't want to be alone. Anyway, he's not sure what people do on dates these days, and he feels silly at the thought of having to ask. Besides, who would he ask? His twelve-year-old son?

Anneke is shy. She knows she needs practice to bring her social skills up to par, but the thought of plunging into dating situations scares her. She's been wracking her brains to come up with something that isn't a bar, isn't a blind date, and isn't a dud.

One of the best ways to build good social skills, make new friends with minimal risk, and maintain the mental stamina that dating requires is joining a group of cohorts in the same boat you're in. Joining a group isn't exactly a Guerrilla Dating Tactic. It's more of a Guerrilla Adjustment Tactic. After all, there's always something important to be learned from others. In addition, your spirit needs replenishing because everyone has rough days. Enthusiasm wavers. And you can't get your daily requirement for emotional sustenance from Flintstone's vitamins. Life will be easier if you have a solid support group in your corner, urging you forward and cheering you on.

A supportive group is especially helpful if:

- You are coming out of a divorce and are confused about dating.
- You chronically wonder, when you meet someone, if you say and do the right thing.
- You're returning to dating after a loss.
- You lack confidence.
- People don't respond to your efforts in the way you'd hoped, and you don't know why.
- You're doing fine, but you've temporarily run out of ideas.

WHAT KIND OF GROUPS EXIST?

Nationally, adult education centers, YWCAs, YMCAs, community centers, continuing education programs, religious organizations, and private psychotherapists offer groups for single adults with a variety of purposes from building self-esteem to overcoming shyness. You can find a wild array of one-night workshops, or a long-term group that will keep you on your toes and give you something to talk about. Simply call local organizations and ask what kind of programs they offer to the general public. In addition, check listings in singles' magazines and local newspapers. Such programs are often listed in the same section that carries personal ads.

Special interest groups exist, too. If you are widowed, divorced, separated, afflicted with herpes, HIV positive, physically challenged, gay or lesbian, or have a special need, there's a group for you. You may opt for a group that welcomes everyone, or you may prefer to seek out a specialized group. In addition, there are always self-help groups such as AA, OA, ACOA, and others that are open to anyone who needs them. Although the setting certainly was not designed to perk up your social life, Larry Fortensky didn't do too bad meeting Liz Taylor at the Betty Ford Clinic.

If you choose a group with a leader, check out his or her credentials. They can vary widely. If you opt for group therapy, keep in mind that in some states, any Tom, Dick, or Harriet can hang out a shingle calling himself a psychotherapist, even if his only training is watching twenty episodes of "Dear John." Sometimes that's enough, but a licensed therapist is a better bet.

Classes as Groups

A small class delving into a subject you love is also a group. You may opt to sign up for something like that instead. Explore the Russian novel, learn how to change your spark plugs, meditate, master the art of Cajun cooking, or buy some dancing shoes to learn the Texas Two-Step. If you take a large class, or people don't seem know each other, *you can change that.* Invite everyone out for coffee or bring in donuts one night. Often times, lack of interaction stems from shyness rather than lack of interest.

Workshop participants have talked about other beneficial group experiences:

Community theaters
Amateur orchestras
Church choirs
Volunteering to cook dinners weekly at a hospice
Various charity committees
Attending your union's meetings
Local activist groups
Political campaigns
The Chamber of Commerce
Greenpeace and other environmental groups

Starting a Group

You can start your own group with the focus of making single life more user-friendly. Choose three to seven people who will be willing to commit for the duration of the group and work out the details of:

Your purpose for meeting
How often you will meet
How many weeks you want to meet
How long each meeting will be
Whether new members can join once you've started
Where you will meet (make sure you have some privacy)
Issues of confidentiality (don't leave this out)

WHY NOT SHAKE UP THE SYSTEM?

Try making brand-new acquaintances as a way to reexperience yourself, take new risks, and pull out of a rut. Here are ways that a group builds on strengths and improves your outlook.

Brainstorming and Imitating

Two heads are better than one, and ten heads can be better than two. Think of all the great ideas members can give you. Some nights steam rises as the group wracks through strategies to talk a member through a situation. Members tell you what they have tried, and, in keeping with Chapter 7, "Closely Guarded Secrets: Borrowing from the Best," you may even want to copy someone's idea. There is comfort in having so many people working on your behalf. (If the converse is true and it's very uncomfortable to have people working on your behalf, this is just as important to explore. Is it hard for you to accept undivided attention?) It is just as comforting to work on another's behalf. You often end up trying the very things you recommended for someone else.

One group problem-solving technique is what social worker Livia Policie calls Wild Problem Solving Sessions. The purpose of these sessions is to loosen up, to lighten up, and to brainstorm. Wild Problem Solving has rules:

- Generate as many ideas as possible.
- Do not comment or criticize any idea—no matter how silly or inappropriate you think it is and no matter if you've tried it already.
- Write down every single idea that is mentioned.

Instead of trying to come up with careful, rational solutions to a specific meeting dilemma, the group imagines wild solutions—the nuttier the better. Suppose you've noticed a woman in your office building whom you want to meet. You might:

- Serenade her outside her cubicle
- Drop your files when you see her in the hall
- Send someone from your office to her with a note
- Leave a bouquet of flowers on her car
- Have her name tattooed on your arm
- Send a limo to pick her up after work
- Leave a love note on her desk

- Hire a restaurant in the neighborhood to deliver lunch for two to her office, complete with strolling violinists
- Ask her to dance in the elevator
- Hire a skywriting airplane to paint her name in the sky

Imagining yourself doing wild things to meet someone may give you a great idea or it may make hello look like kid stuff, thus helping you to finally say it. And you've got a group who will ask you next week how you've fared. They'll keep you on target.

Ending Isolation

You don't need 1-900-PSYCHIC to tell you it can get lonely out there. Statistics show that there are more than eighty million single adults in the United States, but as your friends pair off, it's easy to feel as if you are the only one. The most frequent comment I get in my workshops as people share their concerns is, "I thought I was the only one who felt this way." Finding others who share your experience is a big relief. And soon people recognize that if most people in the group feel this way, people who aren't in the group probably feel this way too. Maybe others would be grateful to us for reaching out.

Permission Giving

One night in Dallas, Adele, a smart, sophisticated woman in her fifties, arrived to brush up on her flirting. During the evening, the subject of women calling men was raised. With uncharacteristic adamancy, she stated that she would never, ever, under any circumstances, in this lifetime, call a man.

The group ventured that they thought it was okay these days for women to call men. She jumped all over us, swearing that she meant what she said.

The next week we went around the room to hear what progress each person had made. When we reached Adele, she said, "I called a man and invited him for dinner." Her self-aware explanation for this radical change was, "I was looking for permission, and I got it."

What other rules had she been living by that no longer made sense for her life? What rules do you live by that are outdated and overrated? Becoming a member of a group can help you to give yourself permission to try all kinds of things that once seemed out of your range.

Role-Playing

One common group technique for trying out new ways of behaving is role-playing. Two or more people pretend they are in a situation that has been giving them trouble (such as flirting, approaching an appealing person, asking for a date). Then they act the situation out in front of the group.

I asked Penny, a truly pretty and very quiet woman, to do a flirting role-play with Jeff, a photographer. She declined, saying that she had been voted the shyest person in her high school class. I offered to make it simple. She wouldn't even have to stand up.

Jeff rose from his chair and walked to Penny. He spontaneously asked her about the logo on her T-shirt naming a well-known state park. Penny told him she often hiked there, and Jeff was surprised because he had been hiking there only that past Sunday. Penny perked up. So had she.

Penny's end of the conversation was fluid and relaxed, yet when it was over, she explained that she was shaking every minute that she talked. The group pointed out that her anxiety was not noticeable. Guess what:

Penny's experience of herself was vastly different from other people's experience of her.

Role-playing presented an opportunity for her to succeed at what she'd sworn she could not do. It compelled her to take another look at her assumptions about her shyness.

Other role-plays have worked differently. People who have identified themselves as slightly outgoing have come on like the love child of Joan Rivers and Howard Stern. People who have described themselves as friendly have been reticent and unavailable. An awkward role-play can be the result of performance anxiety in front of thirty people, or it can identify areas where more work is required.

Perhaps you have assumptions about yourself, relying on words that labeled you as a child:

The shy one
The moody one
The plain one

I have news for you: These may have been your labels, but they may never have reflected your true self. And even if you were once the moody one, I'll bet you've learned a lot since that

time. Do you really choose to characterize yourself with such outdated classifications?

Monitoring Progress

A common complaint is that people are overworked and don't
have time for a social life. (A social life is something that you must
set time you don't have aside for.) Working with a group is a positive way of reflecting on your progress on a regular basis. You
won't be able to indicate disbelief that you've let another year
slide by. And whenever you get the urge to say you aren't getting
anywhere, you'll have the benefit of testing that remark on the
group to see if they agree with you. Chances are they'll point out
the progress they've seen you make.

Maintaining Humor

One afternoon in Hartford, Hamid and Shirley tried a role-
play where two people were trying to meet in a supermarket at
the checkout line. Even though they knew in advance that neither
would reject the other, they had trouble getting started. Both stood
in complete silence for minutes. Finally Hamid peered into Shirley's imaginary grocery cart and said, "I see you bought eight cans
of cat food."

Shirley answered, "Yes."

Again what seemed like minutes passed. Finally, Hamid
looked at her earnestly and said, "Got a cat?"

It spoke to the clumsy remarks we all make, and the group
couldn't stop laughing. We'd all been there. Groups remind you
that life is filled with icebreaking laughs if you know how to find
them *and* if you can trust yourself enough to let them be funny.

Change and Growth

A group provides a protective environment in which to change
and grow.

Groups support change by offering:

- the opportunity to learn other points of view and to compare
  them to your own
- the chance to test out new ways of relating to others
- acknowledgment of your strengths and where you want to
  work on yourself

MASTER MIND

If you don't want to be in a group or you can't find a suitable one in your area, try the Master Mind, a technique I learned about from my artist friend Mary Jones.

Choose one person who could also benefit from ongoing support and make a pact. Once a month (or more frequently if you choose) each of you gets one half hour of complete, undivided attention. Once a month you call Mary, and you talk. Mary listens with complete attention to your needs. She responds, but only in terms of you. During your Master Mind, she cannot raise issues of her own. She empathizes, offers constructive advice, and mentally pampers you. Mary is entitled to her own Master Mind at another time and on another day.

This technique is a nice boost, offering relief, empathy, and an ear during tough times. It can also be used as a concentrated work session where you map out what's happened and what you plan to do about it.

CONCLUSION

I once heard the following tale touted as an old Korean fable. Years later, I heard it again as an old Talmudic fable. I think this story has been around because it points out so beautifully the benefits of working together.

A revered old Korean man died and went to heaven. The gatekeeper welcomed him and said that he would hold an esteemed place in keeping with his vast accomplishments. The old man replied that since he was already accepted into heaven, he wanted the opportunity to consider hell. The gatekeeper was surprised, but he granted the request.

He led the old man through the center of the earth. Blood-curdling screams could be heard coming from behind a door. Slowly, the gatekeeper opened it to reveal a long banquet table filled with the most fabulous array of delicious foods. Delicacies from many lands sat on large silver platters. The eight dinner guests who sat at the table were emaciated and howling with an eternal ravenous hunger. Each person held a pair of four-foot-long chopsticks. Each could pick up food from a platter on the far side of the table, but when they tried to turn the chopsticks around to eat the food, it could not be done. No matter how they contorted their bodies, the chopsticks were too long to get the food into their mouths.

The old man shuddered and asked to return to heaven ASAP. He was led down a long hall to a wide door. This time the sounds coming from behind it were contented gurgles. When the door was opened, it showed the same-sized banquet table, the same delicious food, *and* identical four-foot-long chopsticks.

The eight people seated around the table were enthusiastically feeding each other.

CHAPTER 16

Undaunted and Undented: Survival Strategies for Rejection

The best hitter in baseball fails nearly 70 percent of the time; the best team in baseball loses between 40 and 60 games during a season. At the end of the day, as Earl Weaver sagely observed, "We gotta go out and do this again tomorrow." ... Life is like baseball at least this much: It isn't about winning, it's about learning to live with losing.
—GEORGE ROBINSON AND CHARLES SALZBERG,
"On a Clear Day They Could See Seventh Place"
Baseball's Worst Teams

My friend Donna heard that the best place to meet men was in a bar during baseball playoffs, so in 1986, during the notorious Mets/Red Sox World Series, we headed for a local bar to watch the sixth game on TV.

As we walked down the street, Donna rehearsed the sum total of her baseball expertise. Over and over, with varying inflections, she uttered, "Nice play."

Upon our arrival, we saw approximately one hundred men and three women. Now came the hard part. Donna and I split up. I sat at the bar with the goal of smiling at five men. Twenty minutes passed, with me smiling at *no* men. I managed to avoid everyone by obsessively focusing on which men I *shouldn't* smile at and why:

Too young
Too old
Married
Not if I hadn't dated in a decade
Why was I born?
What was I doing here?

Seated across from me at the bar was a young man around twenty wearing a grubby T-shirt and a Red Sox cap. A large tuft of hair stuck out at a ninety-degree angle from the opening in the back of the cap. *I hate it when that tuft of hair sticks out.*

All of a sudden he looked at me and smiled, winning me over immediately. Without hesitation, I smiled back.

"No, not you," he said as he stuck out his finger and pointed behind me. "Her."

I turned around to see a very pretty woman smiling back at him. It was the first time in my entire life that I had returned a smile without first checking all around me to prevent just this occurrence.

I felt like I was drowning as the "No not you's" of my life flashed before my eyes:

No Not You for the volleyball team
No Not You for the prom
No Not You for the raise

I felt ashamed. It became apparent to me that the depth of my hurt was not in keeping with the facts. In fact, it had nothing to do with the facts: A sloppy guy, fifteen years younger (okay, nineteen years) than I am, was smiling at a woman standing behind me when I thought he was smiling at me.

"No" HURTS

"No" hurts. Even when it comes from someone we wouldn't date on a bet. We always want to be the one to say it. We never want to be the one to hear it.

THE TWO PARTS OF "NO"

One part of my response was the immediate disappointment of being turned down. Perhaps this guy only liked tall brunettes, something I'll never be, or women under twenty-five, something I'll never be again. I can comfort myself by saying that it was his loss. It is even possible to talk myself into the possibility that he wasn't saying no to me so much as he was saying yes to her. Maybe he knew her. Maybe he was as big a lug as he appeared, and I was better off for not having met him. When I take a critical look at what happened, I can organize it into something I can live with. And if that doesn't work, I can call him names—that always helps.

But hurt is an emotion, not a rational, logical progression. It has a cumulative effect in our lives. We tend to bundle all the no's we've ever heard together into one painful ganglia, waiting to be poked. Each rejection hits the on switch of a lifetime of memories of rejections. Every single one of us knows the feeling of not getting what we wanted to get.

REJECTING YOURSELF

If you try to avoid rejection by avoiding risks, you probably know already that it doesn't work. Sure, you may not be giving an outsider the chance to turn you down, but you don't have to do that. You've already been rejected by the most important person in your world. You have *rejected yourself first*.

You are rejecting yourself before anyone else has the chance when you:

- Close yourself off to experiences to feel protected
- Stay home every night watching "Leave it to Beaver" reruns
- Hide your interest in someone
- Expect someone else to make the first move
- Think this should be easy and walk away when it isn't
- Dress in unflattering ways
- Anticipate and expect rejection when you do meet new people
- Expect to feel great about yourself all the time and mentally deride yourself when you aren't operating at 100 percent

Before your spot deep in the self-rejecting trenches becomes a second home, read on.

GUERRILLA PROTECTION TACTICS

The way to manage rejection is rarely by remaining passive and doing nothing, unless that is truly, in your heart of hearts, what you want to do. However, you can protect yourself with the dating equivalent of training wheels.

Guerrilla Protection Tactics are steps that lie between complete passivity and asking for a date. Just as with real training wheels, you start off by taking smaller risks on smoother pavement. They prepare you to answer the question:

What can you do when you've had your eye on someone and discover that what you thought was a returned gaze was actually a contact lens malfunction?

You Are: On friendly terms
Guerrilla Protection Tactic: Ask for help with something neutral

Louise took a fancy to Fred during a cooking class at an adult education center. Although he was happy to help her knead dough for her Irish soda bread recipe, he never asked for a date. Each week she found out more about him, including his self-described audiophile status and many other interests he held dear.

Louise wanted to dump the cookbook and preheat Fred's oven in her own way, but not at the risk of being rejected. She decided to tell Fred that she was about to choose new stereo speakers. As he was an expert in the field, she wondered if he might accompany her to the department store to help her pick out a pair in the hundred-dollar price range. After he stopped laughing and recommended she buy a used megaphone for that price, he agreed to go.

Why This Could Work
This gave Louise a chance to meet Fred on new turf. She had invited him out, but in both of their eyes it wasn't a date. If they spent the afternoon together and he still wasn't responding, Louise might choose not to pursue this after all. Though it would still sting a bit, it wouldn't feel like a rejection—more like something that just didn't work out.

How You Can Use It
You can always opt to begin with the low-risk method of getting to know someone. Rather than asking for a formal date, you can make suggestions about a small way to spend time together and wait to see how that goes. Relationships evolve. Spending more time with someone on a non-date is one way to assess if an invitation for a date is in order.

You are: In a singles environment
Guerrilla Protection Tactic: Group insulation

Carl met Edie at a singles party. He couldn't tell if she'd go out with him, and he was afraid to ask. Rather than let her slip away, he used a technique that had worked for him in the past. He invited her to join him and his friends to go out for pizza after the party.

Why This Could Work

Carl has the chance to talk more without having to make all the conversation. He can try to figure out Edie without having to be smooth and quick-witted at every moment because he has friends to pick up the slack.

How You Can Use It

One week in New Haven, a woman who took my workshop told me she had been referred by her friend Dee, who had attended a workshop in Washington, D.C. She related a story about what had happened to Dee during my class.

Dee sat next to a cute man who told us that he had just moved from another city. He stated he was kind of lonely and hadn't made many friends yet. I was telling people to seize the moment, so Dee turned to this guy, told him that she was having a wine and cheese party that Friday, and invited him to attend.

The truth was that Dee wasn't having a party, and now she had to run around planning one. She managed to pull together a nice crowd. However, she had failed to tell this guy that her interest in him was special, and she also never thought to tell her friends. A short while into the party, he met one of her friends and the two of them left together.

Remember: If you have a special interest in someone and you use the group Guerrilla Dating Tactic, you'd better at least tell your friends about it.

THE GUERRILLA COMEBACK

You may decide to counter a hasty "no" with a comeback that will give you a second chance.

You are: Approaching someone
Guerrilla Comeback Tactic: Offering a second chance to loosen up

Lydia was taking the subway home when she noticed a tall man reading the new Robert Ludlum thriller. She asked him about it, and he answered her curtly. Lydia waited a moment and then said, "It sounds as if you've had a hard day."

It worked. It had been a hard day, he told her, and he related every gruesome detail for the next twenty stops.

Why This Can Work

Sometimes it takes two tries. We all have irritable, closed moods. We're thinking about our own lives instead of what's happening out there. If you show interest in someone's irritable, closed moods, it can have the effect of drawing them out.

By the way, take it from Lydia—don't ask if someone's had a hard day unless you're prepared to hear the answer, the whole answer, and nothing but the answer.

GUERRILLA PROTECTION TACTICS AND SAFETY

In her one-woman show, *The Search for Signs of Intelligent Life in the Universe*, written by Jane Wagner, Lily Tomlin called reality "a collective hunch." Safety is a similar concept. It's a shared set of perceptions and rules that we rely on to protect us from a chaotic, unsafe world. These rules don't always work even if you follow each one to a tee.

Rather than alarming you, the lack of safety can invigorate you. Since no matter what you do or don't do, outcomes are unpredictable, why not try what you want to try? The number of risks that you are willing to take make success more possible, not less possible. In addition, taking risks gives you options. You are not limited to whatever fate tosses your way.

Real Safety

Real safety comes from inside—from the ongoing process of developing and maintaining a belief system about who you are. What you want is a self that isn't dependent on acceptance by others in order to be maintained. This self is a tree. It can get rained on, swept by hurricanes, and even be the favorite territorial marker of the neighborhood canine community, but the core is strong and protected by a nice coat of bark.

You need a coat of bark. And you need it in less than the hundred years it took the tree to get it. In many other ways you protect yourself automatically without giving it much thought. You wouldn't go out for dinner without a few bucks in your pocket, thus leaving yourself unprotected against being forced to wash dishes because you can't pay the bill. When the sky is dark, you grab your umbrella. You have all the information you need to protect yourself in the external world.

Have you given thought to protecting your internal world? If you're anything like the rest of us, that part of your education has been overlooked.

When I began to type this section I accidentally made a typo and wrote refarming instead of reframing. It struck me that I might not be off base in pursuing that word.

Putting yourself out there can be likened to growing a garden. You plant the seeds. Sometimes there's a drought and sometimes it rains too much. Your seeds don't grow. At other times, the wind snaps and what you thought would be a tomato turns out to be a green pepper—or a tiger lily.

Remember: No matter what happens, one thing is sure: If you don't plant the seeds, you always get zip.

SEVEN STRATEGIES FOR REVIVING YOURSELF WHEN YOU GET ZIP

Talk About It

Keeping secrets about rejection is like swallowing Drāno. It eats away at you from the inside, causing massive internal corrosion. Tell a friend about your "Dweeb of the Month" award. He may have a story that beats yours hands down. Or she may remind you that the other person was the Dweeb, not you.

When I got zapped by Mr. Hairtuft, I told my workshop about it the next week. It was more contagious than the common cold—*and* more common than the common cold. We shared stories that had us laughing in the aisle by:

- Relieving the burden by sharing it
- Finding someone worse off
- Discovering a great story couched in a painful moment
- Surviving to tell the gruesome tale

Remember: Part of keeping yourself together is recognizing that you are isolated only if you choose isolation.

Identify Rudeness When You Meet It

In every part of life there are clods wearing invisible rudeness sandwich boards across their fronts and rears. When this person rankles you on the job, it may disconcert you at first, but you realize in time that it's them being rude, not you. You didn't do anything to warrant such behavior.

Do the same thing when scoping new dates. There is a difference between being unresponsive and being unfriendly. If someone is unresponsive, you may choose to either pass on them or give them time. If someone is unfriendly (which means actively unkind in word or deed), you can say so long and walk away . . . physically and mentally. Don't take on the responsibility of their thoughtlessness.

Peter was at a dance and approached a woman standing alone. He asked her if she wanted to dance. She didn't even bother to say no. She just turned around and walked away.

There are few excuses for her behavior, and Peter needed to remind himself that such unkindness is a rare occurrence that reflects her problems, not his. It may take many self-reminders. That's okay, because the alternative is feeling low all night.

Return to Rational Self-Talk

When you are rejected, say the following kinds of things. Say them firmly. When you feel you've said them enough, say them one more time.

This reminds me of other hurts. In and of itself, what happened wasn't so bad. I can live with it.

I hate when this happens, but it will pass in a few minutes.

I'm going to give myself time to bounce back. I can be proud of that because once upon a time it took years to bounce back. This is small potatoes.

Maintain perspective on the rejection. Don't let it grow from a dinghy into the *Titanic*, unless you know *all* the words to "Nearer My God to Thee."

Take Time Out

Rejection is the ouch that Curad hasn't made a bandage for. At a dance or party, where you don't want to lose the whole evening to an unkind word, take twenty minutes to feel better. Take a brief walk, get another soda, go talk to a friend. Involve yourself in something that will take your mind off what happened. Some people hurl themselves back into the throes immediately. That's fine if you are that type, but don't worry if you aren't that type. Do it your own way, but don't let yourself become absorbed with the rejection and slink off into a corner like a consumptive field mouse.

Borrow the Wisdom of Others

At the end of my workshops I always ask group members if they have any words of wisdom that have helped them through tough times. Here are a few of my favorites:

- Develop a silicon attitude: Let it all roll off your back.
- Every no brings you closer to a yes.
- If you feel like a loser for taking a chance, ask yourself this question: What did I lose?
- Imagine that you are a ray of sunshine trying to melt an ice cube.
- Role-play rejection with a friend so you won't be thrown by it.
- It's better to be one for ten than zero for zero.
- Think how you felt when you did nothing instead.

Practice the First Five Techniques

Reframing rejection takes ongoing practice and takes time to integrate into your life. You can be successful at dealing with it with one person and later find yourself sliding back into old habits. Keep reminding yourself and keep trying. Don't beat yourself up if, once in a while, it clips you in the jugular.

Long-Term Practice

When I first began teaching my workshops in Boston, I decided to smile at everyone I saw in the halls, in a cheery but not too cheery fashion. Sometimes people smiled back and other times I was completely ignored.

The first time a guy looked at me as if I were a carrier of the bubonic plague or, possibly, the river rat herself, I asked myself what I'd done wrong. I worried that I looked like one of the three witches in *Macbeth.* I kept expecting someone to ask where my cauldron was.

Though part of me wanted to stop smiling, I wasn't in a position to do it. How would it be if the instructor of a class on meeting people was a grim reaper? I forced myself to keep on smiling no matter what. Eventually I realized that some people are easily friendly, some aren't, some probably don't like the way I look, some think I'm cute . . . but along the way, something changed:

> When people didn't smile back, I used to ask myself, "What's wrong with me?" Today, when they don't smile back I ask myself, "What's wrong with them?"

I no longer jumped to assume complete responsibility for their responses.

A FINAL NOTE

I wish I could tell you that if you diligently practice diffusing rejection by moving in and among the ideas offered here, it won't hurt you. It wouldn't be the truth for you, and it's not the truth for me. But you can bounce back sooner when you refuse to be a willing partner. After all, do you really want to give that much power to someone who just passed over the best thing that would have happened to them that day?

VI.

Coopting Internal and External Conflict: Late-Night Thoughts on Preparing to Date

17

Equal Partners:
Who Pays for Dinner

Frank, an adjunct professor of music at a New York college, invited Ruby, a Wall Street secretary, out for a drink. The server brought the tab to their table, but Ruby didn't make a move. Frank paid for the drinks and said cheerfully to Ruby, "The next round's on you."

Ruby blanched. It was clear to Frank that no one had ever said anything like that to her before. He felt as if he had landed from a neighboring planet and taken an alien out. Her response mystified him.

Yet he said nothing.

The rest of the evening Frank felt like he was bench-pressing with a slipped disc. The subject of the drinks and another date were never raised again.

Darlene, a managing editor for a major magazine, ran into a different problem when the check came and Trevor, an account executive she met at a friend's party, immediately picked it up. Darlene responded with, "I'd really like to share this." Trevor quickly said, "No. I've got it." Darlene countered by saying, "Oh no. I want to do this."

She was thinking, "I really like him. I want to show him how much by sharing the bill." He was thinking, "She doesn't like me. She doesn't want to feel like she owes me anything."

They had no language to discuss it. They never went out again.

Henri and Lola also lost something with potential to silence. She really liked him, although he was much shorter than she. It didn't bother her at all. Lola had a good job and was still living with her parents. Henri was just beginning to sell his art. They went out on three dates. On all three dates, Lola never offered to share or pay ... not even the tip. One evening, the bill sat in the middle of the table for a full hour before Henri ended up reaching for it. He began to feel irritated with her assumption that he would pay.

Lola was doing what she'd always done. It never even occurred to her that he might feel differently.

Henri never said a word. He just stopped calling.

When I ask workshop participants to list dating concerns, this one always appears:

On a first date, who pays for what?

True, we've come a long way. But when it comes to a date, how equal is equal? Should men and women split the bill or take turns paying?

Considering that, by a shrinking margin, men earn more, do we adjust the bill accordingly? Perhaps we could bring a calculator on our dates—your gross adjusted income divided by dinner for two at Enrico's divided by an order of Chicken Vesuvio and a glass of red wine equals $14.63 plus tax and parking. That may sound fair, but it sure doesn't sound romantic.

Deciphering who pays and how to do it gracefully is, in part, symbolic of larger concerns that encompass how men and women interact. In the dating arena, we're trying, generally in a date-by-date way, to reinvent rituals and/or traditions of dating that are no longer functional. Unlike the cast-iron roles our parents assumed (or we assumed in the past), this can mean that two people who have vastly different beliefs about men, women, and money may end up sitting across from each other on a date.

The easiest dates are the ones where you are in tacit agreement. Or where you make several stops and comfortably take turns. Or where you both feel so relaxed with each other that you figure it out together. Most couples come around to a satisfactory way of paying for dates by the time they've gone out a few times. It's on that first date, when trying to make a good impression, that people are likely to withhold responses to what might be a touchy situation. The very nature of a first date is such that two people usually don't know each other well. We are about as relaxed as a turkey on the second Thursday in November.

THE BALANCE OF POWER

New dating rituals reflect the changing balance of power. And we all know that money is power. In fact, in couples therapy, money issues come in on top as the biggest problem area.

Money can have tremendous meaning for two people on a date. As women become a more recognized part of the work force, it's logical for them to assume some of the economic burden of dating. It's logical, but for some of us it goes against the training of a lifetime. Some women, eminently comfortable negotiating a labor contract or piloting a 747, are uncomfortable reaching for the tab. Some men who have spent years racking up costly credit-card statements by spending more than they can afford on dates still shift uncomfortably when a woman reaches for her wallet.

THE OLDEN DAYS

When I dated in the sixties, in a small town far from the feminist movement, we had a strict code of how things got done, which I learned from my mother who dated in the forties.

1. The man pays
2. You repay him with
   a. a kiss (in the forties)
   b. a French kiss (in the sixties)
3. The more expensive the dinner, the more he expects you to put out.
4. After three dates, you
   a. invite him over and cook him a meal.
   b. purchase a small token of your affection, such as a Spiedel money clip or cuff links
5. If he invites you to a drive-in, put the complete works of Shakespeare in your pants. Since you were unable to get through that, maybe he won't be able to either.

Certainly, such arrangements are outdated. Today we have many more choices. When we talk about new ways to pay the check, we are talking about new ways to share the balance of power. Carrying the power for two can be just as great a burden as giving all your power away.

Here are some situations frequently presented in workshops as the kind of dilemmas that come up over and over again.

CAN I HELP YOU WITH THAT?

Derek says he hates it when he reaches for the check and a woman says, "Can I help you with that?" He says he doesn't need help, although he might value a cash contribution. He says that framing the question in this way makes him feel that the woman doesn't want to help, but thinks she should.

If she wanted to pay her way, she'd say, "I'd like to split it," "I want to share that with you," or "Here's my portion."

CREDIT CARDS

Alison says she is always ready to pull out cash if the guy pulls out cash, but if he pulls out a credit card, she lets him pay. It's just too complicated to figure out how to share a credit card payment. However, she says, "Thank you for treating me. It's my turn next time."

Frank disagrees. Even if he pulls out his credit card (because he's cash-light that evening), he appreciates it if a woman offers to pay her share. He says that pulling out a card is not a clear sign that he wants to pay 100 percent.

I INVITED YOU

Michelle believes that whoever asks is the one who offers to pay. When she invites a man to dinner, she plans on paying. If he reaches for his wallet, she tells him she invited him and wants to treat him.

Michelle knows that different men have different feelings about this. She tries to get a sense about them by raising the subject during the meal. She introduces the story of a friend who experienced a difficult time with this. She states that lately this has been a confusing subject for her too. This generally leads to a discussion that allows both people to begin to share their views comfortably because they are talking about someone else.

It's great to be treated, to have someone pay every last cent, right down to the tip. I think it's generous, friendly, and, with someone you like, romantic. It's just as romantic to treat . . . to not let him touch a wallet all evening. If you've never been the one who pays for the date, you may be surprised at how strong and sexy it can make you feel. Myth has it that men expect sexual favors if they pay a woman's way. I wonder if the truth could be that paying, in and of itself, is an aphrodisiac.

DISPARATE INCOMES

Carla earns more than twice as much as Jay. She's used to the finer restaurants, but when she invites Jay to one, *she makes sure he knows in advance that it's her treat.* Otherwise she fears his pride might get in the way of his good time. He'd feel awkward nixing her choice, yet it's way out of his price range even if they split the bill. Letting him know when the plans are made that she intends to pay makes it easier on both of them.

I've personally been in this situation more than once. A new man in my life invited me out to a fancy place that I couldn't afford on my own. All night I wondered if I should offer to split the bill, knowing it would be a hardship on me. It's much smoother when someone says, "I'd like to treat you to dinner" if that's what they plan on doing. (If I'd known that in advance, I wouldn't have ordered cinnamon toast.)

COMFORT BEFORE POLITICS

Bennie waits until the check comes and sees what feels comfortable. He doesn't feel that the policy on the first meal together needs to be written in stone, because it is an ongoing process. He checks out the situation before he decides on the most comfortable way to proceed.

GUERRILLA FINANCIAL TACTICS

It is a mistake to think that there is one right way to handle who pays what. On a first date, comfort is what counts. Being equal partners is not contingent on one dinner check. If you think you like someone, maintaining flexibility early on makes sense, even if:

- He insists on paying, and that's not your style.
- She excuses herself to the Ladies Room when the bill comes.
- He assumes you'll kick in half when he invited you and such a thought never even crossed your mind.
- She grabs the check when you'd planned to grab it.

Here's how to open a dialogue about it.

The check has just arrived:
Your goal: is to decide what to do about it together because you'd like to split it.
Guerrilla Financial Tactic: "Here's the check. How do you want to handle this?"

Many people will readily offer to pay half. Some will fidget. I know of at least one woman who won't bat an eye when she says, "I want you to pay." What you are saying when you use this Guerrilla Financial Tactic is that payment for the date is an active decision that the two of you will make. However, you may be with a woman who has never thought of dating as a two-person decision-making process. Her past experience may be that the man always pays. If you like her and you really want to see her again, even if she seems to take it for granted that you will pay, then you may decide to pay now, talk later.

When you get to know her a little better and you are both feeling more comfortable, say, "I enjoy being with you so much, and I want to spend more time together. I've been used to taking turns treating or splitting the check for dinner. It seems as if you do these things another way, and I thought it might be helpful if we could both talk about our feelings on that subject." Then give her the opportunity to do so, without criticism or judgment. When she's had the time she needs to amplify her thinking, tell her your thinking on the matter. Surely a comfortable arrangement can be worked out.

The check has just arrived.
Your goal: is to treat tonight, but not forever.
Guerrilla Financial Tactic: "Tonight, I'd like to treat."

While many people will happily say thank you and let it go at that, some will insist on chipping in or paying themselves. If you really like him, let him pay now, and you can talk about it later. As you come to know each other better, you can say, "It's fun to treat you to dinner. I enjoy doing it. It seems as though you aren't as comfortable with the thought of that as I am, so I hoped we could talk about it. I'd sure like to know your thoughts on the matter." Then let him tell you his thoughts. Maybe he's not used to it. Maybe he thinks it makes him look like a wimp. Reassure him that it is something he can learn to enjoy from time to time, just as you have learned to enjoy it with him. Encourage him to consider the idea of letting you express your caring and your independence in this way.

WHEN THINGS AREN'T GOING SMOOTHLY

Once in a while, no matter how thoughtful you've tried to be about the check, you'll get the impression that your date has other ideas. The only way to salvage the situation is to raise the subject:

I noticed that you seemed uncomfortable when I suggested that:

- I pay for dinner
- We split the dinner check
- You buy me dinner

I realize that people think differently about this. Why don't you tell me your thoughts, so I can understand how you see it. I'd like to also tell you what I was thinking.

Now you have a chance to clear the matter up. However, you can't please all the people all the time. No matter what you do, someone may think you're cheap, controlling, macho, nutty, wimpy, bitchy, or one of a thousand other slurs. Know in your heart that you've done what you can. Don't start jumping through hoops on date one if it doesn't seem to be enough because by date three the hoops just get smaller.

THE BEST WAY TO HANDLE THE CHECK

After listening to thousands of adults struggle, wonder, and argue about this stuff, I've come to the only conclusion that seems to make sense for the vast majority, regardless of their personal preferences in this matter.

Whenever possible, the best time to handle who will pay is when you make the date.

WHEN YOU ARE TREATING, TRY THESE:

- I'd like to treat you to dinner one night next week.
- I just heard about a great new pasta restaurant. Would you join me as my guest next Thursday?

You'll have a good idea immediately as to how he feels about this.

WHEN YOU WANT TO GO DUTCH, TRY THESE:

- Let's buy each other dinner. You pay for mine and I'll pay for yours.
- Want to have dinner? Let's find someplace we can both afford.

In keeping with the theme of Guerrilla Dating Tactics and the element of surprise, deciding to go dutch before dinner can actually foster a dashing romantic opportunity. If you really like her, when the check comes, *grab it* and say: "I know we were going dutch, but I had so much fun that I really want to get this."

C H A P T E R 18

The Hamlet Syndrome: I Came, I Saw, I Thought About It for Three Acts

COACH: I wish there was some way we could go back.
CHRISTINE: Funny, I was wishing there was some way we
could go forward.
—an episode of the television sitcom "Coach" in which
Coach and Christine discuss their recent break-up

DO YOU KNOW ANY OF THESE PEOPLE?

Three-Date Sue

She's a whiz at getting dates. Divorced for one year, Sue wonders where all the fuss about locating available men comes from. She attracts more than her share wherever she goes. She wouldn't admit it to you (because you might hate her), but she averages three dates per week.

But she never gets past the third date.

Ready Eddie

Eddie is an open book about his yearning to be in a relationship. When you go out with him, it is the first thing you will hear out of his lips. He is tired of dating and eager to settle down and start a family. He's played the field all his life, but at forty-two he's ready for more. He'll look you straight in the eye and tell you so. And even though you're convinced he had as much fun as you did, you never hear from him again.

Polly the Postponer

After a dateless year, Polly decided to relocate to Boston—where the men were. Three weeks before she was scheduled to move, she began a torrid romance with someone she met at a party. Bad timing. No sooner did she get to Boston than she read that the ratio of women to men there was three to one. Too much competition.

A friend recommended that Polly move to Austin, Texas, saying that it was filled with available men. One month before the movers were coming, Polly fell in love. She moved anyway. Several dreary months with a few bad dates went by when she turned on a talk show that recommended that single women move to Alaska.

Sue, Eddie, and Polly suffer from full-blown cases of the Hamlet Syndrome, the umbrella for neurotic ambivalence that leaves you executing soliloquies instead of dialogues. Ambivalence means having multiple thoughts about the same thing that result in wavering opinions. Hamlet is a classic example of ambivalence gone wild—a man tortured by the inability to make decisions.

In moderation, ambivalence is a healthy sign of intelligence that is apparent in the many ways we can think about the same thing. It provides the opportunity to explore a variety of scenarios and fantasize outcomes without taking any action. It appears nearly everywhere in our lives.

Take something as simple as choosing dinner off a restaurant menu. Some people can't order until they know what everyone else is ordering. Some people always wish they'd picked something else and will feel that way no matter what they choose. Some people order things they know they shouldn't have and end up feeling guilty all day. Others make a choice, then spend the meal picking food off your plate. As we factor cost, calories, mood, time, and whether our choice will fit what others are eating, we are caught in one of the most common exercises in ambivalence.

UNDERSTANDING AMBIVALENT DATES

The ambivalence that your dates may experience about you can be the reason you are zonked with mixed messages and the thwack, thwack, thwack of confusion. It is important to consider what is going on with Sue, Eddie, and Polly. Otherwise, if you become involved with one of them, you risk erroneously blaming yourself for the inability to connect when, really, there would be little you could do to change their present behavior. Each one of them has a different dilemma on their table.

Time-Limited Ambivalence: Sue

When you hear that Sue never gets past the third date, you might guess she's so fussy that no one could ever please her. Or perhaps she does something stupid with each person over and over again. In Sue's case, neither of these guesses are true. Sue doesn't lose interest, and she has never once pulled an obnoxious Jerry Lewis routine on a date. It's just that the third date is the point when she discovers that she's dating a person who comes complete with quirks of his own. Does she really want to take on his oddities, she asks herself? Can she be bothered with making something work that promises to be less than perfect? The answer is always no.

As stated above, Sue was divorced a year ago. She has demonstrated the capacity to form and maintain a relationship in the past. She hasn't quite recovered from that hurt, but she isn't in touch with that as an issue. Her mind believes that she is ready to try again.

Her gut rejects everyone as imperfect.

One day her mind and her gut will concur that she is sufficiently healed and ready for new risks. At that point she will begin to date in a more serious fashion. Until then, nothing will feel worth pursuing.

Chronic Ambivalence: Eddie

Someone like Eddie can be painful to date because he thinks he means what he says. When he takes your hand and tells you that he is delighted that he found you, he means it. In fact, he comes on stronger and sooner than most people.

While he talks the language of someone who wants a relationship, he demonstrates a terrible way of trying to get it. He disappears. If you call him, he is vague, unavailable, or on the other line. He'll promise to return your call, but he won't. And yes, your suspicions are probably right. He's playing out the same scenario with others.

You may doubt reality. You were certain that you both had fun. Well, you're right. The fact that you did have fun is the reason you'll never hear from him again. His ambivalence about relationships is played out in that he never lets himself get close enough to find out what could happen. He likes 'em and leaves 'em because he is afraid to love them.

Eddie is charming, but he has a track record that shows a dearth of connections with one person. He views women as interchangeable—all wonderful. The fantasy of settling down thrills him, but the reality of relating one-on-one terrifies him.

Approach/Avoidance Ambivalence: Polly

Polly can't *be* in her life. Romance only makes sense for her when it is an idea—when she is pursuing it. Therefore, she must constantly move around looking for an environment where it can happen. While she lives somewhere, she is inaccessible. Only when she knows she is leaving can she be free enough to get attached.

Polly can't tolerate the anxiety of a permanent relationship. She copes by orchestrating a life in which romance is temporary, with a dramatic built-in escape.

Polly thinks it's a coincidence that she falls in love before skipping town. She thinks it's chance that she lives hundreds of miles away from any guy she ever really cared about. Polly's fear of love (and the possibility of losing it) drives her to keep moving. She seeks a fantasy and leaves the breathing, loving man behind.

What a disappointment to date people who are not in touch with their own ambivalent feelings. Things seems to start off so well that it's hard to accept how quickly they fall apart. Please don't make the mistake of blaming yourself for why things didn't pan out. It's not your fault, but you do need a framework in which to think about it so you don't end up feeling used. And now to the important question:

Can you ever win over someone who has a severe case of the Hamlet Syndrome? Maybe, if:

- You are a habitual rescuer
- You can direct the person into counseling
- You can tolerate the hot/cold feelings you'll get from them
- You can hang on long enough for them to become attached to you
- You can live like a Ping-Pong ball

If so, you may be able to help him/her develop the desire to make a lasting connection.

Then again, you may not.

MILDER FORMS OF DATING AMBIVALENCE

I have certainly dated an Eddie or two in my life and spent a few weeks completely confused about what happened. I've also struggled with my own ambivalence about men I've met.

Dating ambivalence comes with the territory. Perhaps you aren't sure if you want to ask a certain person out or whether he or she is worth a second date. Perhaps you had a good time, but don't know if you feel ready to enter a relationship. If these things happen occasionally, they are no big deal. We rarely are 100 percent certain of our feelings toward those we've known all our lives—not even our own parents or siblings—so why would we be certain of our feelings toward someone we've recently met?

However, if you're seldom sure about whether or not to ask someone out, if you're always thinking things through instead of acting, if you find that your ambivalence is a very old story, if you ultimately talk yourself out of every idea you have, you may want to give it further consideration. If your overly oscillating thoughts impede your chances of getting something going, you're a definite nominee for this affliction.

If you're ambivalent about where you stand, take this quiz.

I don't know whether or not I want to date someone.

___Often ___Sometimes ___Rarely

After asking for or accepting a date, I have second or third thoughts. They don't let up, and I begin to dread the date.

___Often ___Sometimes ___Rarely

After one date, even though it was fun, I don't know if I want a second date. It could go either way. I don't seem to care.

___Often ___Sometimes ___Rarely

As soon as I begin to like someone, I want to bolt.

___Often ___Sometimes ___Rarely

When someone whom I like begins to talk about "us," I sweat buckets.

___Often ___Sometimes ___Rarely

My good feelings about someone die quickly—almost as quickly as they appear.

___Often ___Sometimes ___Rarely

If most of your answers fall into the Sometimes/Rarely categories, you are experiencing the usual levels of ambivalence that come with the uncertainty of dating. However, if you find yourself answering Often to more than two of these questions, you may wish to probe your thinking.

Here are six steps to begin learning more about your own ambivalent feelings.

Ask Yourself What Might Be The Source

Sources of the Hamlet Syndrome can range from early childhood traumas to more recent hurtful events such as divorce. The general theme of your past experience would have to do with something unpleasant that happened when you trusted someone. It could be as ancient as a parent who was not available when you needed them or as recent as a spouse who broke your heart.

Of course, there's no way to be certain of the source of your ambivalence. All you can do is see what strikes a chord that rings true for you. You can ask yourself two questions:

When have you had these same feelings in the past?
Who do you think has had these feelings about you?

Answering these questions may point you in the direction of giving you food for thought. Self-knowledge leaves the healthy mind in a better place than you were when you lacked understanding.

Separate Past From Present

People aren't born with mixed and confusing thoughts about others. This is something that accumulates through life experience. We develop ambivalence as a coping mechanism to fend off fears about being hurt.

However, once you have tried exploring the historical origins of your ambivalence, you need to separate past events from your present situation so that you build your repertoire of ways to contend with the uncertainties of life. It's difficult to move past our history and do this, but most things worth having are difficult.

When you find yourself with mixed feelings about someone new, remind yourself that you still have very little information about this person. Tell yourself that although being with him stirs uncomfortable feelings that remind you of something that has happened in the past, he is actually someone you've just met. Unless his behavior is unacceptable, you may need more time to get to know him better before making a decision about him. While he may remind you of someone else, he is not that other person. If you treat him like someone who will let you down, you risk creating a self-fulfilling prophecy.

ONE DAY AT A TIME

While it's natural to take quantum leaps in time and fantasize what might come of this, for now, try and stay in the present and see if it is possible to enjoy your time with this person.

Allow for the awkwardness and discomfort, but don't try to turn him into your history or your future. Jumping to the past or the future is often a method people use to cover up the tension of the present. After all, if you can decide the outcome, you won't have to stick around for the main event. I will be talking further about this subject in Chapter 22.

WHEN IN DOUBT, TRY AGAIN

If she's mean to you, don't see her again. If, instead, you know that you tend toward ambivalence and premature judgments, then think about how long it's taken you to get past that point in the past, and see her that many times plus two (if she'll see you). Don't pretend to be offering more than friendship, and don't make promises you aren't sure you can keep. It's fine, as you get to know her, to tell her that you haven't been the best at getting something going and sustaining it. It's not the kind of thing you should be announcing before your first dinner together, because that would make many people feel irritated and defensive. But why not openly let her know where she stands? It gives her the chance to decide whether she wants to proceed or not, and it will save you some guilty feelings if you break it off.

MONITOR YOUR FEELINGS

If you are overly ambivalent, recognize that you have developed this as a way to protect yourself from what you fear can hurt you. Strive to look for what would be there if the mixed feelings were taken away, and you may begin to touch on what you are really afraid of. Don't be angry with yourself for your mixed feelings. They are serving an important function for you or they wouldn't be there. Be as gentle in exploring your ambivalence as you would be with a really close friend.

Do the best you can to maintain a dialogue with your feelings. One common feeling that ambivalent people experience on a date is boredom. They have difficulty tuning in and often find themselves off in another world when they have a date sitting across from the table. If this describes you and you want to work on it, ask yourself certain questions:

What is making me feel bored right now?
What is the most boring thing about this person?
What is the least boring?

See if you can focus on bringing out the most interesting and spontaneous parts of the person you are with as an exercise in dealing with your boredom. This will demand that you focus on the conversation. You may even discover that you're having more fun than you thought.

TAKE ACTION

Without experimenting with new ways of behaving, you cannot integrate new learning and new ways of experiencing into your life. Action will help you work through your impressions, feelings, and beliefs. The key to working through an unrewarding behavior lies in doing something to change it.

Chronic ambivalence can improve simply because you stopped to take a look. You may want to talk with friends about it to find out how they have dealt with similar feelings—to reassure yourself. Take your ambivalence out of the closet. Talking about it helps. If it doesn't, consider professional guidance. Your situation needn't be permanent.

The prototype ambivalent discourse is the famous Hamlet soliloquy, "To be or not to be." After three acts of trying to figure out what to do, he is tortured with indecision, and finally he goes berserk and murders everyone, including the wrong man.

Don't you wait that long.

CHAPTER 19

Low Morale and
Battle Fatigue

It pays to know when you're worn out. Dissipated romance seekers come as close to a George Romero film as you can get without actually walking like one of the living dead. If you push yourself too far and too hard, you may find yourself increasingly irritated at having to put on a front while wrestling with the downside of mood swings. Battle fatigue can make you negative, disagreeable, and cranky. Suddenly one night, as you resist the impulse to fling your chicken tostadas at your date's head, you realize something drastic is happening.

In case you aren't sure this means you, soldier, here is a test designed to define the need for PTI, or Psychic Time Out.

Do not ignore these warning signals.
Signs of Low Morale and Battle Fatigue

You blame yourself for everything that went wrong by saying: "If only I hadn't said that, we'd still be together," or "If only I'd taken her someplace else, I would have impressed her."

I feel this way ___always ___sometimes ___rarely

You find yourself forming a relationship with a personal ad when you haven't even spoken to the person yet.
Your life insurance salesmen has such a great a voice on the phone, that you buy a new outfit and redecorate your apartment for the day he delivers the policy.

This happens to me ___frequently ___once in a while ___rarely

You find yourself feeling discouraged most of the time. You begin to believe that no matter what you do, it never pays off.

___always ___sometimes ___I'm disappointed you asked

You go on dates, but feel as if it's not really you who is there. Somehow you have the disconcerting sensation of observing yourself rather than being yourself.

This happens ___frequently ___sometimes ___are you speaking to me?

No matter what he says, it annoys you.
No matter what she asks, you find it inappropriate.

___always ___sometimes ___you have a nerve

I hate men, you think. *They just don't want commitment.*
Women can't be trusted, you tell your friends. *They use and abuse me.*

___I have a variation of this that I believe.
___Yes, I'm bitter, and I know it's a problem.
___Hisssssssssss!

You show up for the date, but forget the tickets to the concert. She comes to pick you up for the pool party and finds you dressed in a tuxedo.

This has happened ___frequently ___from time to time ___I thought the tux was fine

You don't remember a thing he said.
Your mind wanders off and you call her by your last partner's name.

___frequently ___rarely ___huh???

You're too tired to make the effort. Everything is too complicated, and makes you feel sleepy.

___always ___sometimes ___Oops. Was I snoring?

If you temporarily find yourself on a first-name basis with these symptoms, you may have a whopping case of low morale, the leading cause of battle fatigue.

There are three types of low morale. Read on to figure out which type describes you:

- Growing Pains
- Insulation by Chronic Complaint
- Fatigue: Pure and Simple

Growing Pains

Sometimes you try everything you can think of diligently, but you still haven't connected with someone. You've set a regimen for getting out, you've asked friends to fix you up, you've even made a stab at the personals. Nothing has worked. Moreover, you've dated someone who was perfect for you, but she didn't think you were perfect for her. Although you've mentally mapped out the next five years, the rest of the world doesn't react to your script.

Terrible as this feels, it is a common point of new beginnings for many people. In psychotherapy, clients often feel worse after starting treatment. When they return for their next visit and wearily state that therapy has made them feel awful, a therapist might counter, "Good. That shows you're working."

You may be at a point where you are about to "start working." If you chronically attract clods, or if you're doing everything and nothing works, you may decide to take a long, hard look at yourself. It signals new experimentation with the ways in which you meet the world. You may consider your contribution to the difficulties, and look inward for reasons instead of blaming the world.

Without minimizing how disappointing a bout of low morale can be, it can also be the best thing that's happened to you in the long run. Life is a process whereby people change and grow, but because it hurts, people rarely opt to do it until they have no other choice. People change because *they have to.* Life has become too intolerable not to do something.

If you perceive this as a time when you want to work on yourself, remember: Whatever your age, that's how many years it took you to be who you are. It's pretty silly to think you can change that overnight.

Have patience, and don't forget to congratulate yourself for starting. You're assuming more responsibility for your life and reflecting on the style you employ to engage the world.

Insulation by Chronic Complaint

For certain people, low morale is a style of presenting themselves. On almost any day you approach them, they invent a variety of ways to tell you that life stinks. So adamant are they in their belief that if you hang around them too long, you may end up agreeing because low morale is contagious.

One night Darcy, a tall woman with new-wave two-tone hair, entered the workshop announcing that she felt discouraged most of the time. Randy jumped in and agreed, saying that no matter what he did, women dumped him. In no time, three other group members were moaning collectively about the horror, the horror. Transported into the heart of darkness, I listened while everyone got it out. No one wanted to budge from their unhappy position. I was sitting in a roomful of cranky adults when Darcy stated loudly, "It's not worth it."

Jon, who hadn't said a word until that moment, replied, "Then why are you here?"

Then Why Are You Here?

Whatever you find unfair, whatever hurts, whatever has sapped your strength, you're here. It may not be the best place you've ever been, but it's all you've got to work with.

We tend to lump negative feelings together into one big ball that rolls downhill picking up anger, ambiguity, speed, and size. Eventually it takes on a life all its own, making greater demands upon your time and energy. Soon you can wind up using your energy to fuel your bad mood instead of problem-solve it. Before you blink, you're enmeshed in an ongoing bout of chronic battle fatigue. Even the simplest day-to-day activities betray your irritation and turn people off.

Cindy met a man in the bicycle shop where she was having her bike repaired on a Saturday afternoon. She noticed him looking at bikes. Thinking he was cute, she sauntered over to try and sneak a peek at his ring finger. He started speaking to her. He told her he wanted a bike so he could escape the rat race of the city and ride through the country. He told her how much he hated being single, hated riding his bike alone, hated city people, and hated weekends. He was attempting to engage Cindy in a conversation, but she couldn't escape fast enough. Fifteen minutes of talking to him exhausted and depressed her.

Over and over, I have seen this type of low morale in action. A man (or woman), scared of the risks, insulates himself from his fears by making chronic complaints. He relies on low morale to cope with problems. He constantly blames others for what's unrewarding about his own life. This means he is off the hook. Now he doesn't even have to try. He can alienate people before they fulfill his worst fears. Now he is relieved of the burden of self-examination.

Chronic complaints are one way to cope in the short run. Who doesn't enjoy a laugh as you sit around a table with your own gender and tell horror stories about why the other gender is some kind of mutant Dean Koontz goon? Bitching and moaning can provide short-term gratification and ego protection, but the long-term effects are devastating. Optimists don't want to hang around you, and so you attract other negative types. You end up living in the land of the lowdown, buoyed by like-minded souls—and it's not a happy place.

Low morale clouds your effectiveness in connecting with others. You can't force yourself to be cheery, because it doesn't come from the heart. So it leads to more disappointment, which leads to lower morale. You end up in a vicious cycle that can damage you. If this describes how you feel, don't get discouraged; keep reading. We're coming to the section on what you can do to begin interrupting this cycle and making more comforting choices in tackling the lows.

FATIGUE: PURE AND SIMPLE

If you aren't having growing pains and you aren't misusing your bad moods, you could be experiencing a bout of pure and simple fatigue. It's appropriate and normal to have low morale some of the time. The pressure of trying to appear at your best takes it toll. Ignoring these feelings rarely makes them go away, and can actually exacerbate the condition. Even when you successfully control them, they can become reinflamed from time to time—just like athlete's foot.

Whichever type of lows you suffer, the following nine tips can reroute you back on target.

Admit You're Temporarily Derailed

Acknowledge and accept your slump. Don't fuel it by resorting to platitudes such as, "That's how my life goes" or "I never get a break." Don't ignore it by telling yourself everything is fine and believing that you can magically make the problem go away. Neither should you feed a fear that falling off track means you'll never get back on. This is a temporary setback, and it happens to everyone. Stop to consider recent events that led to the straw that broke the camel's back. You probably have good reasons for feeling bad, so let yourself off the hook.

Vent

Venting is what it sounds like—reducing pressure by letting the bad feelings out the steam valve. It is not the same as complaining because it happens in a discrete, identified time frame rather than being chronic and ongoing. You tell a friend you want to vent for fifteen minutes. Then rail at the world. Tell why you can't stomach the gender you are attracted to and why you never want another date as long as you live. Let it all hang out with no holds barred. Be inconsolable, angry, and unreasonable.

When your time is up, so is your venting. By giving your complaint a beginning, middle, and end, you get it off your chest and move on, instead of dwelling on it in a way that is ultimately unproductive.

Give Yourself Permission to Rest

Ball games have built-in time-outs. Players need to rest between sets, innings, and quarters. At work we get weekends and vacation time. You may not rest on the weekend, but the mere fact that you are doing something else is restful.

Factor in time to relax. Do not initiate conversation with anyone. Scowl at puppies. We are like wells, and sometimes the well runs dry. Rest. Let the well fill again. And when you are resting, please don't say, "I should be trying to meet someone."

Describe Yourself Kindly

When something runs amok, see it as an occurrence rather than a diagnosis. For example, if you go on a date where you are irritable or critical, and you realize it later on, frame it appropriately. Say, "On this date, I acted unkindly," instead of making generalizations such as, "I'm a lousy person." Say, "On this date, I asked a few too many questions," not, "I'm a beast."

Use a self-description of what you did, not who you are. What you did can be corrected next time. Who you are is ongoing. Don't turn mistakes into artillery that you use on yourself.

Coddle Yourself

Actively do things to keep from getting depleted. Treat yourself to a massage. Throw out all the soap-on-a-ropes you got last Christmas. Set up candles and wine in the bathroom and soak in the tub. Go to the best barber in town. Throw a birthday party for yourself even if your birthday is six months away. Organize a treasure hunt. Volunteer for your favorite charity or cause. Buy yourself a chocolate Easter bunny.

Whether alone or in the company of others, make choices that direct positive attention toward yourself. Go that extra mile to remind yourself how important you are.

Avoid All-or-Nothing Thinking

Are you prone to statements such as, "I never get a break" or "Why do these things always happen to me?" Whenever you find yourself using words like "never" and "always," little alarm bells should vibrate inside your head. Remember, life is not black and white.

Reframe Tasks

Instead of asking how life is treating you today, ask how you are treating life today. Are you treating it like one insurmountable problem? If so, then reframe your outlook by partializing. Break down challenges into manageable tasks. Instead of trying to meet the love of your life by next Wednesday, take smaller steps like saying hello to five people. Don't try to accomplish everything at once, and don't compare yourself to others and decide everyone else is doing better than you are.

Challenges are met in steps, not leaps. It's possible that part of your morale problem stems from overwhelming yourself with the big picture rather than reducing the picture into a smaller, more manageable game plan.

Exaggerate How Bad It Is

Purposefully make everything as dim as possible, like this:

It's awful out there. I'm doing a lousy job. No one will ever want a loser like me. And anyway, it's useless. Books like this never work. I never have a good time no matter what I do or who I meet. Only the creeps are left. It's beyond me why I bother to get out of bed.

As you listen to your negative self go on and on, your positive self should rally by recognizing that not only is this onslaught unpleasant to listen to, it's also irrational. Moreover, it's no way to make friends and influence people unless you're trying to influence them to ignore you.

Keep a Journal of Your Progress

Be wary of falling into the "I'm getting nowhere" trap. Chances are that if you are applying Guerrilla Dating Tactics to your life, you are meeting new people. Nonetheless, when we experience low morale we tend to minimize our accomplishments and maximize our flaws. A journal of your progress can be a helpful reminder of what is fantasy and what is real. Write down the things you like about yourself and the positive responses you've received from others. Write down what you've tried and how it felt to tackle new territory. Write down your personal insights as they happen. On low days, read back and surprise yourself with how far you've come. You may find that even your agonies are funny one year later.

Variation

Elly, a woman from Providence who lost fifty pounds and began dating, attributed her ability to maintain a positive outlook to what she called her New Attitude tape. It started with Patti LaBelle singing "I've Got a New Attitude" and continued with other powerhouse performances and personal affirmations. Her friends loved it so much they requested copies. You could make a New Attitude tape of your own.

CONCLUSION

No matter how much momentum you build up, lows come with the territory. Learning to tolerate the lows is just as important as learning to create the highs. *You aren't a machine.* Accepting down time is part of accepting yourself. Soldiers are confined to their lookout posts for seemingly endless hours that may exceed their abilities to be competent. They may be forced to skirmish even when they are depleted, exhausted, and scared to death. You, on the other hand, are looking for love. You may experience this search as a contest, but in reality it isn't. If you're suffering from low morale and battle fatigue, put your uniform in storage and take a nap. No marine sergeant will insist you do one hundred pushups before breakfast. You can rest, regroup, and rally at your own pace.

VII.

How to Get More Than Name, Rank, and Serial Number: First Dates

20

How to Get More Than Name, Rank, and Serial Number: What You Can Learn from a Good Talk Show Host

When sparks fly, you immediately recognize the feeling. You say hello to a total stranger, and within five minutes you feel like you've known him or her all your life. Conversation pours smoother than Napoleon brandy. Eventually you glance at your watch and discover that what seemed like six minutes has become six hours. It's 2:00 A.M., and you have to get up for work at seven. Even so, it's hard to tear yourself away.

Then, there's that other familiar feeling. You say hello to someone you've never met ... she says hello back ... you ask her where she works ... she tells you ... seconds plod by like aging tortoises. Your instincts tell you that you'd like to get to know her ... but how?

It can be tough to maintain relaxed conversation with someone new. Many people find that they can gab on the phone to a friend for two hours yet feel depleted after two minutes with someone who piques their romantic interest. Talking that is second nature with friends feels awkward and strained with strangers. If sometimes it clicks but other times you feel stuck, you've got company. In the nine years I have been leading workshops, I have never led a group of singles where this subject has not been raised. It is almost always raised by a man, although women readily relate to the strain.

Solid communicative skills are not a mysterious gift that you either possess or lack. Scintillating conversation is not a deft gift relegated to turn-of-the-century British playwrights. The plain fact is that while conversation can attain the level of high art, many of the skills are more like basic math. You can learn them, practice them, and call on them when you need them.

Breaking the code of good conversation lies not in inventing witty things to say, but in learning the essence of good talk: Listening! Yes, that's right. A person who listens will rarely run out of things to say. Since this sounds strange, let's explain it by calling on two trained professionals who earn their living by being good listeners: the Good Talk Show Host and the Psychotherapist.

WHAT YOU CAN LEARN FROM A GOOD TALK SHOW HOST

Several years ago an article appeared in the monthly cable television guide rating talk show hosts by creating mock interviews. The author used these interviews to demonstrate the difference between the Good Talk Show Host and the Bad Talk Show Host. Here is an overview:

The Good Talk Show Host

A guest walks on stage and is seated. The Good Talk Show Host says, "I'm delighted that we could finally get you on the show. Tell me, where have you been hiding?" The guest replies, "I just flew in from Paris." The Good Talk Show Host says, "Paris? *Ooh lá lá!* Tell me more."

The Bad Talk Show Host

A guest walks on stage and is seated. The Bad Talk Show host says, "Tell me, what have you been doing with yourself?" The guest replies, "I just flew in from Paris." The Bad Talk Show Host says "Paris? Did you say Paris? Did I ever tell you what happened to me in Paris one day during lunch at Maxim's? Well, I was seated at my table when . . ."

The difference is clear. A Good Talk Show Host uses the guest's response as an opportunity to show interest. A Bad Talk Show Host uses the guest's comment as an opportunity to elaborate upon his favorite subject: Himself.

A date is not the same thing as a talk show interview. In fact, if you've ever been the victim of twenty questions at the hands of someone you've just met, you can swear to this fact. Still, some of the Good Talk Show Host's skills can help you. In addition to obtaining information from a guest, a Good Talk Show Host helps a guest relax. A Really Good Talk Show Host helps the guest to feel confident about himself by listening carefully and providing relevant feedback. A Good Talk Show Host talks *with* a person, not *at* him. She demonstrates an ongoing interest. And, as if that weren't enough, a Good Talk Show Host makes it clear that, for the moment, even if Mother Theresa and Michael Jackson are waiting in the Green Room, this guest is the most important person on earth.

You may not have the opportunity to observe many Bad Talk Show Hosts (except on public access) because no one is renewing their contracts, but you can observe real pros at work. For example, tune in Barbara Walters on a night when she is doing a one-on-one interview, not with someone in an adversarial position, but with someone she likes. Observe her intense level of interest in her guest. She's done her homework and remembers what her guest said the last time they met. Still, have you ever wondered why celebrities speak so openly with her in spite of the klieg lights and camera crew, not to mention the fact that what they reveal will be aired on national TV? Celebrities talk because Barbara Walters has mastered listening. What could be more compelling than the genuine interest and acceptance she shows? Put at ease by Walters's sincere desire to hear and understand, the guest feels safe, and safety leads to generous displays of feeling.

You can learn a great deal about the basics of good listening skills without ever turning off your television. Tune in a respected talk show host and concentrate on his *techniques* instead of the latest Hollywood scandal as told by the ex-maid of a movie star.

WHAT YOU CAN LEARN FROM A GOOD PSYCHOTHERAPIST

Showing an ongoing interest is hard work, and while it can't be faked, it can be learned. Trained therapists spend years developing their listening skills. They strive to hear what is said, as well as the messages *behind* what is said. We aren't therapists, and we definitely shouldn't be doing therapy, but we can benefit from an understanding of a therapist's listening skills.

Don't make the mistake of thinking that to listen is to be passive, as in one person talks and the other person waits. One of the best ways to keep someone talking is to use the techniques of *active listening*, which are anything but passive. Active listening involves specific procedures to maintain talk. As an active listener, we are purposefully involved with each twist and turn in the conversation. The following is a partial list of active listening techniques as they might apply to dating situations. Although I hope you won't be dating for the rest of your life, unless you want to, you *will* be listening for the rest of your life. That is a very good reason to learn how to do it well.

BODY LANGUAGE

A good listener uses more than his ears to hear. He hears with his entire body. Good listeners use relaxed posture, gaze, and gesture to show interest. For example, leaning slightly forward when someone makes an important point is one posture that shows you are intent on listening. However, this maneuver should be handled carefully if you've been drinking because you don't want to end up in someone's lap. That would be overdoing it.

If you want to find a soulmate, remember that the eyes are the mirror to the soul. Maintain natural eye contact while someone is talking—which means look, don't stare. No feature is more capable of conveying understanding. If you have not been used to maintaining eye contact in the past, this may feel uncomfortable at first. Practice with a friend, or even your dog. Your friend may get bored after ten minutes, but your dog will probably be happy to go on for hours.

And speaking of your dog, keep in mind that he has always known your moods without your having to utter a word. Up until now, you may have thought he is the Einstein of Dog World. I'm sorry to tell you, but that's probably not it. The truth is that much of what we communicate, we communicate without uttering a single syllable. Your dog isn't reading your mind, he's picking up on your observable cues. When you look at people on the street, you can generally tell what kind of mood they are in. When you walk into your boss's office, you know whether to expect a raise or a pink slip before she says a word. Body language is a powerful communicator that reflects mood and level of involvement. Think of yourself as a mirror reflecting back the tone of the speaker. Imagine the different ways you can show someone you understand without once saying, "I understand."

VERBAL GESTURES

Ernie met Lena at a coed volleyball game. They struck up a conversation, and Ernie asked her how she became interested in volleyball. As Lena spoke, Ernie listened intently, yet after a few minutes, Lena said, "Am I boring you?"

Ernie was baffled.This had happened to him several times before with others, when, just like this time, he really was interested. When he attended the Guerrilla Dating Tactics workshop, he asked for feedback on what might be going on.

We discovered that Ernie doesn't make a single utterance as he listens. He sits in stone silence, which a woman may misinterpret as boredom. With other men, silence might be a sign of respect, but with Lena, he could benefit by making *verbal gestures*. These consist of offering minimal encouragements while someone talks. For example, as you listen you can go "uh hum," "I see," "mmm," "and then . . .," to encourage the speaker to continue as well as to show you are engaged in active listening. Women tend to naturally offer verbal gestures. Men often don't. When social workers are trained in listening skills, verbal gestures are part of that training. These gestures tell the person that you want to hear even more of what they have to say, as well as affirm your ability to relate to their feelings.

PARAPHRASING

Paraphrasing is a skill that can build rapport and lead to trust. It is a verbal technique in which you restate what someone has just said to you, but in fewer words. It plays back the heart of someone's statement and encapsulates his or her thoughts without adding new thoughts of your own or major interpretations.

Often it's hard to understand what another person means. Paraphrasing leaves ample room for illumination of a comment because you don't jump to any conclusion in your response. You simply reflect back to that person what you think he's said and let him tell you if you're on the same wavelength. Paraphrasing conveys understanding. When you think of how good it feels to you when someone understands the heart of your message, you can get an idea of how powerful paraphrasing can be. Here's an example of paraphrasing in action:

ORVILLE: So I told this person that I was certain I could build an airplane that would remain airborne. My brother and I had been working on it for years. We experimented with winged bicycles and gliders. Day after day, we planned it and replanned it.

WENDY: (paraphrasing) You've put in a lot of time developing your ideas.

ORVILLE: You got it! We've spent hours and hours watching birds glide. It's time to move on to something bigger. We think we understand conceptually what makes something stay in the sky.

WENDY: (paraphrasing) Sounds like you're making progress.

ORVILLE: Progress, not perfection, but we're on our way.

WENDY: (paraphrasing) Any day now.

ORVILLE: Could even happen next week.

WENDY: (changing subject) By the way, is your brother Wilbur single? I have a friend, Juanita, who gives new meaning to the word "airborne."

Here are two more brief examples of paraphrasing:

ROSELLE: Um . . . I'm free this weekend. My plans changed at the last minute. I thought I was going to have to work, but now it looks like it can wait until Monday. I heard that Irish band at McGloughlin's is great. I know you like Irish music. I saw all those tapes at your house.

BRAD: (adding a low-risk interpretation) So you want to get together.

JOHN: You're terrific company. You're smart and funny. Every time I'm with you, I enjoy myself more and more. In fact, I can hardly remember a time when I didn't know you.

HEIDE: You're overwhelmed by my incredible charms.

Learning how to paraphrase and integrating it into your repertoire will keep conversation flowing. Your date will feel that you understand, and understanding is one bridge to building a relationship.

EMPATHY

Empathy encompasses the ability to put yourself in someone else's shoes and feel what he or she is feeling. This is different from saying, "I know how you feel." Actors do it when they pretend to be a character. It is a method for feeling along with someone by tuning in the mental dial just as you tune in a radio dial. You do your best to eliminate static and get as pure a sound as possible.

Without empathy, relationships rarely form. Before giving you examples of empathy in action, take a look at how lack of empathy plays out:

Jackilyn was seated at a lunch counter when a nice-looking man with a cast that went from his foot to his thigh sat next to her. Jackilyn thought, what a perfect conversation starter, and began by asking him what happened. He looked a bit sheepish as he told her that although he'd like to be able to say he broke it mountain climbing, the truth was he broke it running for the bus. Jackilyn responded by telling him he should never run for the bus because there is always another one soon after.

Benny met a woman at a convention and invited her for a drink. As he asked her about her job, she told him that she hated it. She was having ongoing conflict with her boss, and basically she'd like to put a stink bomb in his files. Benny told her that life was much too short to be in a job where you are unhappy. He told her he knew of several employment agencies that could help place her somewhere new and he would go right now and look them up in the phone book. She said thank you, but he noticed that she began fidgeting.

Jackilyn and Benny tried to help, but they both responded in ways that showed a lack of empathy. Both gave advice. Giving advice to people you don't know well can be tricky. In fact, they have probably thought of most of what you'd tell them to do and have reasons, sound or unsound, for not having done something about their situation.

An empathic response for Jackilyn might have been, "That sounds painful. I'm sorry that happened to you." An empathic response for Benny might have been, "It sounds awful to work for someone you can't stand." These responses acknowledge the feelings without offering interpretations or claiming to know how the other person feels. Usually you only know how someone truly feels when you've been through it yourself. Even then, we bring our individuality to each experience.

The ability to empathize is one that can be developed. It is working right when your date tells you something important and she knows immediately that you truly understand. A real connection is made. Trust is born in such moments, and to build trust, concentrate on these points:

Don't imagine what you'd feel like in her situation. *Do* imagine what she feels like.

Don't give advice. *Do* help to lessen his anxiety about revealing something important to you by conveying that you have no intentions of judging him or telling him what to do.

Don't insist on eternal optimism. *Do* let her know that it's okay for her to express unpleasant feelings.

Don't jump to conclusions. Find out if you are taking in information in an accurate way? Empathy depends on perceiving the other person accurately. If you aren't sure, ask a question to clarify.

Practicing Empathy

If you meet new people you like but, over and over, things don't pan out, it may be an empathy misfire. To check out whether or not this is true, try practicing empathy with a friend. Sit facing your friend and let him tell you a story about himself where he felt strongly about something. It could be a very old feeling of worry, discomfort, upset, or sorrow that happened a long time ago. It could even be a very current feeling about how ridiculous it feels to try an empathy exercise.

After he's finished, take a minute to relate his feeling to one of your own experiences, even if it means digging way back. When you have found a feeling of your own that seems to match the feeling he's expressed, sit with it for a moment and then tell him about it. When you have finished, let him say if the feeling in your story matches the feeling he had. Try again and reverse roles. Another way to practice is this: Instead of going back in your past to come up with a matching experience, look for the words that would comprise an empathic response. How can you respond to what somebody tells you in a way that allows her to feel closer to you than she did before?

> ### Note to Women
> If you think men don't care about this stuff, you are wrong. In the past few years, my workshops that focus on probing empathy have had *more men signing up than women.* I've actually sat in a room observing large groups of men working on empathy exercises with the same vigor and commitment they bring to programming the VCR. Don't underestimate anyone!!

CLARIFYING

Clarifying means knowing when to ask a question if you aren't sure what someone meant. If your date begins to ramble, or if she loses you somewhere, ask rather than assume. You can clarify by using questions like these:

- Could you run that by me again? I think I lost you somewhere.
- I think I understood what you meant. (Paraphrase what you think you heard) Is that right?

Through clarifying, you can verify your perceptions and avoid incorrect interpretations. It is yet another technique that encourages the other person to continue talking by showing you are listening carefully and want to understand.

When you begin to try active listening techniques, they feel awkward because they ask you to listen in different ways than you usually do. Why not, as suggested earlier, practice with a friend? You can take turns and offer feedback on each other's performance. Think of it as a way to check out if someone said what you thought they said, as well as encouragement. Many communication problems arise from assumptions and misunderstandings about what someone meant. Paraphrasing and clarifying give you the tools to avoid guessing wrong.

In addition, try practicing in your everyday life when you talk to people. These are skills that can be illuminating anywhere. Don't save them for someone who attracts you. Indulge in regular active listening workouts.

OTHER CONVERSATIONAL GAMBITS

One of the most feared moments on a date is the lull—that moment when you've both run out of things to say and feel overwhelmingly self-conscious with the silence. Here are techniques to banish it from your vocabulary, along with thoughts on avoiding distractions and taking turns when you talk. They can even turn a dull date into a dramatic one, because dull dates don't necessarily signify dull people. Frequently they are the outcome of two strangers who don't understand each other's talking style.

Lull-Busting by Bridging

Tony and Tina sat in a restaurant on a blind date arranged by a mutual friend. They found themselves off to a great start. They discovered that they both loved scuba diving and they both loved *everything* on the dessert menu—from the mud pie to the carrot cake. However, somewhere between the main course and the time dessert was served, they became silent. If Tony and Tina were in a relationship, they would identify this as one of their precious "quiet times," a time when there was no need for words. But on a first date, two stomachs churn as they enter the zone of the dating dead, otherwise known as a *lull*. With each passing second, anxiety builds as neither can come up with something new to say. Tony begins to examine specks of food on the tablecloth. Tina's critical self nixes every suggestion she thinks up while a little voice in her head starts saying, "I told you that you should have stayed home and rented *Barbarella*."

Don't panic! Lulls are the easiest thing to get past. The reason people don't do it is that they wrongly believe they must constantly come up with fascinating new material to discuss. Not true. *Bridging* is the perfect lull-buster. When you bridge, you return to something that has already been discussed *instead* or searching for something new.

In Tony and Tina's case, there is always more to be said about scuba diving. Tony can say, "So you said you love scuba diving. Have you ever had a scary encounter? What is the most interesting thing you ever saw under water? Do you subscribe to any scuba magazines?" Certainly Tina has something to add about her favorite sport. Return to a subject the person has already demonstrated that he or she is passionate about. An open-ended comment that goes back to a topic your friend enjoys can lead you in new directions. Simply memorize the word and build a *bridge* that connects a previous subject to the current discussion.

Lull-Busting by Identifying the Lull

Doug, a talented musician and a consummate conversationalist, uses a system of identification to nip the lull in its bud. When an extended silence prevails, he comments in a good-humored way, "Oh, I recognize this. This is a lull. Don't panic. It will pass." Doug swears his dates smile because his comments break the tension. Verbal identification of an awkward moment can keep it from becoming an awkward hour. He has also been known to say at the end of a date, "Is this the place where I ask you if we can go out again and you either say yes so that I leave feeling elated or you say no and I act like it really doesn't matter but it really matters?"

Don't underestimate acknowledgment of awkwardness as a way to end it, but keep it in a light, humorous vein. If you don't *act* like it's traumatic, it won't *be* traumatic.

Avoiding Distractions

Sam learned how easily distracted he was the hard way. Because he liked Cindy so much, he took her to his favorite hangout on their first date, a little neighborhood bar and grill. He wanted to be seen with her. Every time the door opened, he looked to see if it was someone he knew. Several friends sauntered over and, after introducing Cindy, he spent quite a chunk of time exchanging hellos and relating recent events Cindy knew nothing about. In addition, the noisy marguerita machine forced them to shout part of the time. Cindy reached a point of utter exasperation and snapped at Sam, telling him that he seemed more interested in who was walking through the door than he was in her.

Now Sam works hard to avoid being distracted on dates. Since it is his natural tendency to look up at everyone who walks in (and never even realize he's doing it), it was important to find a way to keep himself from doing that. These days Sam always takes the seat facing the back of the restaurant or the wall so he can minimize distractions and maximize the attention he pays to his dates.

Taking Turns

Remember, a date is not an interview, talk show, or therapy session. You are not supposed to spend the entire evening asking questions and reflecting on every answer. Take the case of George and Lucy to heart. George, a radio personality with hundreds of interviews under his belt, uses excellent listening skills. He made it easy for Lucy to talk about herself, and talk she did. She told him about her job, her tap dance lessons, her belief in reincarnation, and even about her ex. When the end of the evening came, Lucy realized that she knew little about George, but he could be certified as an expert on her. She even told him things she had promised herself never to discuss on a first date, like the fact that she still sleeps with a teddy bear she's had since she was seven years old. By the time she got home, she felt uncomfortably vulnerable about all she'd said because George had not matched her revelations. George, believing he had successfully demonstrated great interest in Lucy, actually left her squirming.

Taking turns is just as vital to a satisfactory evening as good listening. You aren't doing anyone a service by encouraging them to share unless you share, too. When someone talks to you, listen to what he or she says, but don't hold back your responses. At some point, tell the other person you know what he or she means.

Tell him or her you had a similar experience. Let your date know you are in this together and you share common ground.

THE REST OF THE WORLD

It is incorrect to assume that because you are working at improving your conversational skills and know when to take turns, your date has done the same. You may have to help him along. For example, perfectly nice people can monopolize when they get nervous or sense an impending lull, and some perfectly nice people simply talk a lot. Don't assume he has an ego that wouldn't fit in China because he isn't taking turns, and don't just zip your lip and give up without trying to even things out. More important, don't give all the responsibility for conversational balance to the other person.

Many people have come into my workshops complaining heartily about a date who wouldn't shut up. When I ask what they did to correct this situation, their answers are uniform. Most say they gave up after the first five minutes and tuned out. It rarely makes sense to give up your personal power so easily by opting for remaining irritated and silent. After you have played the Good Talk Show Host, wait until your date pauses, jump in, and take your turn. Since people's conversational tempi and styles vary, don't wait too long or he may start off on another subject.

If someone doesn't pause, jump in anyway and gently cut him off even if this makes you cringe. Firmly state, "I have something to add" or "I need to stop you." Should this tactic fail, borrow a pen and write on your napkin, "Thirty seconds till my turn." Hold it up. He'll get the message. If this doesn't work, then you can consider chalking this one off.

Remember, upgrading your conversational skills takes time and sweat. They don't appear because you read a chapter about them. They need frequent exercise, so go ahead and work out. Practice with a variety of people in different environments. Keep yourself in tip-top shape for the talk that really matters.

21

Taking the Trauma
Out of Talk

―――――――――――

Most of our transactions with each other are rooted in talking, the high octane of getting-to-know-you. Talk breaks the ice, conveys the tone of our emotional life, and inquires about the emotional lives of others. We talk to gauge if a person is interested in us, to plant the seeds of intimacy, and to establish rapport. The kind of talk that leads to dating happens in stages, and Stage One is small talk.

SMALL TALK OVERVIEW

Dan walked into my Boston workshop announcing that his goal was to eliminate small talk altogether and move straight to mid-talk. Lynn swears she is a small talk klutz who only shines when discussing important matters. Raelene said that she hates small talk because it wastes time and tells her nothing about the person. Many single adults share these opinions. They see small talk as an unrewarding enterprise that gets in the way and slows you down.

They're mistaken. What eye contact is to initial nonverbal behavior, small talk is to initial verbal contact. The fact that it's uncomfortable does not mean that it should be skipped.

REFRAMING SMALL TALK

Rethink small talk as your first tentative step in the ritual of exploration with someone new. Its importance lies not in relying on it as a source of gathering information about the weather, but as a source of getting a mental take on someone. Small talk is process-oriented instead of content-oriented. In other words, what you talk about is irrelevant—it's the message you send each other ("I want to keep talking to you") that counts.

Small talk is made up of queries and replies about innocuous topics like the weather, who else you know at the party, how your donut tastes—subjects where no one will thrust an opposing opinion at you and expect you to debate, defend, or come up with a Pulitzer Prize–winning response. Focus on nonthreatening common knowledge and/or the immediate environment:

I can't believe this line is so slow.
It looks like rain.
Is this the bus stop?
Doesn't that woman look like Shirley MacLaine?
What are you eating? It looks delicious.
Where did you buy those sneakers?

Don't try to be brilliant! Think of it as a polite precursor to the next phase. While you may prefer more provocative openers such as those in the chapter on pickup lines, you will undoubtedly notice charming people in places where pickup lines aren't appropriate. So even when your goal is to leap beyond small talk, don't avoid it, because:

Small Talk Lets You Regain Homeostasis—As I discussed in earlier chapters, meeting someone interesting throws the organism off-balance. You feel awkward, even stupid. You think you're stupid because you're talking about the weather, but the truth is that you feel stupid because you're off-balance. Small talk is an ideal skill for maintaining a connection while you regain balance. This takes some people longer than others, but you can't regain balance when you try to talk about something that makes you feel prematurely challenged.

Small Talk Lets You Experience Another Person—You've seen Delilah across a crowded room, and she's an MGM minx. Your visual sense of her arouses the Samson in you, but at this point you have no idea if she's as nice as she looks. Small talk lets you find out. You will discover her emotional tone. Does she laugh easily? Is she nervous but receptive? Does she start off the conversation by telling you that you need a haircut? Small talk offers you information about what it feels like to be with her instead of look at her.

Small Talk Lets You Experience Yourself—Give yourself the opportunity to find out if talking with him is what you thought it would be. Do you want to keep going, or do you want to move on? Do your instincts tell you that something nice could happen here? Don't put all your energy into how he feels about you. Ask yourself how *you* feel about *him*.

Small Talk Offers a Breather After You've Shared Something Private—In relationships, we share secrets, histories, and troubles. However, after telling him a secret, you may want to go back to something banal for the next few minutes. We can't always take risks. Revert to small talk until your pulse slows down.

Small talk only lasts from three to five minutes. The trick is knowing when to move on rather than risk small talking another to death:

"What a lousy day."
"Yeah. I'm glad I brought an umbrella."
"Me too."
"Yeah."

VERBAL FLY-FISHING

The first sign of a slump signals the time to move to Stage Two: Verbal Fly-Fishing. When you fly-fish, you cast a line in several directions until you get a bite. Verbal fly-fishing works the same way. The purpose is to reel in a talk bite, to find something that is of mutual interest. Just as with real fly-fishing, don't expect to get a bite on the first try. Here are some actual excerpts of workshop participants enacting verbal fly-fishing role-plays:

BOB: I'm a little sore today. I went skiing this weekend—took a fall. (VFF #1) Do you ski?

CAREN: No, I never have.

BOB: It's fun. Although I'm a beginner.

CAREN: Uh huh.

BOB: (VFF #2) What sports do you like?

CAREN: I like roller-blading.

BOB: I've never done that.

CAREN: (Pause) It's fun.

BOB: (VFF #3) Where do you roller-blade?

CAREN: Down by Haynes Auditorium.

BOB: Haynes? (VFF #4) There's a really good Mexican restaurant near there.

CAREN: Casa Mexico?

BOB: Yes.

CAREN: I love it there.

Bob sought to engage Caren with sports. They couldn't seem to connect on this subject, so after a few tries he threw her another line. She picked right up on it.
Here's another example:

SAM: You look great in that dress.

FELICE: This?

SAM: Absolutely.

FELICE: I made this dress. I sewed it myself.

SAM: I'm impressed. I can't even sew on a button.

FELICE: It takes concentration.

SAM: I have no concentration.

FELICE: I sew to relax. (VFF #1) What do you do to relax?

SAM: I lie in front of the television and watch videos.

FELICE: (VFF #2) What's the most you ever watched in a row?

SAM: Would you believe me if I told you seven?

FELICE: (VFF #3) I've done ten.

Remember:

- Actively seek to hook someone by throwing out lines.
- Don't expect immediate success.
- Be prepared to jump around between subjects until you find mutual ground.
- Mutual ground can be a shared love for Mozart or a shared love for vegetarian chili.
- Avoid heavy political talk, religious discussions, and previous wounds.

FURTHER SMALL TALK TECHNIQUES

Small talk guidelines help create a pleasant ambiance. There is no one right way to have a conversation, but here are helpful hints for encouraging prolonged contact.

Greetings

All approaches begin with greetings, but not all greetings are the same. "Hi" can seem abbreviated, as if you are about to take off. "Hello" lingers, as if you plan to stay around and continue after you've said it. "Hello" lets the person listening experience you as someone with time to talk.

Identify Yourself First

Offer your name before you ask for a name. If you do, you can find out her name and start calling her by it (a sexy thing to do). If you ask her name first, she may experience you as intrusive, asking too much too soon, or she may feel a small discomfort as she tells you. If a few minutes pass and you haven't exchanged names yet, stop and say, "Oh, by the way, my name is Drew." Even if you have met him briefly in the past, offer your name anyway. He may have forgotten it. You'll spare both of you an awkward moment.

Shake Hands

Even this brief physical gesture is a way to show interest. If he really moves you, take your free hand and place it over both your hands. Shake slightly longer than necessary. No knuckle-breakers or wimpy wrist wriggles, please.

Offer Your Number First

The hint about your name applies to the exchange of numbers. Offer yours as you ask for hers. If she hesitates, acknowledge her hesitation and replace your request with one for her number at work. You may tell her you'd like to call her, but you understand if she would prefer to call you. Then stop. Let her tell you what she wants.

Make a Counteroffer

In his excitement over meeting you, perhaps he makes a premature request:

- Let's get out of here and find someplace quiet to talk.
- Would you like to come back to my place?
- Are you free next Saturday night?

If you knew him better, you might want to do any of these things, but at this point he's a little pushy. Don't let the moment slip away without making a counteroffer of what you *can* do:

- Let's just walk over to the bar. It's quieter there.
- How about going out for coffee instead?
- Suppose we got better acquainted over lunch this week first.
- I don't usually meet men in a supermarket, but I always do my shopping at the same time. Maybe we could meet and exchange those recipes here next week.

For Men—Frame Yourself

She doesn't know you from Adam, so she will have safety concerns about talking with you. Frame yourself as decent by offering pieces of information that substantiate you as "safe" early on. Don't overdo it, but you might mention where you work, work out, eat dinner, buy the newspaper, hang out with friends ... anything so she can begin to see a life instead of a lifer.

Comment About the Here and Now

"You look like you're in a good mood."
"You look like you've had a long day."
"You laugh easily. How nice."

Notice something about how the person responds to the world and let him or her know you are intent on noticing. Such comments are more personal than "nice day" and direct any exchange into more intimate territory. Use lighthearted observations, not heavyhanded interrogations.

Here and now statements also include a running commentary on the environment:

"They always serve the same hors d'oeuvres, but I've never seen a single person eat one. What do they know that we don't know?"

"I love these paintings. He has wonderful taste. That one looks familiar. Do you know who painted it?"

Pay a Compliment

Pay a personal compliment, making sure he knows you mean him and not his suit. Tell him the suits looks great on him instead of the impersonal, "Nice suit."

Don't make comparative compliments. Don't tell him he's the best dancer in the room. He'll be looking around trying to figure out if it's true rather than basking in the compliment (and he'll be sure to see someone he thinks dances better). Instead say, "I love dancing with you." This is indisputable. He can't argue with it, and he can't counter it with fact.

Take a Compliment

Imagine that he's gathered his courage. He takes a deep breath and says, "That dress looks great on you." Should you reply, "This dress? I never liked this dress," it's not encouraging. When someone takes the time to compliment you, don't deflect it. A lingering "Thank you. It's so nice of you to notice" will suffice.

Search for a Level of Entry

As in the early example in this chapter between Bob and Caren, your opening may appear unexpectedly. You may steer talk toward one area while she remains unresponsive or steers it to another. Look for what is called a Level of Entry. This means the place where you can jump in and turn a statement or response into a conversation. When she tells you where she takes her class, latch on to something new if you're batting zero. Note geographical location, who you know who lives in the area, nearby restaurants, what used to be on that street thirty years ago—anything that could provide a connection. Careful listening leads to unexpected avenues.

Make Him Laugh

Nothing joins people like laughter. If you can make her laugh, take two steps forward. Tell a great joke—be slightly silly. When her smile reaches her eyes, you're on the right track. Remember the 3 D's of joke-telling: Nothing derogatory, dastardly, or dirty.

A combination of small talk, verbal fly-fishing, and active listening techniques will help you start a conversation and keep it going. So let's move on to the next step, because when men and women talk, there are multiple considerations. Life will be easier if you are aware of them.

GENDER-BENDERS AND SPEAK SNAGS

If you feel off the mark half the time, it's no wonder. Take a gander at what we lug to each and every conversation:

Self-perceptions
Needs
Values
Feelings
Experiences
Problems
Expectations
Expertise
Gender*

Each sentence that someone speaks is understood through the lens of our personal histories. They say the words, but we fill in the meaning. It's a wonder anyone understands anyone else.

Talk gets more complex when it is between gender. Men and women think about talk and like to talk in vastly different ways. When men get together, you often find them discussing objects (cars, VCRs, computers) and numbers (scores, percentages). When women get together, you often find them discussing feelings (troubles, impressions) and relationships (familial, working, romantic). In addition, men tend to value talking in authoritative tones, while women seek talk that emphasizes how we are like each other. Men frequently feel most helpful problem solving, while women usually feel most helpful empathizing. Both use talk to connect, but they tend to rely on different material and different talking styles.

Consequently, when we talk to each other, we hit snags. We can end up confused, mystified, and misunderstood—not to mention irritated, angry, and hurt. When we meant to be friendly, we are perceived as being pushy. When we meant to be tender, we are perceived as being needy. When we meant to be charming, our date got insulted. When we meant to be strong, we were perceived as withholding. And when we meant most to be understood, men and women are likely to feel the frustration of our two distinct languages, without the benefit of an interpreter from the U.N. Peacekeeping Council.

*Based on a model from *The Helping Relationship* by Lawrence Brammer.

RASHOMON

In the Japanese film *Rashomon,* a group of people witness a crime. When the authorities arrive, each person is asked, one by one, for her or his version of the event. Although it was the same crime witnessed by the same people, their stories are vastly different. The same exact scene is described in various and opposing ways. No one is lying. Each person's reality is their own. Talk operates the same way. Each person hears within their own frame of reference.

Here are examples of male and female perspectives, taken from tales told in my He Says/She Says workshops. They occur after the beginning stages of a relationship, at points past our discussion of meeting and going on first dates. Nonetheless, they indicate grounds for confusion that can percolate from the first hello.

Dave and Cassie spent an afternoon together exploring antique shops, something Dave knows plenty about. Walking down a quaint street, Cassie spied an outdoor cafe. She asked Dave if he'd like to stop and have a cup of coffee, and he said yes. When the coffee arrived, he drank it. Cassie sipped slowly and talked. Thirty minutes later, Dave was ensconced in a wave of irritation. For Cassie, coffee was like those droning General Foods International Coffee commercials. For Dave, coffee was just coffee. He couldn't understand why she dawdled. She couldn't believe how he rushed her. Dave feels frustrated. Cassie feels pressured.

Gender-Bender Explanation: Dave feels comfortable getting to know Cassie when they are focused on the activity of antique hunting. He knows about antiques and he can talk about them, thus providing a service to Cassie, who knows little about antiques. He uses talk to offer information. He likes that they have set the task of visiting several antique stores before calling it a day.

Cassie enjoys hearing Dave tell the history of a canebacked chair, but she wants to get to know Dave in a way that is more meaningful to her, a way in which they are relating more to each other. The day would not be complete for her without sharing thoughts and feelings—without quiet time.

Certainly there is crossover and even role reversal among men and women. Still, many men view a connection as beginning through an offering in the *external* world of information and advice or while engaged in an activity. Many women view a connection as beginning through the offering of the *internal* world of feeling detail and tone. To borrow a quote from Fred Friendly, I offer this discussion "not to make up anybody's mind, but to open minds."

Evelyn was eager to see the new Martin Scorsese film playing at the Regency. She had a date with Jack for the following Friday night. When they talked on the phone about what they were going to do, she queried, "Have you heard anything about that new Scorsese film?" Jack said he hadn't and immediately suggested the Robin Williams movie. Evelyn said okay, but felt slightly hurt at having her wishes passed over. When the movie ended, she told him how she felt. Jack was floored. He never had a clue to Evelyn's feelings. And he couldn't believe that a phrase like, "Have you heard anything about . . ." could really mean, "I'd like to go see. . . ." Evelyn feels ignored. Jack feels hurt.

Gender-Bender Explanation:

Evelyn uses a technique to express her wish that another woman would have picked right up on. Her question is not a question at all—it's a suggestion. When women make decisions together, it will generally happen after each nuance of possibility, be it question or suggestion, is thoroughly explored. This isn't because women are wishy-washy. It's because a) women prefer consensual decision making, b) the process of coming to an agreement furthers closeness and connection among them, and c) women have been socialized to approach things indirectly as a way of avoiding conflict. Evelyn's remark, among women, would be considered a first step in what will be a discussion—not as a closed yes or no question.

Jack is hurt. To him, questions are discrete and concrete. When someone asks a simple question, they are seeking information. He does not assume that he will have to interpret what Evelyn means. He takes her at face value. He would have been happy to accommodate her, but he's no mind reader. So he's even more hurt that he disappointed her when he thought he was pleasing her.

Evelyn is mystified by the concrete yes and no of Jack. Jack is confused by the way Evelyn dances around the point.

Joe says that by the time he says something, it's his final thinking on the matter. He has done all the work internally, and the case is closed. Yet when he articulated one of his decisions to Susie, she wanted to discuss all the options. He's done that already. He thinks Susie talks in an exploratory fashion—thinking out loud. He thinks in his head. It's incomprehensible, he says. He can't understand this thinking out loud business. He describes himself as the walking space shuttle disaster—a man whose O ring isn't perfect.

Joe feels put upon. Susie feels excluded.

Gender-Bender Explanation:
Joe's internal life, that which is uncertain and makes him feel vulnerable, is a personal matter for him. Socialized to be sure of himself, to maintain status as a fast-thinking, sure-footed guy's guy, Joe presents his thoughts only when they are clarified and conclusive. He does not want to put the process of his thinking on the table for view. He prefers to present the bottom line.

Susie considers decision making as more than a singular process. She seeks ongoing feedback and reality testing. She isn't looking for people to tell her what to do. She will make her own decisions, but she likes to feel connected to others by sorting through ideas. When Joe tells her his idea, she automatically believes he is asking for the same process. She feels cheated out of a certain closeness when his thoughts are not up for discussion.

> Reams have been written about what he says and what she says. If you want to read two books that explore the etiology of these differences, take a look at *Men: A Translation for Women* by Joan Shapiro, M.D., and *You Just Don't Understand* by Deborah Tannen, Ph.D.

SURPRISE, SURPRISE: WE ARE DIFFERENT

These differences show up even in the way in which we describe our dating lives. In a recent workshop series on communication, here are just a few of the interesting distinctions that came up. Men used violent language to describe dating. Joe said he was a walking space shuttle disaster. Alfie tells of being shot down so often, he feels like a duck flying into a duck blind. When I questioned John about how he was doing in a small group exercise he looked me in the eye and said, "I ate dirt and died." Women rarely express confusion or rejection in these terms.

Initially, I separated the men into one group and the women into another. I asked them each to come up with a definition of intimacy. The men stated that it was based on shared goals. The women said it was based on shared connections. Men expressed allegiance to task while women expressed allegiance to relationships. Nowhere was this particular difference more obvious than in how men and women went about coming up with these definitions in the first place. In addition to the definition of intimacy, I also ask them to make a list of what they find most confusing about the opposite sex. Absolutely no instructions are ever offered about how each group is to do this. Yet nearly every time, the men do it by taking turns. One by one they speak and tell each other what confuses them. The women, on the other hand, always work together—all speaking at once, interrupting, and validating each other—coming up with a list based on what they all think together. The men's list represents a compilation of what each one thinks as an individual.

Michael, an astute Washington, D.C. workshop veteran, made a very interesting observation. He pointed out that the concept of woman as nester and man as hunter can be seen at a singles dance where women plant and wait, while men track and pursue. Michael also stated his burning desire that the man (of course, we don't know that it *was* a man at all) who invented shopping malls rot in hell. He said men go to the mall to buy something, while women go to the mall to "experience the mall."

In short, don't expect the opposite sex to talk like you talk, think like you think, like what you like, relate like you relate, or share like you share. Instead, cultivate an awareness and a sense of humor about our differences. Instead of insisting that he or she "get it," maybe it's really time for you to "get off it."

In the past, it's seemed as if women have been more willing than men to work at improving communication. If this was ever true, it no longer holds up in the groups I've been leading. Today, almost across the board, my communication workshops have more men signed up than women. In two New York workshops, all the participants were men. In Washington, D.C., I ran a group that was 98 percent men. In many other cities I've been in lately, more men are signing up to learn how to improve communication, dating, and conversational skills. The time has come to drop those "all men . . . all women" black-and-white statements we've used to characterize each other in the past. Take a good look and take heart. We are heading down the *right* path.

Our task in caring for and about each other is to view differences as something that may intrigue, enhance, frustrate, and irritate us, but also as something that will not cut us off from each other.

So don't be surprised if:

He calls to say hello during the last thirty seconds of his coffee break. (To him, calling you is the connection. He doesn't need to keep talking to maintain it.)
She's hurt that you called as your break was ending. (The amount of time you talk to her correlates to how much you care about her.)

She probes you about your feelings even after you've sworn that you don't have any. (She would love to have you share as she shares.)
He tells you everything you never wanted to know about single-malt scotch. (He connects with you by providing information and advice.)

He invites you to sleep over, prepares breakfast, and then reads the paper during it, never glancing in your direction once. (Proximity *is* the intimacy for him.)
She invites you to stay over and asks you to put down the paper and talk to her. (Connection *is* the intimacy for her.)

Again, this is stereotyping. It is not true for all men and all women. Many comedians use this material as the basis of their routines (and we laugh till we cry or cry till we laugh). Here's what Jerry Dugan, a comedian, said on a recent HBO special: When women say, "We have to talk," what men hear is, "Hotel fire. Head for the nearest exit. Keep low to the ground. Do not take the elevator."

As our relationships progress, we can work at finding a common arena of communication that is more satisfying for both genders, since these differences can cause confusion and discomfort. This understanding often happens after we've become part of a couple who have the time, sense of safety, and desire to understand. But, meanwhile, while you're out there dating, take care not to turn the discomfort into stop signs. Don't make something that is gender-based and cultural into something personal. Next time you run into a snag of this nature, see if you can reframe it in a way that will make you smile rather than blow up.

Understanding communication along gender lines will help you frame your reality, but it will never make life between men and women friction-free. Maybe that's not the point. Maybe understanding the principles of talk between gender is simply meant to free up more time and energy to argue about something else . . . like housework.

22

Growing Bold Together: Building Rapport

You've sailed through the small talk. You've been promoted to sergeant for your ace listening skills. You've passed Go and collected $200 for your Verbal Fly-Fishing. You've weathered gender-benders that have sent others back to basic training. It's time to enter new territory because you can't grow old together without growing bold together.

RAPPORT VERSUS CHEMISTRY

Rapport and *chemistry* are two words we hear all the time and, sometimes one is mistaken for the other. Chemistry is the glorious shock to the system—the undefinable crescendo of being drawn to someone. It goes way beyond looks. Rooted in the realm of subconscious and genetic puzzles, we can never completely explain why the whole is greater than the sum of the parts. Chemistry, with its far-reaching whammy, vibrates just beyond our grasp of understanding.

Three Observations About Chemistry
- It's out of our control, and that's the pleasure *and* the pain of it.
- It does not discriminate between signs that read ROMANCE AHEAD and signs that read DANGER AHEAD.
- Though myth would have us believe otherwise, it's not always "at first sight" and has been known to spontaneously combust after days, months, and even years of knowing someone.

I hope that every person experiences chemistry for another at some point in life. Without it, who would write our love songs?

However, we realize as we grow older that chemistry alone is not enough. It makes us fall in love, but it won't make love work.

Rapport, on the other hand, is not a first-sight phenomenon. Described as the state of being in harmony with another person, it nurtures safety and trust. When we are in a state of rapport, we demonstrate a willingness to take risks in revealing ourselves. Having a rapport does not mean that a relationship will form or endure, but not having it makes it impossible for two people to "know" each other in the deeper sense of the word. Developing your rapport skills opens communication lines and clears a path for increased chemistry.

GUERRILLA RAPPORT TACTICS

The following are ten observations on rapport that provide a framework for understanding the components that enter into building it. If you are talking with someone and the rapport feels automatic, just keep going (you might review this list later and see if you can pick out what made it so easy). But if you're in an on-going struggle to establish rapport, consider one or more of these building blocks as being out of sync. In the past, when you weren't on her wavelength from day one, you may have said that it wasn't in the cards for you two, that it wasn't fated. I hope the following tips will help you see the point where your rapport got stuck in the conversational mud.

> Occasionally, even with all the rapport techniques at your fingertips, things won't gel. If things refuse to click, recognize that you can't build rapport without a willing partner.

Pick Up on and Accept Cultural Differences

A recently widowed woman started "seeing" her dead husband at different times during the day. At the market or in the dentist's chair, he would suddenly appear. This continued until she was referred for a psychiatric evaluation because her physician thought she was delusional.

She wasn't. She belonged to a Native American culture where the appearance of a deceased loved one was the cultural norm. In fact, not to see the deceased was a sign that the dead person was not missed. There was a positive correlation between frequent sight-ings and the amount of love that existed between the couple.

On a date, you're likely to face something this unique, but don't underestimate the impact of cultural differences on the bud-ding relationship. Perhaps in your family people showed affection with touch. My friend Erika is like that. She doesn't consider that she's talking to me unless she is pulling lint off my jacket and fluffing my hair. At first it made me uncomfortable. Then I met her mother, who heartily kissed me as she smoothed my lapels. What struck me as odd about Erika was suddenly understandable.

Dating parallels for cultural clashes might include:

- Someone who likes to kiss in public when you think kissing should be done behind closed doors.
- Someone who invites you home to meet his parents much sooner than you would think is appropriate.
- Someone who asks you very personal questions on a first date.
- Someone who invites you to his home for dinner but doesn't serve it until three hours after you've arrived (extra points if you starved yourself all day).
- Someone who gets annoyed for a minute, blows off steam, and forgets about it while you're still reeling.
- Someone who withholds feelings when you like to lay the cards on the table.

Differences in background can affect everything from where we like to go on a date to what we share, how we show anger, and what we perceive as appropriate first date behavior.

When your date acts in ways that seem foreign to you, don't automatically write him off. Consider that he may be acting appro-priately within his cultural identity. Postponing judgment of unfa-miliar attitudes or behaviors gives you time to understand. Of course, I'm not referring to accepting the unacceptable, aberrant behavior—merely those irritations that set us off.

Mirroring

Put a person at ease by mirroring back their body position to them. If she crosses her right leg, cross your left. If her body po-sition is open, with her arms and legs uncrossed, keep yours open, too. If she leans forward, you lean forward. But don't overdo this. Your goal in mirroring should not be to mimic someone. Leave that to the old Groucho and Harpo Marx routine. All you want to do is establish a harmonious balance of body parts.

Encourage Simple Symmetry

Simple symmetry means likes and dislikes we have in common, such as a shared love for Rottweilers or Whitney Houston. It doesn't form a basis for a relationship, but it attracts us to each other and helps us hold each other's attention. It gives us something to talk about that lets us feel that we have things in common.

You often hear of couples with a favorite song. Sharing it binds them to each other. We actively seek things that make us like the other. It can be thrilling to find that your date shares your passion for something as mundane as pancakes.

Caution: Once I dated someone with whom I had the *Guinness Book of World Records* record when it came to symmetry. We liked the same food, the same wine, and the same music. We also shared the same favorite poet, whom few had ever read, and the same favorite female jazz singer, whom nobody else I knew had ever heard of. I remember sitting across from him in a restaurant that we both loved, drinking our favorite wine and nibbling at our favorite cheese spread. A little voice in my head said, "What's wrong with this picture?" It took months before I knew. We were aces in the symmetry department, but that was all. I made the mistake of believing it was a sign that we would fall in love.

Awareness of Advanced Symmetry

Couples can run into trouble when months fly by and they never get past simple symmetry—a mutual love of pepperoni pizza. He never found out that she doesn't want children while he wants at least five kids. She never found out that he wouldn't consider marrying outside his faith, and she's outside his faith. Certainly people change their minds about such things all the time, *but not without a commitment to the relationship.*

Advanced symmetry exceeds preferences. It is the domain of values involving shared views about how we approach our lives. These aren't the subjects you raise on a first date. They come up as you get to know someone. So even if you want to ask such questions right up front to save yourself time, don't push it.

However, when they do come up, it makes sense to find out more. You will see glimmerings of whether or not your advanced symmetry matches up. You may choose not to push the point right away. Maybe she thinks this way because she hasn't gotten to know you ... yet. But don't put talk about important matters off forever, hoping that he will magically end up agreeing with you. If three months of steady dating pass and you still haven't gotten around to discussing vital matters, it's time for a friendly, nondefensive heart-to-heart that sounds like this:

> I remember, shortly after we met, that you said that you didn't want a serious relationship at this time. Well, with all the time we've spent together, I find that my feelings for you are growing and they are getting more serious. It seems like something that it would help to talk more about.

> Once you said you didn't want children. If there's one thing I know, it's that I do want children. Let's talk more about it so we're both clear about each other's feelings.

Don't expect to share all of someone's values or to convince him that you've got the right idea while he's got the wrong one. In every relationship, you'll have things you agree on and things that you are at odds about. If you want someone exactly like you, start hanging around at the nearest pool, and on a clear day you might fall in love with your own image.

Complementary Relationships

In addition to what people share, rapport builds because of how people fill in each other's gaps. For example:

He hates to kill bugs	She buys steel-toed roach boots
She hates instruction manuals	He finds programming the VCR more fun than sex
She loves to eat	He loves to cook
He can't do his taxes	She carries a calculator everywhere

We like to feel that the other person rounds us out, and that we can be more efficient as a couple than we have been as an individual. We like to divvy up tasks to make life easier. It reinforces our value to each other. When couples have been together for a while they get complementarity down to an exact science. If the plan is to go to a movie, he parks the car while she purchases the tickets. She finds a seat, and he buys the popcorn. He repeats the lines she missed. She explains the ending to him.

There is also emotional complementarity, which means that your schedules for feeling depressed are different. You can encourage him during his down cycle, and he can build you up during yours. If you both get depressed at the same time, life is harder.

So if your date mentions she hates washing her car, let her know that it's your little passion. Just don't let on that it takes you eight hours to do it, you do it every Sunday afternoon—come rain or come shine—and that you wouldn't let anything come between you and your favorite Sunday ritual.

Balance

Keep a reasonable level of equality and balance in shared information. Rapport won't build unless one person in the couple takes a risk and shares vulnerable information about himself. If that person is you, then tell your date about an event in your past . . . a secret . . . a feeling that you have about being on a date . . . any story that conveys an authentic, heartfelt moment in your life.

Then stop.

Let your date balance your disclosure by sharing something of his own. He may not immediately follow your lead. After a revelation you may both revert to Small Talk, Verbal Fly-Fishing, or Symmetry Talk for a while.

If you don't keep on an even keel with revelations, you can feel overexposed at the end of the night. You've shared your heart and soul, but all you know about him is the name of his favorite rockabilly band. Kermit asked Charlene about her sexual past. Instead of denying his request, or telling him one small story, she related everything she'd ever done. If she wanted to share this information at all, it might have made sense to tell him one small story and then let him match her with a story of his own. Don't sit with a balancing scale, but, as explained in Chapter 20, maintain awareness of taking turns. For Charlene, it did not make sense to offer up so much personal material.

Maintenance of the Self

As you seek to find out what your date likes, don't forget to be a person of your own, with your own opinions, wishes, and needs. Frequently, daters make the miscalculation of being overly agreeable. They go where their date wants to go, eat where their date wants to eat, and claim that whatever their date wants to do is fine. They mistakenly put such behavior under the umbrella of being "nice." This isn't nice, it's wimpy.

If you want someone to fall for you, let her know that there's a person in there—a person who has preferences, a person who can disagree, a person who can develop a thought, a person with a mind of his own.

You win someone's affection by demonstrating that you had a life before you had his affection. Your search for a relationship shouldn't turn you into a doormat.

Negotiation and Compromise

Trina told Elaine that she had to break up with Patrick, a man she'd been dating for two months. They had started to sleep together, and she discovered that he liked sleeping on his side of the bed, while she liked being held all night. In addition, his idea of foreplay did not exceed the length of your average television commercial. It turned out she hadn't talked to Patrick about this, but she believed that they weren't a good match. Elaine's first words to Trina were, "Welcome to the world."

Harmony is won. It doesn't automatically appear except in small stuff like chewing the same gum or loving the same author. Or if it naturally appears in some areas, it will be lacking in others. On your first few dates with someone you like, you may think she is a perfect match. That's because she has not yet become a fully dimensional person to you. In time, she'll become more real than you may have hoped for.

In Elaine's words:

> Everyone you like will be 80 percent gold and 20 percent dirt. Look for the 20 percent you can live with.

Trina needs to talk to Patrick and convey, in a loving manner, what she needs, find out what he needs, and develop a communicative environment where they can find ways to get these needs met. When she realizes that Patrick has different ideas about sex, her impulse is to dump him and search for someone on her sexual wavelength. She could find a man like that, but something else would be out of whack.

There are no perfect matches or perfect situations. Expect to compromise, communicate difficult material, and negotiate in a solid working relationship to keep it that way.

"Where I Am" Statements

One big concern on a date is the feeling that you have no idea where you stand. Because it's uncomfortable, many people prematurely reach for feedback about how they're doing. He'll ask if she's comfortable in that seat over and over again (when he's really asking if she's comfortable with him), or she'll ask if he likes his meal over and over (when she's really asking if he likes who he's sharing his meal with).

It's not surprising that this happens. On dates we can operate like we're tethered by a thin rope to a space capsule hovering between Venus and Mars.

Everyone wants to know how they are doing. Nonetheless, you can't find out by asking.

Instead, tell your date how *he's* doing and where *you* stand by making simple, clear "Where I am" statements from time to time. Say:

This is great fun.
or
You're easy to be with.
or
You're thoughtful and I appreciate that.
or
I feel like you understand.
or
Cool. (if you're under twenty)

In keeping with the previous section on balance, don't keep offering praise until there is balance. Let your date know where you stand once or twice and wait for him to match your display during the evening. If he doesn't, it could be that his sense timing is different, his feelings are different, he's oblivious, or he is less comfortable with this process. Either way, be moderate with praise.

Trust the Process

People have different concepts of timing and self-disclosure. Some let themselves be known easily, while others need substantially more time to open up. Be prepared for telling, waiting, wondering, worrying, asking, not knowing, and respecting our differences in how we do this. This is a time-consuming process, so:

- Don't try to peg people within minutes of meeting them.
- Don't judge one action as a reflection of 100 percent of that person.
- Don't try to put someone in the box of relationships you've had in the past.
- Don't view one small piece of the puzzle and think you know what the finished puzzle looks like.

While it may temporarily relieve your anxiety to decide you've got someone all figured out, you may pass over someone special in the long run.

ADDITIONAL RAPPORT CONCERNS

Certain questions about tampering with rapport may float through your mind, especially if it's something you've taken for granted as being out of your hands in the past.

Won't Thinking About It Take Away the Mystery?

You may believe that if you have to be conscious about building rapport, it won't be natural. Not so. Knowledge of rapport techniques offers insight into how it happens and how to re-create it. You won't have to approach relationships in a hit-or-miss fashion, and it won't detract from the mystery of another person at all. In fact, *Increased awareness lets you look deeper and paves the way to discovering deeper mysteries.*

Understanding rapport won't mean that you can always build it or that you will always want to do so, but you may be less apt to blame yourself when it doesn't work out. (You might blame yourself a little—it's human nature). You will be equipped to see what went wrong and understand it and, if you so choose, decide what can be done. This puts you giant steps ahead of where you were when you dealt with such situations by saying things like, "That's just my luck."

Caution

Rapport can be practiced, but it shouldn't be faked. People can master the motions yet never be emotionally connected to the process. Certainly, you can use rapport techniques to make a sale or land a new client, but when you want to connect with another person for a personal relationship, building rapport is to be taken seriously. It is a powerful tool. Schools of thought that promise instant rapport or instant intimacy need the critical eye that watches to see that we talk not only about techniques, but the real emotions of real people.

Should You Have to Work at This?

I was in a long line in a crowded New York clothing store waiting for a dressing room to try my clothes on. The woman in line directly behind me was standing with her husband, who was keeping her company. They both appeared to be in their early fifties. Because we'd waited for so long, she suggested that he go browse in the men's department. He said he'd stay and hold her clothes for her if she wanted because it looked like all those hangers were getting heavy. She thanked him for offering, but sent him on his way. A moment later he returned with a basket she could rest the clothes in. When he left this time, a woman behind her said loudly, "Where did you get him and do they come in my size?" We all laughed. After the laughter, the first response from this woman was, "We've been married for over thirty years, and we've worked very, very hard at it."

In most areas of your life, you already know that good things come as a result of hard work. Establishing relationships is no different. In fact, working to keep relationships healthy and happy is some of the most demanding (and most rewarding) work you'll ever do. You may as well start from the moment you say hello by mastering how to build rapport.

VIII.

Sabotage, Insurrection, and the Double Bind

Your Survival Kit: The Date of the Living Dead

JOHNNY CARSON: Well, how do you feel about dating?
JUDGE RHEINHOLD: About the same way I feel about oral surgery.
> —from a 1991 "Tonight Show" interview

"I turned down a date once because I was looking for someone higher up on the food chain."
> —comedian Judy Tenuta

You know you're on The Date of the Living Dead when:

You tell him he looks familiar, and then remember where you've seen him before: On "America's Most Wanted."

You tell her she looks familiar and then remember where you've seen her: In a photograph on your boss's desk.

He shares with you that his last seven wives died of mysterious stomach viruses.

She meets you at the door wearing a wedding gown.

Yes, there are circumstances where you'll never want to give a second chance. Instead, you call a cab or the police, or recommend counseling. These dating horrors keep the television tabloids in business.

The bad dates you'll go on will most likely be garden-variety flops. You'll be bored, grossed out, miffed, or miserable (maybe all four), but your life won't be in danger. One tier below the Date of the Living Dead lies the Saturday Night-mare.

Johanna tells the story of when Ed picked her up for their second date and told her he had a big surprise for her. Instead of a movie, he was taking her to his therapy session. If the therapist thought the relationship could work, Ed wanted to move forward.

When Carla sat down in "Cologne Man's" car on their date, he opened his glove compartment. There sat six bottles of cologne. He asked her which one she preferred as he proceeded to put a bit of each on his wrist and took her for a long drive. Carla has been unable to stand the smell of any perfume whatsoever since.

Daisy took Ralph up on his offer of a home-cooked meal. As he served the grilled chicken, he explained that an old flame was moving in with him for the summer. She traveled a lot, though. As far as he was concerned, he could still see Daisy when his live-in was out. Shortly thereafter, Ralph said he couldn't understand why Daisy hadn't eaten a thing.

Seth, a shy computer analyst, hadn't been on a date in years when he asked Annie out to dinner. During the first course she invited him home to meet her family, attend her class reunion picnic, and be her Valentine (it was only July). When he commented that she was moving fast, she stood up, told him he was just like all the rest, and stormed out of the restaurant.

Welcome to the World

Bad dates come with the territory. One of yours is bound to have bad hygiene, bad judgment, or bad manners. Of course, instead of putting energy into finding dates, you could put it into avoiding bad dates, but that means sitting home more. In addition, along with successfully skirting disaster, you are likely to miss out on something that could have been lovely.

The question is not how to avoid all bad dates. Ask instead:

How can I have fewer bad dates?
How can I tell if he's a gem in jerk's clothing?
How can I tell when to give a second chance?
How can I get a second chance when I'm the jerk?

We can answer these questions by exploring reconnoitering operations, retreats, and reevaluations as we move through the following guidelines for:

DISMANTLING HOSTILE FORCES

Nobody asks someone out because he anticipates a dreadful evening. We ask because we hope that the date will be a pleasant experience. Nobody accepts a date who makes her stomach crawl. Sometimes you know enough in advance to be reasonably certain about what kind of night you'll have, but at other times (blind dates, sometimes you've met briefly, the personals) you operate with limited information. You rely on feelings, intuitions, what your friend told you, compatible interests, great looks—all the surface symmetry stuff that attracts people to each other, but may not mean that this is someone you could love or even like.

When you aren't quite sure what lies ahead for you, keep these guidelines for planning the date in mind:

Make Appropriate and Familiar Requests

If you met her in your bowling league, you know she has clothes she can bowl in. So, unless she's expressed a mutual passion for parasailing, the Pirates, or Puccini, don't invite her somewhere when you aren't sure she owns the gear, the desire, or the gown. Some people love to be thrown into alien environments, but not always with a stranger. Since she hardly knows you, she may not tell you that she'd rather have her tooth filled without Novocain than fly through the air strapped in a lightweight contraption or sit through nine innings or three acts of Italian lyrics. First dates make people nervous enough. Throw in a tight tux, a low-cut gown, or an unfamiliar environment, and you can have more to squirm about than you need.

Don't Spend a Bundle

Show him you like him without springing for beluga caviar at the Ritz. You may think you're letting him know he's special, but when you spend too much:

- The pressure is on to make the date great.
- What will you do for an encore?
- He'll wonder what you think you're getting for dessert.
- She'll think you're trying too hard to impress her.

Talk on the Phone

Women tend to like talking on the phone. Men tend to use the phone as a vehicle to provide or seek information. But both sexes may want to talk more than once before making a date ... especially when you barely know each other. You can call just to say hello, just to touch base, or to let her know you are tied up at work for another week but wanted to keep the connection. With a few telephone conversations under your belt, you will have a much better sense of the person and what he'd like to do. You may or may not want to ask for that date at all, depending on your "telephone reception."

Caution: You can have a great talk and a bad date, especially when you meet through the personals, so:
- Even if you're sure that you know what you're doing;
- Even if it sounds like a match made in heaven;
- Even if her voice sounds like Lauren Bacall's;
- Even if she's told you she's mistaken for Lauren Bacall on a regular basis; follow the next tip.

Try the Short Date

The best way to avoid a bad date is to never sit still long enough in one place to have one. Don't guess what a whole evening with him will be like. Rely on the time-tested method for surviving the first night: The short date. I think it's the answer to avoiding bad dates forever.

When you call him, say:

I'll be in your neighborhood for a meeting Thursday at eight o'clock. Would you have an hour to meet for coffee before it starts?

I'm on work overload, but I'd like to get together anyway. Do you have time to have a drink next week?

I'm going to a lecture or reincarnation. Cleopatra will be there. I wondered if you'd like to join me.

The short date provides a graceful exit after an hour or so. Anyone, even you, can be charming and friendly for that length of time, even with an inappropriate match. If you like him, make a second date. If you don't, thank him and move on. If he adores you but the converse is not true, go back to the section in Chapter 6 on the art of disengaging. If you adore him and your desire goes unmatched, return to Chapter 16 and survival strategies for rejection.

Warning: Don't fall into the short date trap of zipping in and out as you search the coffee shops for "your type." This is the dating plague of the nineties.

Don't Attend His College Reunion

He may have an important function coming up—one for which he needs a date. If it's the kind of function where you'll be surrounded by all his old buddies, where the liquor will be flowing, and where everyone will be telling the kind of stories that seemed hysterically funny at the time but "you had to be there," you could age ten years in four hours. Unless you are absolutely wild about him and therefore able to tolerate this ordeal, decline the invitation and go back to the short date.

Don't Attend Uncle Luigi's Birthday Bash

She may ask you, on a first date, to accompany her to a family function. I'd think twice before sitting around the dinner table with her family before you really know her. Her sister may have four kids who want to use your tie as art canvas. Her uncle may pull out the slides of Sarasota. Her cousin Schlomo may look at you as her fiancé, even though you've just met her. UFO's (Unknown Family Oafs) can make for scary, awkward evenings. There'll be time to face the crew when you both decide what you and she have going.

Don't Go on All-Day Dates

Suzanne met a guy at her health club. He invited her to Newport, Rhode Island, (a two-hour drive) for a picnic in the forest followed by dinner with some of his friends. She accepted. Upon entering her apartment his first words were, "Nice place. What do you pay?" Then he took a slow, panoramic view of her cleavage and sighed. When they got in his car, he emitted a loud belch as he told her he'd decided that rather than pack a lunch, they could pick up something in the park. There was no food sold in the park. Suzanne was starving by the time they went to meet his friends, but his friends showed up two hours late. He wanted to wait for them. By the time they arrived, the kitchen was closed. And she still had a two-hour car ride home to look forward to.

Don't accept all-day dates with people you don't know. There will always be time to plan such a date if you hit it off.

When in Doubt, Opt for an Activity

If you hate first dates, but you don't want to schedule a short date because you aren't comfortable with the concept, you have options. If you know that you both love tennis or you both love pool, do the activity you both love. Many find first dates far more comfortable when engaged in an activity that throws the focus off internal anxiety. Plan a date that keeps you moving instead of obsessing.

Caution: If you play a sport, avoid going heavy with competitive spirit on a first date. Don't try to show her your great slam-dunk shot, and don't try to show him you can outswing Jack Nicklaus or any other man. At the same time, don't purposefully lose the game. Simply remember that you got together to learn more about each other—not to show who can clobber whom. The competitive spirit can be all-consuming and is completely inappropriate on a first date.

Be Careful About What Movie You See

Movies can be too distancing and too intimate at the same time: too distancing because there is no interaction between you during the film ... too intimate because of your proximity during potentially sexy scenes that could leave you fidgeting.

The same goes for watching a movie on the VCR. When Phil invited Jody for dinner, she thought it was very sweet. After a delicious meal, he told her he'd rented a movie. The movie turned out to be *9½ Weeks* and the television turned out to be in his bedroom.

Break Every One of These Rules at Least Once

The whole theme of Guerrilla Dating Tactics is encouraging you to dump the rules and invent your life in your own way as you go along. Once you have guidelines for avoiding bad dates, I hope you'll listen to your heart and take a few chances. Otherwise, you'll be forced to sit silently while your friends have brutal bad date stories. Otherwise, you'll be conservative when it's time to let loose your wild streak. Otherwise, you'll ignore the song in your heart and opt for a tune that's B flat.

Take a hot-air balloon ride with a stranger. Rent a rowboat and picnic across the lake. Stay out all night. Opt for occasional derring-do.

THE ONE RULE NOT TO BREAK:
If Need Be, Go Home

Domenic invited a woman to dinner at an arty New York bistro with a jazz trio. He made a comment about how few women jazz musicians there seemed to be. His date responded to his comment with rage. She lumped him in with the worst patriarchal, dominating, insensitive men she'd ever met ... the ones who'd barred women from the jazz scene. He feebly tried to defend himself. When that incited her further, he asked her to stop. He excused himself to the men's room and tried to give her time to cool off. Somehow he had pressed a button, and she got really, really mean. Upon his return from the men's room, as she picked up where she left off, he told her he was sorry but he had to leave.

Candice met a man from out of state who was visiting for several weeks. He invited her to have dinner with two other couples, old friends. Things began smoothly, but soon he began to drink quite heavily. He became loud and obnoxious, and he embarrassed the entire table with his antics. Candice endured it, but, in retrospect, she wished she'd up and left.

You should not endure cruelty, substance abuse, or antisocial behavior from your date. If s/he behaves irresponsibly and becomes out of control, go home. If you are worried about his safety (and the safety of others) in getting himself home, take the car keys and call him a cab.

Never leave your house for a date without enough money to call a cab or pay for your meal. If you must, call a friend or relative to come get you. It is better to be embarrassed at having to do so then to put yourself through hell or danger.

Gems, Jerks, Second Chances

Following the above guidelines will help you avoid prolonged bad dates, but remember: Many wonderful people don't come off as wonderful first dates. A case of full-blown first date heebie-jeebies can temporarily transform a gem into a jerk.

Maria had a car, so she picked Carlos up. As she waited for him, she listened to her favorite FM station. Carlos jumped in the car, and without so much as asking, hit the button and changed channels.

Paul invited Claire to dinner, expecting to treat her. She grabbed the check and, ignoring his protestations, dropped a fifty-dollar bill on the table. When Paul attempted to explain his discomfort, Claire told him he was making a big deal out of nothing. When he made a second stab at discussing it, she dismissed his feelings entirely.

Liza met Don at a restaurant. She was unable to smell her burger over his body odor.

Debby had to leave her phone off the hook because Joe called her so much. She'd accepted one date with him, and now he wouldn't go away. If this kept up, she was going to have her number changed next week.

What separates these bad dates from the preceding stories is that each of these couples ended up getting married to each other. Every day good relationships emerge from the rockiest of starts. Here are just four of the ways in which two perfectly nice people can rub each other the wrong way.

Power Plays

When Carlos changed the station and Claire plopped the fifty on the table, both were attempting to recapture some of the control they felt like they lost in a first encounter of the hormone-hopping kind. If Carlos couldn't control his nerves, at least he could control the radio station. If Claire couldn't know if there would be a second date, at least she could control doing all she could on this date. Unfortunately, they tried to win back their balance at the expense of their dates.

Both are good people who momentarily acted out their anxiety unpleasantly. It's easy to make a snap decision about them, but it's a mistake.

When someone makes a power play early on with you, you will have to evaluate whether this is temporary anxiety or a pervasive personality trait.

Hygiene

Nothing is a bigger turnoff than bad hygiene, but even here, people self-correct with guidance. Don grew up in a home where his dad never wore cologne or used deodorant. Consequently, he ended up being a nice guy who smelled bad when he got nervous. After a few dates, Liza bought him a bottle of roll-on. She gently explained that she really liked him, and that he needed to use deodorant. He was very, very surprised and a little hurt, but he got over it. How sad it would have been if she hadn't done this and stopped seeing him instead.

When someone's hygiene is not up to your standards, you will have to evaluate whether you should never see him again or get to know him well enough to tell him. A close friend of mine married a man who never wore deodorant in his life until she gently pressured him to try it. His first response was that no one had ever complained about his odor in the past. His second response was irritation at her persistence. His third response was to try it.

Overzealousness

Persistence can be admirable, but pressure is not. With Debby on his mind, Joe just couldn't distinguish between the two. She often left the phone off the hook so he couldn't bother her. Debby finally gave in to a date because he depleted her, and she decided to get this last encounter over with. She was surprised at the delightful evening.

Someone who keeps asking you might just deserve two short dates before you decide if you want to give him the standard brushoff or the deluxe Fuller brushoff. Or you could end up like Debby and Joe—hitched.

You will have to decide whether you've attracted a pest or whether he knows something you don't know. It can work either way. I know countless tales of people who fell in love with someone who hung around, maintaining interest even after they'd been turned down a few times. My friend Mindy referred to one persistent admirer as "the thing that wouldn't go away." She married the thing.

Insecurity

Talking too much
Talking too little
Too many questions
Too many giggles
Too many interruptions

Insecurity on a first date breeds any one of the above behaviors, which can erupt like Mount St. Helens all over your good time. Just as you practice rational thinking when you goof up, give your date the benefit of your rational thoughts:

- This behavior doesn't reflect 100 percent of who she is.
- He deserves the benefit of the doubt.
- Snap judgments can be rash judgments.
- When I think of all the times I needed a second chance, I can certainly give her one.
- Boy, is he nervous.

If you are wondering why you should do this, I'll tell you what Virginia Satir, the gifted family therapist, had to say:

We are all flowers in a garden and we blossom at different rates.

You may be dating an annual, a perennial, or a load of ragweed, but you can't be certain till you sprinkle on a little friendly fertilizer and wait.

SPECIAL REPORT: WHAT TO DO WHEN YOU'RE THE JERK

You will invariably have the sinking sensation at least one time that you are the jerk. This revelation may come to you at one of two points, On the Date or After the Date. Here's how to try and recapture his positive feelings.

On the Date

Rita is great on a mediocre date. She's charming, witty, and her mediocre dates are wild about her. Yet when Rita goes out with a man she really likes, she's a nervous wreck. Recently she spent the first half hour with Rob nervously kicking her leg. She barely spoke. She could see Rob retreating but felt powerless.

Al made a comment. Lois took it the wrong way. Before he knew it, he could feel her palpable irritation. He immediately changed the subject.

Don't try to gloss over, ignore, or do a patch job on awkward moments. People are very forgiving, but not when you try for the supreme cover-up. Look at what happened to Nixon!! If you goof up, don't act like the tape was erased. Directly acknowledge what is happening. As always, humor helps.

I've suddenly realized that I've been kicking my leg for the past hour. I must be nervous. Believe me, my batteries will run down soon.

I can see that our wires got crossed. I sure didn't mean to put my foot in my mouth for at least another twenty minutes.

The moment I said that, I could see it bothered you. I didn't mean to upset you.

Acknowledgment of your clunker projects your personal awareness and willingness to concede reality. You also allow room for clarification, understanding, and working through a difficult moment, all of which can further closeness. If, however, you put all your energy into holding your leg still or changing the subject every time things feel difficult, you will have no energy left to be a good date.

After the Date

You toss and turn all night long realizing that you blew it. You pushed sex too soon or said something alienating. And you really like her. Must you disappear into the woodwork, or is there hope?

If you want to try again, you can, but only if, as in the above examples, you acknowledge the misfire. Call her and say:

I've been thinking about our date. I was nervous and realized too late that I'd monopolized the conversation. I wanted to call you. I could see that I hurt your feelings. I got so flustered I didn't know what to say—so I said nothing. I could have handled it better.

I didn't mean to make that crack about your ex. Maybe I was projecting my own feelings about my ex.

Sorry! I can't believe I did that. Maybe I never should have sent away for that "How to Be a Don Juan in Three Easy Lessons" tape.

After acknowledging what went wrong, wait and see what she says. She may appreciate your owning up. She may be willing to talk about what happened. She may give you a second chance, and she may not. The best way to get it is to ask for it. Perhaps you could ask her for a short date in a week or so.

The key to acknowledging your mistake lies in your ability to separate (in your eyes and in her eyes) your behavior from who you are:

- What you did was inappropriate, but you are not inappropriate.
- You made a goof, but you are not a goof.
- Your behavior was foolish, but you aren't foolish.

Sometimes you can turn a bad date around, and sometimes it can't be done. Either way, it's cleaner all around to have closure on it and to feel that you did what you could to make things right.

On a personal note

I'd like to share my all-time bad date with you. After my divorce, I was asked out by someone I'd known in high school. It was one of my first post-divorce dates, and I was very excited. I thought he was really funny and really cute. He arrived over a half hour late. I jumped into his car and saw a beautiful bouquet of flowers on the dashboard. At least he'd done something to make up for his tardiness, I thought. "The flowers are beautiful," I said, reaching for them. "They aren't for you," he responded. Then he explained that they were for another woman he was meeting after he dropped me off. They'd had a fight last week, and he was a wreck about it. Did I think she'd like them?

24

Taking the Court
Out of Courtship

Make love in the microwave.
Think of how much time you'll save.
—Carly Simon

Life is like McDonald's. You don't have to get out of your car
to live it. You can even order it through the window.
—a Rhode Island workshop participant

A first date occurs when two people agree in advance, and for the
first time, to coanchor a designated amount of time together.
Do not confuse first dates with chance encounters, where you
bump into her in the market or pick him up at a dance. It is not
a real first date unless it is mutually agreed upon in advance. But
here are some exceptions:

- If you have a chance encounter with someone and during it,
  one of you utters the words, "I guess this is our first date"
  and the other person nods, it becomes a first date.
- If you get drunk on New Year's Eve, meet someone smashing
  or, like you, smashed, and elope that night to Las Vegas, your
  wedding doubles as your first date.

The singular purpose of a first date is to decide if you want a
second date, but the goals of dating are endless and ever shifting.
They can include any combination of the following:

- not wanting to be alone
- finding a suitable partner
- sex
- fun
- the tradition of twos

- marriage
- children
- pursuing a mutual interest
- status

It can get confusing because two people on a first date may not have a single shared goal.

SUBGOALS OF DATING

Beneath the goals lurk the subgoals, the unresolved emotional jigsaw puzzles of our psyches:

- I want to marry my mother or father.
- I want to marry myself.
- I want to marry the opposite of everyone.
- I hate myself, and I want to marry someone who agrees with me.

DATING AGENDAS

Each person also brings an agenda to the date. The first part of a dating agenda is the one we share out loud (the *purpose* of the date):

"I'd like to get to know you better."

The second part of the agenda is kept secret (the hidden goals of the date). After all, it is not polite on first dates to say:

"I want sex with you."
"I want to get married."
"I'm lonely, and I think you could put an end to that."

> *Second agendas you should carry to your grave:*
> "I'm going out with you because my VCR is broken."
> "I'm going out with you because you're paying."

Because we keep part of our agenda a secret, the second agenda becomes what is commonly called a hidden agenda of urges, needs, and personal game plans.

During the date we juggle the first agenda, the Miss Manners of who we are, with the second agenda, the Sidney Sheldon of who we are. We are forced, like aquarium seals, to keep several balls in the air since we have no idea what the other *really* wants out of the date.

Your date responds to how your statements hook up with his *hidden agenda,* the part about him you don't know yet, while you respond to how his hook up with yours, the part about you he doesn't know yet. This bumbling maneuver requires enough ducking and shuffling to confuse the Pentagon (then again, something as simple as the appropriate price for a toilet seat confuses the Pentagon).

How this Differs from the Old Days

Years back, daters had two goals: marriage and sex. In the forties and fifties, men knew where to find women because, by and large, women stayed put and married right out of high school. In the sixties and seventies, many of us went off to college, but it didn't hurt a thing. College was a four-year mixer, and we found each other there.

The kind of dating we did in the high schools and colleges of days gone by gave us time to hang around each other. We figured out the answers to life's big questions (such as how to buy beer when you are under twenty-one), but, underneath that, we knew what was expected of us: marriage. So we built relationships, and we got married—even when we didn't want to.

The film *It's a Wonderful Life* is a perfect example of this. Jimmy Stewart's character, George, is planning his trip around the world. Then his brother convinces him to dance with Donna Reed's character, Mary, at the prom. Although George is very clear about what he wants—a lifetime of exotic travel—he falls for Mary, marries her, and lives out the rest of his "wonderful" life in the town he was born in.

Today I envision a very different premise. Mary would be an accomplished executive, dancing not to the beat of a vintage band, but to the tick of her biological clock. After hearing George's dream of living out of a suitcase, she would have nixed him on the spot as an unsuitable match, made the brave decision to become a mom anyway, and headed for the nearest sperm bank. Voila! A whole new movie, directed by Barry Levinson instead of Frank Capra. Throw in kinky sex and Laura Dern, and you can hire David Lynch.

How Nineties Culture Has Affected Dating

Today the roles, expectations, and life-styles of men and women are vastly different. After we go away to college, we are less likely to settle back home. We're bicoastal. We're career-oriented. We're on frenetic deadlines. Many of us are much, much older. We've been divorced, burned, and co-dependenced ad nauseam. *And* we aren't all dating to get married.

Some of us just want to live together and some of us just want sex. Some of us just want to date. Some of us don't want children and see no reason to marry. Some of us want children and see no reason to marry. In the nineties, you could be dating *anyone*!! And who has time to figure all this out? *No one*!!

In fact, recent innovations that were designed to give us more time seem to give us less time. Fax machines, microwaves, cash machines, and fast food (which you wait in line twenty minutes to get) all mean we can work longer hours, eat hurriedly, take the kids to the extra ballet class, and still make it to the gym.

Life seems so much faster and tougher. We no longer ask for a raise, we swim with the sharks. We no longer sweat out staff conflicts, we use the one-minute manager. We are breathing hyperboles on a collision course to the bottom line.

I consider the most serious side effect for single adults of our fast-paced life-styles to be:

BOTTOM LINE DATING

All this emphasis on saving time has spilled into our personal lives. We are so intent on collecting vital information about our dates ASAP that we have endangered the art of how to build relationships. This pressing need to avoid wasting time and find out about people quickly makes us unlikable, unattractive, and uptight—the very qualities that we avoid in others become exaggerated in ourselves.

Industrial Dating Side Effects

Following industrial trends, we've applied advanced technology, technophilosophy, and the entrepreneurial spirit to dating. The massive singles scene of events, cruises, personals, and dating services can put us in contact with countless others in a few hours.

These inventions need to provide manuals that teach us healthy ways to use them, because they have created new difficulties of their own.

> Think of medication. It heads straight for the sickness and cures it—but often at a price. You can cure a fever, but get an ulcer. You can cure an infection, but get a sour stomach. Even the most prized lifesaving devices often bring on unwanted side effects.

Bottom-line daters, with their glazed eyes and torn checklists, are the casualties of the nineties and can be likened to sitting under a lone dangling light bulb in the back room of police headquarters while a bad cop picks his cuticles with a Swiss army knife and snaps:

What do you do?
Where do you work?
Are you divorced?
How long?
Kids?
Car?
Co-op?
Blood test?

You thought the definition of the *court* in courtship had something to do with wooing. Instead, you learn that the court in courtship is criminal court and your date is the prosecuting attorney, judge, jury, and executioner all rolled up together.

QUALIFYING MATCHES

Hallie tells of attending a singles gathering in Norwalk, Connecticut. No sooner did she meet a man than he tried to determine her status through a series of nosy, premature questions. She felt like she'd been transported back to third grade where the currency of exchange was pass/fail.

I had a similar experience years ago with a man I'd met through the personals who qualified me instead of talking to me. It was our first phone conversation, and within two minutes he asked me about what I wanted for myself and where I saw myself in five years. When I couldn't answer in twenty-five words or less, he told me that he was sorry I didn't know myself yet because I seemed like a nice person. Then he hung up.

One male client told me that he received a call from a woman whose personal ad he'd responded to and her first question was, "What brand of shoes do you wear?" On the basis of that she planned to decide whether or not they should meet.

There are four major myths about dating that make us qualify people:

Myth: I have standards.
Reality: You cannot date a résumé, and standards don't make a person lovable.

Myth: It's a timesaver in weeding out unsuitable matches.
Reality: You are often weeding out yourself.

Myth: Other people ask lots of questions.
Reality: If you saw them all jump off the Brooklyn Bridge . . .

Myth: When I say I've met someone I like, friends and family grill me about them. When I don't know the answers, I feel foolish.
Reality: Let your friends and family get their own dates.

> BUILDING RELATIONSHIPS IS LIKE
> MAKING WINE. IT CAN'T BE RUSHED.

Here are some tips for getting to know people and forever taking the court out of courtship. Read them three times before you go out on a date or to a singles event. They may just save your evening.

CURTAIL INVASIVE QUESTIONS

A barrage of questions is unsettling. It's like a baseball player during a practice who gets "peppered," a drill that entails having ball after ball hurled quickly and relentlessly at him. Don't pepper someone with questions, and keep in mind that personal questions asked too soon are a turnoff. Think twice before asking a new acquaintance why his last relationship bit the dust. Allow people to reveal themselves on their own timetable. In addition to what you ask, consider how you ask. Nothing is a more powerful communicator than the style you employ to frame questions. When you begin with innuendos such as,

Why did you?
How could you?
Why won't you?

you are not asking a question at all. You are making a judgment.
For example:

Question: Why did you stay in that job for four years?
Translation: Any schnook would have quit after four months.

Question: How could you have bought that car?
Translation: I have a "Bozo the Clown" sign you can borrow.

If someone is not responding to your questions with more
than a word or two, there are four possibilities:

1. You're asking closed questions—these are questions that
   have yes/no answers. Instead of asking, "Do you like Italian
   food?" ask, "What's your favorite Italian restaurant and what
   makes their food so good?"
2. You're treading on delicate territory by asking questions that
   are loaded. Back off a bit and see what happens.
3. You're being put off. This person does not want to know
   more about you.
4. You've met a shy person who needs longer to warm up.

For each of these situations, don't increase the questions to get
more of a response. Change strategies (reread Chapter 20).

DON'T OVERREACT WHEN YOU'RE THE TARGET OF INVASIVE QUESTIONS

People ask too many questions because they think that's how
to show interest, because they're anxious, or because they would
rather focus on you than on themselves.

If you are the target of an interrogation, invent a few
counterquips:

Bomb: What happened to your last relationship?
Guerrilla Dating Tactic: I was just about to ask you the same
thing.

Bomb: How come you're still single?
Guerrilla Dating Tactic: Lucky for you I am or I wouldn't be here.

Bomb: Where do you work? What do you do?
Guerrilla Dating Tactic: Please slow down. We can take turns finding out about each other.

All these quips should be said with good spirit. See if you can't redirect someone along a more comfortable path.

KEEP IT IN THE HERE AND NOW— DON'T SAY "WHAT IF"

Ginger met a man in the elevator while he was moving into her apartment building. She left him a note under his door telling him where to find the cheapest dry cleaning, the best Chinese food, and, of course, her. He called and asked her to try the Chinese food with him. During their phone conversation, he mentioned that there was a chance he would have to move out of state in three months.

Ginger was a wreck. Should she cancel the date because he might ultimately leave town?

In addition to the fact that Ginger had just abdicated 100 percent of her control to this man by giving him the power to like her or abandon her while never once asking herself if she liked him, Ginger has forgotten all about the here and now.

In the here and now, she's going on one date. If Ginger can invest in the *process* of getting to know her neighbor without leaping to the *outcome* of getting to know him, she might actually stand a chance of *really* getting to know him and even having fun. How can she have fun when she is already worrying that he might leave her?

Her worries have meaning for her. They are not trivial. But she needs to explore them in the appropriate setting. Coincidentally, Ginger works for the airlines. If anyone stood a chance of exploring a bicoastal romance, it would be someone who can fly free—someone like Ginger.

DATE PEOPLE, NOT RÉSUMÉS

I frequently have the fantasy of people exchanging résumés before they decide to date. Judging from the way people describe their experiences, I'm not far off. Most people hate the feeling that you are trying to find out what they do and where they work so that you can decide if you want to pursue them. Anyway, what a person does may or may not have bearing on who they are. We all know high-ranking slimeballs and true saints sweeping floors. You could be nixing the best thing that ever happened to you if you are overfocused on professional accomplishments.

It's perfectly natural to imagine what the person you want will be like or what she will do for a living or how much he makes. We're human. We do this. Just don't turn this into a way to step on your own toes. When you are on a date, try to find out *who this person is*, instead of how close a match they are to who you *thought you were going out with.*

LIMIT EX TALK

At a first meeting, answer questions about previous relationships briefly and nondefensively. Not having read this book yet, your date may grill you.

This happens for several reasons:

- She really wants to talk about *her* ex.
- He wants to know if you are really available because his last three dates went back to their exes.
- You've pulled out your wallet and shown pictures of your ex.
- You've taken her to a restaurant where your ex is the hostess.

> Let the platoon medic tend your wounds, not your date.

Exception 1

You are about to run out of the house for your date when your ex calls. Or he zaps you by backing out as babysitter at the last second, forcing you to ask your mother . . . again. Or you are recently divorced or recently widowed and still have a great emotional connection that plops itself on your lap during the date. Then you discover your date had a similar experience and it turns into your common ground. You both share experiences and offer each other support, humor, and a belief that things will get better. This is a whole different phenomena than ex-bashing or ex-glorifying. This is sharing.

Exception 2

You pour out your heart, and it doesn't matter because you are with someone who is already crazy about you or a truly understanding person. When you start making ex talk, pay attention to the cues of your date. Does she squeeze your hand or do her eyes start frantically darting around the room?

DON'T RUSH TO JUDGE

Each of us shares the same fear: Being judged. We fear that we will be undervalued, passed over for someone else.

We act on that fear in different ways. One person says nothing all night so that they don't say the wrong thing. Another never shuts up because they just want to get it over with.

We can be on our best behavior, we can try our hardest, but we have limited control over how we are judged. That doesn't mean we have limited control. We have ample say over how *we* judge others. Think of the ways in which you can help someone feel that you are on their side, rather than using your radar to pinpoint their weak spots. Your generosity will likely inspire theirs. Whatever you can do to help someone feel a little bit safer on a date can only make that date a nicer place to be.

Remember: If you want to be in court and you aren't a lawyer, volunteer for jury duty. Don't put your date on the stand.

IX.

Reframing Romance for the Nineties: Tender Treaties

Peaceful Takeovers: The Pre-Date, Post-Date Dope

You know how to act *on* a date, but did you know that a date begins before you go on it? The moment:

You decide to ask someone out
Your thoughts turn to what she's doing next Sunday afternoon
You suffer over what you'd wear
You daydream yourself dizzy

you are mentally starting the date and wondering how you will come across.

If you like this person, the excitement is unparalleled, the jitters one of a kind. Feelings flourish that we never even knew we had or that we were sure, at this stage of life, we'd never feel again. (Romance is never age-specific. Couples get lost in love at all ages.) But before we get lost in love, we frequently feel just plain lost.

You can face helpless feelings head on, the Guerrilla Dating Tactic way, by learning the Pre-date Post-date Dope, solid know-how about asking, showing up, ending the evening, and following up.

GUERRILLA TELEPHONE TACTICS

Unless you already know she's crazy about you, getting a date can depend on good asking skills. These are especially helpful if you are someone who:

- stares at the phone twenty times before picking it up
- stares at the phone number but never makes the call

- calls and hangs up
- hallucinates while dialing
- forgets your name when she answers the phone
- attempts to convince your roommate to call and pretend he's you

How Long Till You Call?

Charles met a woman at a party on a Sunday. He mentioned an upcoming film festival in which she sounded interested, so they exchanged numbers. He was excited, so he called his friend Caroline to tell her about it. Caroline sternly warned him that he must observe the Three-Day Rule—do not call the woman for at least three days after the first meeting. Charles was surprised. He didn't want to wait three days, but he didn't want to screw things up.

The Myth of the Three-Day Rule

Caroline's Three-Day Rule has gone by other names such as the Seventy-Two-Hour Gestation Period or the MHS (make her sweat). The rule developed because men and women feared that if they seemed too eager, they would come across as needy or as having nothing else going on in their lives. Somewhere someone planted the notion that such a perception could be altered by waiting three days. (Although I recently met a man who says that he always waits for seven days.)

The underlying principle of the Three-Day Rule makes vague sense. We are *all* needy to a certain extent, and we may choose not to share this until we trust someone. That does not mean we have to act falsely, like a pretend-person. Purposely postponing a call you want to make in an effort to manipulate that person's feelings is a really negative way to look at forming a relationship. It perpetuates the fear of showing who we are and being ourselves. It causes us to hide our true selves. It also nips the precious spontaneity of that enthusiastic phone call in the bud. Anyway, our desire and our search for closeness is a cause for celebration, not repudiation.

There is no need to wait three days if you don't want to. The key is not how many hours until you call, but how you sound and how you express yourself when you do call. If you want to, you can call the next day, make small talk, and say:

I enjoyed meeting you. I'm looking forward to getting together.

THEN WAIT.

Make an assessment of the response. Is the enthusiasm equal to yours? Does s/he hedge? No response at all?

Guerrilla Telephone Tactic: If Your Enthusiasm Is Matched

Make a date. If it's really matched, you can make a date for the next night you are both free. If it's really, really matched, hang up, walk out the door, and meet her. Go with your heart. Let yourself be swept away.

When relationships don't pan out, people like to put in their two cents about why. They may try and tell you it's because you didn't observe the Three-Day Rule. They are most probably wrong. Your success will be based on matched enthusiasm, not how many hours you wait.

Guerrilla Telephone Tactic: If You're Uncertain Whether Your Enthusiasm Is Matched

If dating is new to you and/or signals are unreadable, consider one or two of these tips:

- Talk on the phone for a while to gain clarity about response. You may even talk on the phone a few times before asking.
- Ask for a weeknight rather than a weekend, or ask for the Short Date, as described in Chapter 23.
- Offer two choices: Instead of asking for Tuesday, say you are free on Tuesday, and if she's busy then, on Sunday afternoon. Ask her if she can join you on one of those days.
- If he's unavailable then, see if he offers alternatives.
- If she doesn't, be friendly and take the hint . . . for now.
- You may try again in a few weeks. Keep it low-key, as in, "I was thinking of you and wondering how things are going. Thought I'd call and say hello."
- Now there's been time to think about it. You ought to be able to make an assessment of the enthusiasm for getting together at this point.
- If you still aren't sure, disclose: "I was hoping to get together sometime, but I can't quite tell if that's something you'd like to do."
- WAIT.
- It is perfectly okay to say you are disappointed if he says no. State your feeling without fishing for his response.

- As always, try to make her laugh. Nothing breaks the ice and moves her to accept a date better than thinking she might actually have fun or being humorously pointed in the direction of observing what silly, uptight creatures we can be.

Guerrilla Telephone Tactic: If Your Enthusiasm Is Unmatched—How to Handle Lame Excuses

Be gracious and friendly when turned down. People do change their minds. Once a man asked me out a few times, and I turned him down because I thought he wasn't my type. Cheerfully, he told me the next move was mine, and I should call him if I reconsidered. One month later I did, and we ended up dating. I called him because he was so gracious about my not accepting a date that I began to think I'd nixed someone really neat. I was right.

I learned two very important lessons from him, although the relationship didn't work out. I learned that I had more than one type, but my experiences had not yet pointed that out to me, so I was concentrating on what was familiar. I also learned that you can call someone after a month or so. If they like you, they'll be glad to hear from you as long as your previous conversations were friendly, if not productive.

Guerrilla Telephone Tactic: Asking for a Date: Plan A

Don't ask someone to get together without a plan. Men and women don't like it if you are vague and they aren't sure what they are being asked for. Be ready to say:

Let's have dinner.
I have two tickets . . .
My friends are having a party.
I had this nutty idea . . .

It is fine to ask if what you have to offer sounds like fun. If it doesn't—

Guerrilla Dating Tactic: Revert to Plan B

If you invite someone to a museum exhibition that it turns out he just saw or to participate in a sport that she doesn't know how to do, you need, like a Cub Scout, to be prepared (on the spot) with an alternative. Keep an ace up your sleeve if you want that merit badge.

BIGGEST ERRORS IN ASKING FOR A DATE

- Do not say: "Let's get together. What would you like to do?"
- Do not offer more than two alternatives: Oh, I dunno. A movie, a walk, a champagne cocktail, just hanging out . . . shopping?
- Don't say, "Let's have dinner. What kind of food do you like?" Have restaurants in mind. Certainly, you may ask for additional suggestions. Maybe he's a vegetarian, maybe she's allergic to fish . . . you don't know. Many people, when asked what kind of food they like, feel the burden of choosing the right price range, geographic location, type of food, and ambiance. This is your burden if you are asking for the date.

Vagueness is the number one dating damper. Preplan your requests. It takes extra work on your part, but things will run smoother and mixed cues will diminish. Your date will appreciate that you've put thought into how your first evening together will be spent.

FACE-TO-FACE TACTICS

You won't always be leashed to a phone to ask for a first date. Sometimes you'll face the music and dance. Here's what you can do when you're face-to-face with him and you know you want to ask him out.

Face-to-Face Tactic: Matched Enthusiasm—Desire to Ask on the Spot

Just do it.

Face-to-Face Tactic: Don't Leave It Hanging

Look for a level of entry in the conversation, something that you both enjoy or something that you've talked about and he's shown interest in. Then *suggest you do it together.* If he tells you that would be neat, complete your move by suggesting a day.

Don't leave things hanging, as in:
SHE: I can't believe it. You love pinball too.
HE: Yup.
SHE: Maybe we could hit an arcade sometime.
HE: Great.
SHE: Yeah.

If you haven't found a level of entry, ask for a date and tell him you will call him to talk more about it. Don't put pressure on yourself to invent a sound idea at the moment. You've already exerted yourself just getting the courage to ask. Now you need time to rack your brain and make yourself crazy deciding what you want to do.

WHAT SHOULD YOU ASK SOMEONE TO DO FOR A FIRST DATE?

The possibilities are unlimited:

Spelunking
Picnicking
A historical neighborhood walking tour
Take in a museum exhibition*
Pick blueberries and bake a pie
Dinner
Coffee and fattening desserts
The samba
Tennis
Make your own ice cream sundaes
Fishing
Breakfast at a lovely hotel restaurant
Bowling
A protest march
A lecture
Test-drive a Jaguar
Play pool
A poetry reading
The zoo
Pinball arcade playing
Make a snow person
Open-air concert in the park

---

*Harry, a D.C. radio producer, takes the museum tour twice in advance before he invites a date, so he'll impress her by sounding well-informed.

Sunset watching
Having your Tarot cards read
Scrabble
Invite him to join you at volunteer work
An Ethiopian restaurant*
    See if you can't come up with a date that leaps out of a life-time of dinner-and-a-movie.

GUERRILLA RESPONSE TACTICS

When you are the one who is asked, choose from a repertoire of responses, remembering that your response has meaning. Your friendliness helps her feel confident. Your hesitation or skepticism makes him wish he'd never asked. Go ahead. Give him a chance!! You may discover something you didn't know was there.

Guerrilla Response Tactic: When You Are Asked and You're Delighted

Say:

It's so nice to hear from you.
Yes, I'd really like to get together.
I was hoping you'd call.
I was just thinking about calling you.

Thank heaven she got up her nerve first. Boost her confidence.

Guerrilla Response Tactic: When You Are Asked but Busy That Night

Offer an alternative. Melissa tells of a time that a man she was dying to hear from called to ask her to a ball game on a night when she already had plans. She turned him down, hoping he'd make a counteroffer. He didn't. She never heard from him again.
    Always be ready with a statement such as:

I'm so sorry. I'm busy tonight. Let's make plans for next week.
I'm busy this Saturday. What about next Saturday?
I'm already tied up, but I was looking forward to our getting to-gether. When are you free?

---

*Traditionally, Ethiopian restaurants serve without utensils, and you eat with your hands. (To find out how sexy this can be, rent the film *Tom Jones*, starring Al-bert Finney.)

Statements such as these are much stronger than the old "How about another time?" That tired phrase is yet another way to leave things hanging.

GUERRILLA IMPRESSION MANAGEMENT PLOYS

Since dates start before you go on them, some men and women opt to begin making their impression before you have time to put on your coat and walk out the door to the restaurant. It's certainly not necessary to do so. However, if you are so inclined, creative dating techniques abound.

Guerrilla Impression Management Ploy #1

Do you remember the ketchup commercial where Carly Simon sings her hit song "Anticipation" as the ketchup slowly drips out of the bottle? Well, when Caroline arrived home the night before her first date with Carl, there was a bottle of ketchup sitting on her doorstep with a note that read, "In anticipation of our first date."

Guerrilla Impression Management Ploy #2

Jim met Louise, a writer, in a nightclub a few days before he was scheduled to leave town. He called for a date when he returned. When she opened the door, he handed her a little green clothespin painted to look like an alligator. He'd seen it used as a paper clip in a store and thought that Louise might like it.

Guerrilla Impression Management Ploy #3

During Elise's first conversation with Bob, he mentioned his undying love for pumpernickel bagels that were made at a deli near Elise's home. She arrived on their first date with one gift-wrapped bagel and a twinkle in her eye.

Of course, you can always bring flowers, if you want to—or *you can send them in advance:*

Guerrilla Impression Management Ploy #4

I used to work for a dating service fixing people up. I was at my office on a Friday afternoon, clearing my desk and day-dreaming about later that night, when I was to go on my first date with Boots. At 3:00 P.M. I received a delivery from the florist—

beautiful flowers with a note that read, "I'm looking for a strong, creative, beautiful woman for a late-night rendezvous. Can you help?"

Did this schmaltzy trick work?
I married him.

Giving Flowers to Men

I've asked roomfuls of men how they feel about having a woman send them flowers. In these roomfuls, less than a handful had ever had this experience. While men admit they have taken a bit of office ribbing when the flowers were sent there, all but one were tickled pink. The one man who didn't like it stated that he just couldn't feel comfortable with what he perceived as a role reversal, nor could he ever let a woman pick up the tab. Old warhorses are everywhere.

Beyond Flowers

One unforgettable afternoon, a first date walked through my door and produced a wild orange flowering potted begonia. I was floored and utterly taken. Be creative and hand him:

a flowering cactus
a baby aloe plant clipped from your own
a thatch of pussy willows
flowers you picked in a nearby field

Guerrilla Impression Management Ploy #5

Amanda is standing at a bus stop with Sal waiting to take the bus into town on their first date. She walked over to the curb and pulled up a few sickly daisies. She presented them to him with flair.

Or, for something completely different, bring:

a balloon
a lighthearted card you picked especially for the occasion
a Mallomar
a book
a magic trick

Any pre-date gift must be given lightly, warmly, and in a friendly manner. Don't go making goo goo eyes, overload compliments, or get gloppy on her. Let the gift speak your enthusiasm.

Otherwise, you can easily overwhelm someone. And remember, every pre-date gift must be *cheap*! Flash your creative spirit, not your bankroll.

GUERRILLA GOOD NIGHT TACTICS

In the late seventies, Mae had a date that didn't end for three months. She was catching a salad in a restaurant when a man asked if he could be seated at her table. The restaurant was full, and she had the only seat left. He introduced himself as George and proceeded to order a banana split with two spoons. They began talking and discovered they both loved rhythm and blues. She invited him to join her that evening at an R & B club. One thing led to another and she went home with him. After two days, she returned to her apartment, packed up, and moved in with George hook, line, and mournful R & B riff.

You will, most probably, end your dates within one calendar day of starting them—and that only because as adults we get to stay out past midnight.

Some dates you will want to end sooner than others.

Guerrilla Good Night Tactic: Bad Match

Bad matches happen most often with blind dates, dating services, and personal ads. I'm making the assumption here that you are two nice people who aren't cut out for each other, and you both know it. One nice way to handle this is to face it directly by saying:

> You're really one of the nicer people I've met lately, but I guess we can see that we aren't quite right for each other. Still, I wonder how you'd feel about my keeping you in mind to fix up? Or if I heard about an activity that I thought you might really like and wanted to call and tell you about it?

In this way, you've let someone know you value them, but you won't be dating again. You've also created a new resource for yourself.

Guerrilla Good Night Tactic: Lopsided Match—Your Call

You can see her going gaga while you're going gag-gag. It's awful, it's uncomfortable, and you scan the driveway for a hole to drop into. Seeing none, you thank her in a friendly way for the evening. *Period.*

She may counter with when you will call or if she can call. Bite your tongue, chew your cheek, or pinch your arm before lying.

We have all been on both sides of the lopsided encounter. Women complain about men who say they'll call and don't call. Men complain about women who give their number and then make lame excuses when called for a date. Both complain when after a date they get vague postponements, mixed cues, and never know which end is up.

You can't control how others handle such awkward moments, but you can control how *you* handle them. Remember: THE BUCK STOPS HERE.

Guerrilla Good Night Tactic: Lopsided Match—His Call

Comedian Rita Rudner said it best:

"My boyfriend and I broke up because he wanted to get married and I didn't want him to."

You may meet someone you think is perfect for you, but he won't know it. You'll want another date, but you'll know he doesn't. Be gracious. Check out your intuition—don't make assumptions.

SHE #1: I had a lot of fun and would enjoy seeing you again.
HE #2: Thanks, but I just got cable TV. Tomorrow night they're showing *Attack of the Killer Tomatoes,* and I expect to be fixated nightly on quality programming such as this.
SHE #1: Hold on to my number. Give me a call if time passes and you'd like to try again.

A friendly good-bye without a sour note may generate second thoughts on his part.

Some people opt for persistence—winning her by wearing her down. As noted in Chapter 23, I've met countless couples who ended up together because one of them kept calling, even when they knew their calls were not warmly welcomed. This is a matter of individual style—a case-by-case situation. It is quite possible that these pursuers detected something in the pursued's voice that the pursued didn't know was there. It brings to mind the old joke about chasing her till she catches you.

At the same time, if someone directly tells you not to call, stop immediately. Not to do so constitutes harassment. It's only when signals are wishy-washy that you may want to keep trying.

Guerrilla Good Night Tactic: Good Match

Strike up the band, and offer something better than "I'll call you soon."
What is soon?
Tomorrow?
Next week?
Does that mean I shouldn't call you?

Offer clarity at the end of the date:

This was fun. I'd like to go out again. Can I call you on Wednesday to make plans?
What a nice evening. There's a concert I've been planning to go to next week. Would you join me? I could call you on Tuesday with the details.
What's the best time to reach you?

Then *call when you said you'd call.* By doing so, you set the tone of early trust, the key building block of healthy relationships. Do this even if you

1. have to call from your mother's house
2. have to ask a total stranger if you can borrow her mobile phone
3. have no change and are forced to stand on the corner and say, "Spare a quarter?"

If you forgot to call when you said you would, make certain to acknowledge it:

I ran into a snag last night and didn't get the chance to phone you until now.
I know I was going to call you this morning. Then I got stuck in a meeting. I hope now is a good time for you to talk.

Guerrilla Good Night Tactic: Great Match—Follow-Up (Optional)

In addition to making plans to get together again, you may have the urge to do more. Here's what others have done in the past when they just had to sing or dance or do something extra.

Send a Report Card

I know both a man and a woman in two different states who followed a great date by sending mock report cards. They only graded the best points of the dates. Designations included: good night kisses, dressed to kill, scintillating talk, hand-holding potential, and chance of a second invitation.

Leave a note on the seat of the car

Leeza had a great time with Ramon. While in the Ladies Room, she decided to write him a note on a paper towel. He'd mentioned how much he loved dancing, so all she wrote was, "Wanna go dancing?" Before he walked her to her door, she left it on the car seat.

Send a lighthearted note or card

Silly or warm is fine. Heavy-handed or flowery, such as, "I'm dying to see you again" or "I never believed a first date could be so wonderful" is too much.

Follow-up Flowers

Irv sent Dee a yellow rose and a note that read, "I'm a hostage to your charms."

It's not necessary to go to such lengths. But if you do, think of something that fits your style. Be bold and funny, and don't take yourself too seriously.

ERROR IN ENDING A GOOD DATE

Occasionally people don't know when to stop. Lingering over dessert, standing at her door for twenty minutes, even coming in for coffee are the wonderful perks of a great first date. But when it's 3:00 A.M. and you are nodding out, or your defenses are down and you begin rambling, or your libido is in overdrive and you begin twitching: Get up and go home. You can always make another date right away. Don't overstay your welcome because you are just too darn tired to think straight.

Remember: the last thing you do on a date is say good night. What kind of good night do you want him to remember?

How Often to See or Call

Again, no hard and fast rules, but if you are a person who has the urge to call ten times a day, ask yourself this question:

Am I calling to make a genuine connection or am I calling because I'm entering my neurotic mind-set?

Reemergent Adolescence

When I was in high school there was a boy (well, several, actually) I really liked. I showed him in a typical way. I called frequently and hung up when someone answered the phone. I couldn't help myself, I couldn't stop myself. The impulse to call was too strong, and at that stage of life, I was a slave to my hormonal tidal waves.

I could only trust that he liked me when he was right in front of my face. As soon as he walked out the door, the connection was broken and I felt the loss.

As adults we are still prone to such feelings, especially when we have a crush on someone. The difference now is that we understand the value of controlling impulses. We may want to call ten times a day, but we don't do it.

If you find yourself overwhelmed by frequent impulses to call:

- Remember, you win someone by demonstrating that you had a life before you won them.
- Call a friend instead.
- Force yourself to wait until tomorrow. Give your compulsions time to pass.
- Try a physical activity.
- Go back to Chapter 7 and update your address book.
- Set up an extra therapy session.
- Disconnect your phone.
- Tie yourself to a doorknob.

The key to understanding whether or not the frequency of your calls is appropriate is to ask yourself if they are matched by the other person. If your calls are met with great enthusiasm, quickly returned, and you take turns calling, do what your heart shouts at you to do. If you find that you are the only one calling, asking, and planning, then you may also end up doing most of the hurting. Back off and slow down. You're moving too fast.

There are no prescriptions or secret codes for how often to call or see someone. If you want dramatic cryptograms, buy a puzzle book or join the CIA. In relationships, real intrigue is two people learning each other's secrets. The mystery happens as they discover the essence of each other. Do not confuse this wonderful adventure with manipulation of someone's feelings to get what you want, or mind games. Mind games take you further and further away from the other person and from yourself. They do not foster closeness or any kind of real and meaningful connection. Intrigue is about finding the secret path that leads from your heart to her heart.

Getting Closer: Reframing Sex for the Nineties

A re you struck by the fact that you've just read an entire chapter about first dates with nary a mention of a good night kiss?

TO KISS OR NOT TO KISS

Kissing good night on a first date ain't what it used to be. Long slurpy explorations are out. Kisses don't translate into sexual activity as they frequently did in the past. This doesn't mean, and I hope it never will, that good night kisses are extinct. They are alive and kicking, and whole squadrons of dates await osculation.

Assessing Kissability

You will get signals to advance if your date wants that kiss as badly as you do. Pay attention to nonverbal cues that denote interest:

A gentle nuzzle
Touching your hair
Putting hands on both your shoulders at one time
Taking both of your hands in his hands at one time
Gaze/sigh/gaze conduct
Touching your face
Prolonged parting, including:
  Lingering before getting out of your car
  Lingering at the door
  Lingering on your couch
  Lingering with arms akimbo
  Lingering with lips aquiver

If your date demonstrates these behaviors or makes it easy and tells you s/he wants to be kissed, you can proceed depending on your own instincts and beliefs about kissing. But before you smooch, read the following:

A COMPENDIUM OF OUTDATED FIRST KISS TECHNIQUES

Forehead Kissing—A patriarchal move that sets you up as the daddy. It's perfect for bidding your little pumpkins goodnight—*but not for your date.*

Brush-by Kissing—Sometimes a kiss is not even a kiss. Your lips graze his cheek, but never really touch it. Save this one for third cousins at the family reunion.

Two-Cheek Kisses—Very European. Adjust your monocle.

Hand Kisses—This works best after laying your cape across a puddle on the street in order to keep his Hagar slacks dry.

Butterfly Kissing—Eyelash-to-cheek kissing. If you get pulled to the wrong place, blink your eyes a few times quickly. He'll feel a tickling on his cheek that will tell him there has been a computer error—cancel, retry, abort.

SENSIBLE FIRST KISSES

Cheek Kissing—Friendly, warm, respectfully affectionate. By all means, say you had a ball and plant one.

Light Lip Kisses—Lasts slightly longer than cheek kissing. Should be dry and soft. Don't press your lips together like you are having nightmares of your last dental procedure. Soften up, close your eyes, and relax.

Hugging—Close kissless contact. The old hug and a squeeze. Can mean there is some real bonding here. Very intimate and tender. *No grinding!!*

No Kissing—Many people don't kiss on the first date. It is old-fashioned thinking to wonder what went wrong if your date doesn't kiss you. It is perfectly acceptable to save even this minimal intimacy until you know someone better. In fact, many people prefer not to kiss. They don't want to take one footstep into the sexual twilight zone so early on.

Beyond the Valley of the First Kiss

Remember Sam, the piano player, singing "As Time Goes By" in the classic movie *Casablanca*. He starts off:

You must remember this
A kiss is still a kiss
A sigh is just a sigh
The fundamental things apply
As time goes by.

Guess what? Time went by. The fundamental things have changed. The kiss Sam describes is not just a kiss, it's an invitation to another kiss ... and another ... and another. Before you slide your hand from her shoulder to her waist, before you lean back on the couch and kick off your shoes, you gotta talk.

Sexual Etiquette for the Nineties

Sex needs a book about sex, and this is a book about dating. But it would be irresponsible not to talk about it at all. Even with the tragedy of AIDS and other sexually transmitted diseases that threaten men and women, there is a wide range of sexual behavior out there in the world. Some people remain celibate—pleasuring themselves (the only truly safe sexual act)—some practice safe sex (the next safest choice), and some play Russian roulette, continuing to have unprotected sex as the number of heterosexuals infected with the HIV virus and lesser infections grows at an alarming rate.

Don't put your head in the sand. Current and vital information about safe sex can be obtained by contacting Planned Parenthood, your local Department of Health, organizations devoted to helping persons with AIDS, organizations for the promotion of sex education, or the Centers for Disease Control in Atlanta, Georgia. Most large cities offer confidential, anonymous testing. If you want to be tested for the HIV virus, you may ask one of these organizations to direct you or you may visit your personal physician.

When you are tested, you are asked about your sexual activity for the past *twelve* years, but being tested today may not reflect activity within the past six months. The virus can lay dormant for that length of time. If you are currently in a high-risk group or indulging in high-risk behavior, you should return for a second test in six months to be certain.

No Sex and Dating

People date all the time without engaging in sexual activity. Many have decided that this is the only thoughtful choice to make until they settle down with one person. In addition, no intercourse does not mean people can't give each other pleasure. Instead, people are using their creative skills to come up with safe ways of getting closer.

Common Mistake: Beware of believing yourself to be safe because of serial monogamy, that is, sleeping with one person at a time in sequential relationships. You can end up with four or five serial monogamies per year, leaving yourself completely unprotected.

Sex and Dating

If you plan to have an active sex life, let this one rule guide you through your sexual encounters in the nineties:

> IF IT'S TOO SOON TO TALK ABOUT IT, IT'S
> TOO SOON TO HAVE IT.

Sex is an informed decision that two people must make together. We can find gentle, healthy ways to talk about it, but first let's talk about what *not* to do.

TRULY UNROMANTIC AND UNSAFE WAYS TO ADDRESS THE SUBJECT

Pulse Readings—If Tommy wants to sleep with a woman, he asks her about her sexual history and then grabs her by the wrist and takes her pulse. He says that if her pulse rate shoots sky-ward, he interprets this as meaning she's got something to worry about, so he moves on to someone else. The fact that he doesn't have, at the very least, a perennial black eye amazes me.

List-Swapping—Elsa keeps a computer printout of her sexual partners in her wallet. There are a few names scratched in by hand on the bottom. When she's with a guy she likes, she hands him the list and asks for his. She offers her fax number just in case he wants to send it to her.

Body Exams—Ricky says that when he gets intimate with a woman, he asks if he can take a good, close look where the sun don't shine. He believes he can determine health by a healthy glow.

Unsafe assumptions

A Recent Divorce—Caryn was dating a man who was recently divorced after an eighteen-year marriage. She was sure he was safe. Of course, the reality is that she had no way of knowing what his extramarital activities were during that marriage, not to mention the extramarital activities of his wife.

The Myth of Upper-Class Safety—Sara Beth is an upper-class pro-fessional woman who considers herself and those she dates to be in low-risk categories. How could that Stanford MBA she has her eye on carry even a microscopic genital wart, let alone the AIDS virus? To her, the thought is ridiculous.

Already Tested—Frank told Fiona he was tested last year and he's clean. Since the virus can lie dormant for up to six months, and since she has no idea what he's been doing since he was tested, this test tells nothing!

Avoidance of the Issue—Harry lets his genitals speak for him. He gets carried away with the moment. He waits until the point where he can't stop himself. Then he rationalizes by saying—guess what?—he couldn't stop himself.

Lack of Assertiveness—Carla really loves Jose, but Jose hates condoms. Carla is afraid she will lose him if she presses the point.

> ## THE ONLY INTELLIGENT ASSUMPTION
> You are crawling into bed with everyone both of you have ever slept with and everyone you've ever slept with has slept with. TROOPS!! We are talking *troops.*

RAISING THE SUBJECT

I saw an episode of the television sitcom "The Days and Nights of Molly Dodd" where she brought a new man home. Things got steamy, and you knew where they were headed. She stopped him and went into her bedroom. When she emerged, she was carrying a large wicker basket filled with a wild assortment of condoms. She invited him to make a choice, while pointing out what was available. It was funny, and it got the point across, though it's not for the faint of heart. However, if you are direct and bold about your sexuality, you could do worse than compiling your own condom basket.

> As condom usage increases, the colors, textures, and inventive capabilities of the condom industry know no bounds. A whole new world of fun is opening up, if not at the druggist's counter, then in the pages of certain un-named mail-order magazines.

Not all condoms offer equal protection. Latex is safer than a natural condom. You can buy latex condoms coated with a Nonoxynol-9 lubricant that is even safer. Nonoxynol-9 is also present in water-based spermicidal gels. The failure rate in condoms ranges from 1.5 percent to more than 10 percent. Look for current reports on the most highly rated condoms. *Consumer Reports* has covered this subject in the past. This is important because, for example, a condom labeled extra-strength can actually be one of the least reliable. In addition:

- Never use Nonoxynol-9 in place of a condom.
- Never use an oil-based lubricant such as Vaseline, hand cream, or baby oil with a condom. All of these weaken the latex.

- Because the lubricant in condoms is water-based, condoms may need to be rehydrated to keep them moist during intercourse. Keep a small plastic squeeze bottle of water or a plant mister next to the bed.

The Gentle Approach—There are ways—romantic, loving ways—to raise the subject of sex for the first time. There is a point where you know your feelings are becoming highly sexualized. It can be after a kiss that you wish wouldn't end or after an intimate moment of mutual self-disclosure.

When this point comes, and you believe that you know where this is headed, STOP and say:

- I feel like we're getting closer, and I'd like to get even closer than this. Maybe this would be a good time for us to talk about that.
- I don't want to stop. I really care about you. I guess it's time to talk about sex.

You have gently raised the subject in a way that can effectively tackle the issue from a position of caring for and about each other. It is nondefensive, and it opens the lines of communication.

GUERRILLA CONDOM TACTICS

Just because you wouldn't dream of getting closer without a condom, that doesn't mean that all your partners will be as sexually sophisticated as you undoubtedly are. Certain partners will resist, be afraid to discuss it, or even get surly and defensive. Be prepared, in advance, to deal with resistance so you don't get put into a dangerous position.

You are: In bed
You say: Ooh. Aah. Let me just run to my wallet and get a condom.
She says: That's okay. I'm wearing a diaphragm.
Guerrilla Condom Tactic: You're so thoughtful. We'll use both.
Later: Tell her you always use condoms and tell her why. Let her know it's because you care. Engage her in talking about her feelings about condoms.

When you get up to get that condom, return with
two—just in case.

You are: In bed
You say: Let me open my night table drawer and get a condom.
He says: I hate those things. It's like wearing an inner tube.
Guerrilla Condom Tactic: Not with me, it's not! Just wait till you see
what I've got in mind.
Later: Tell him you always use condoms, and talk about ways to
make it more pleasant and exciting for both of you. Maybe he's
never used condoms in the past. Maybe he's afraid he'll lose his
erection wearing one. Be tender, understanding, and find the adventure.

You are: In bed
You say: Let me put this condom on you.
He says: I never use them. I refuse. Dontcha know I love you, baby?
You say: I'm so glad you love me. Then you'll really want to make
sure I'm protected.
Later: Remind him that the best way he can "prove his love" is to
"wear his glove."

If you meet with resistance, stop and talk it through. Clarify
the objections. When you have a better understanding of your
partner, state clearly how important this is to you. You may decide
to counteroffer other kinds of sexual pleasures that don't include
unsafe sex.

If your partner wants "the real thing" but refuses to wear a
condom, or if your request is dismissed as your paranoia, you've
got a big decision to make. Is this worth your life? If your answer
is yes, get thee to a shrink.

GUERRILLA CONDOM PRACTICE

If you are not yet in the habit of regular condom usage, then
allow me to advise you to do a little "private practice" before taking your show on the road. During a passionate moment, even ripping open the package has been known to confound the finest
scientific minds.

Men: Buy twelve condoms and try them out. Get used to putting one on. Yes, you're right—it doesn't feel the same. Make a few

adjustments. Try different safe-sex brands. You may find it much more pleasant if you use a lubricant with the condom. You can always opt for the old standby, K-Y jelly. However, if you feel more adventurous, try two products manufactured by the Trimensa Corporation, PrePair and ForPlay. These personal lubricants have been around for ten years and have a reputation for quality. Look for them in pharmacies. Try them out. Take all the time you need—after all, this isn't "Beat the Clock."

Women: Practice walking into a drugstore and purchasing condoms and lubricants. You may have cringed at doing something like this twenty years ago, but it's a different world. If it makes you too antsy, bribe your doorman, brother, or fearless friend to buy them for you. Check out magazines that provide advertisements for mail-order marital aids. You can get condoms delivered to your mailbox.

Once you have the condoms, practice putting one on something phallic from the vegetable bin. Become adept at this. A man may ask you to put his condom on, or you may discover sexy and loving ways to contribute to the pleasure of the moment by offering to put it on him. You need to get used to the sight, smell, and taste of condoms.

For men and women: There are books on the market that offer healthy safe-sex techniques. Buy one!!

WHERE TO KEEP CONDOMS

Men, remember that condom you kept in your wallet all four years of high school? This is one case where reverting to adolescent behavior is the healthy choice. You may even get luckier than you did the night of the prom.

In addition to the wallet, sexually active men *and* women should tuck extra condoms everywhere, in your:

raincoat pocket
purse
overnight travel case
bathrobe
night table
glove compartment
aerobics bag
silverware drawer
couch cushions
shoe

Caution: Don't keep condoms in dark, tight places like wallets and drawers for years or decades. They dry out and tear more easily. Check the expiration date before usage and renew your condom supply regularly.

In the old days they used to say, what you don't know can't hurt you. Today what you don't know can kill you. I want you to take good care of yourself and be around for a long, long time. Do your research. End of sermon. On to other sexual issues.

FOR WOMEN: GRABBY MEN

Don't assume that a guy who makes an erotic suggestion much sooner than you'd ever consider it is a pig. If he won't let up, he's a pig. If he makes a sexual overture too soon, don't necessarily dump him, stop him. If you really like him, try some of these lines:

If this happens between us I want to give you the best I've got. It's too soon for that now.

I'm flattered, but you're way ahead of me.

I have the same feelings for you, but it's too soon for me.

Slow down, tiger.

This in no way suggests you should have sex with a man before you are ready. It is simply a framework for you to look at a grabby guy so that you don't make the mistake of assuming he's a heartless, hopeless lech.

It doesn't always work out. Keesha borrowed the line "If this happens between us I want to give you the best, but it's too soon for me to do that now." She reports that Lewis responded, "That's okay. I'll settle for second best."

FOR MEN: WOMEN WHO LUST TOO MUCH

Though less publicized and less frequent, men can be on the receiving end of amorous advances. Gary tells of a woman walking up behind him in a bar and grabbing his buns. Cornelius tells of a first date who got him in a clinch on the couch that almost smothered him. Kim tells a story of a woman walking up to him at a party and sticking her tongue in his ear. You may have to swallow your pride and a lifetime of manly Irish Spring training and use the grabby men lines on grabby women.

THE SEXUAL ACT

If you decide to have sex, keep in mind that just as we learn about romance from the movies, that's where we pick up many of our ideas about sex. We witness selected contortions that match the director's fantasies of what hot sex looks like. It's smooth—without cellulite, scars, and unwanted hair.

Real sex includes negotiating four arms, four legs, two heads, two easily strained backs, and two easily bruised egos. Don't be surprised if the first time it's clumsy, you find yourself feeling self-conscious, and your body has a mind all its own.

Remember that in the beginning:

An erection is like a dog with a concussion; it's just as likely to roll over and play dead as it is to come when you call.

CHAPTER 27

Reinventing Courtship: Daily Workouts

Take a look at your body. You accept the fact that after a certain age, if you want to be in decent physical condition, you have to work at it. I don't mean out-Arnolding Arnold or out-Janing Jane, but whether through low-fat diet, exercise, or both, you will pay attention to your body in new ways.

Your romantic identity needs the same kind of attention. It won't maintain itself (although I believe that the next step in science should be liposuction of the gray matter that remembers heartbreak). Life can wear you down and slap you silly. As you accept your engraved plaque from the "Hard Knocks School of Depressing Divorces and Dorky Dates," you must rigorously exercise your heart to keep it open to romance.

This entails maintaining your spontaneous, playful childlike self—the part of you that laughs easily, can't bear to close your eyes because you might miss something good, trusts people, and enjoys banging pots and pans as much as playing with a real toy. Yet you need to approach romance with the wisdom of the adult who knows that while there are magical feelings, it's not magic and it doesn't happen magically.

Take responsibility for resuscitating your spirit by doing things that give you pure, whimsical pleasure:

Relax in a lavish bubble bath and don't forget your boat.
Throw a coed pajama party with prizes for the best ghost story.
Walk in the rain.
Tickle your friend.
Play hooky and read comic books all day.
Go skinny-dipping.
Rent a Rocky and Bullwinkle tape.
Adopt a kitten.
Organize a softball game.
Run away with the circus (or at least go).

Master a card trick.
Eat a hot fudge sundae.
Go to the kiddie matinee and throw Jujubes at the screen.
Go to the midnight movie.
Go to a toy store.
Go to the zoo.
Learn to mimic Curly, Moe, and Larry.
Learn ventriloquism.
Make a wacky Halloween costume and go trick-or-treating.
Neck.
Giggle.

Reviving your playful, mischievous child resuscitates the playful, mischievous adult. Once you allow yourself to act silly on purpose and realize how free you feel, it will be easier to allow for the silly discomfort of approaching someone. Now the sky is the limit. You've opened the door to recognizing and acting on opportunities.

TRUE GUERRILLA DATING TACTICS TALES FROM THE FRONT

The following stories are responses to my frequently asked question, "What is the oddest way or place in which you met someone?" Each story shows a frisky adult willing to embrace a crazy moment. When you read these stories, you'll know they are true. No one could make this stuff up.

At a Fire

Liam, a television news photographer, was filming a burning Boston building during the dog days of August. In his words, "It must have been one hundred degrees out before the fire." A woman who lived in the neighborhood brought him a glass of ice-cold lemonade with her phone number written on the side of the paper cup.

Wrong Number

David received a phone call that turned out to be a wrong number. After talking to her for a few minutes, he said, "Gee, you sound so nice." He asked her to meet him at a seafood restaurant for dinner. She did.

Scalping a Concert Ticket

Jack's sister couldn't attend a concert they'd already purchased tickets for. Jack went up to a cute woman outside the theater, sold her the ticket, and ended up marrying her.

At a Funeral

Annabelle began dating a man that she met at a friend's funeral. They hit it off royally and managed to allay their guilt by telling each other he would have wanted it this way.

Getting an Allergy Shot

Mike was getting his penultimate allergy shot and talked briefly with a woman in the doctor's office. Later, he called the nurse and scheduled his last appointment for the same time that this woman was coming back. They ended up getting married.

An Eighty-Five-Year-Old Barber

Nathan's eighty-five-year-old uncle had been going to the same barber for fifty years. On one visit he asked him if he knew anyone for his nephew Nathan. It just so happened that the eighty-five-year-old barber had a splendid niece.

Lap Dancing

Bill relies on his wheelchair to enhance his dancing style. He invited Kelly to slow-dance. When she looked at him quizzically, he told her that all she had to do was sit in his lap. He'd take care of the rest.

Paper Airplanes

A woman with the unusual name of Fonda resumed her third-grade tricks. She wrote a note and her phone number on a piece of paper that she folded into a paper airplane. She ended up dating the man she hit with it. Luckily her aim was true.

At a Cemetery

Claire met Sammy while she was visiting her husband's grave at the same time he was visiting his wife's.

Travel Agency Tango

Faith booked a flight for a handsome man headed for Pittsburgh. She looked him straight in the eye and said, "What a coincidence. I'm booked on that same flight. Maybe we could sit together." When he walked out the door, she made a reservation in her own name.

Sneaky Shuttle Riders

Years ago, on the Boston/New York shuttle, a man approached me and said, "You're sitting in my seat." I replied that I thought shuttle seats were unreserved. He explained that this policy had changed, and sheep-faced, I moved in one seat to let him sit. Ten minutes later, he confessed that he was trying to pick me up.

Video Love

Devera was seventy-two and on a fixed income when she joined a video dating service. Every man in her age range said she was too old. Men in the sixties nixed her too. Undaunted, she moved to the men in the fifties and met Roger. Three years later they were still together. She so inspired her seventy-three-year-old friend that her friend placed a personal ad and began dating soon after.

Spare a Quarter?

Joel carries a single bill, *un millon pesos de la República Argentina,* in his wallet. It's actually worth very little, but he uses it to attract attention by asking a woman, "Can you spare a dollar? I'm down to my last million."

Second Chance

Linda was once approached by a man who had a boat. He invited her to sail with him, but she told him she wasn't interested. Several months later she changed her mind. She called him and left a message on his machine that said, "I remember that I promised to let you give me a ride on your boat, but I can't remember if I promised you anything else."

Sketchbook

Dan carries a sketchbook and sketches people he wants to meet. However, he's never let them see any of his work because he can only draw stick figures.

Male Order

Nancy met a man in a restaurant one night. She told him she admired his monogrammed shirt, and she gave him her card. A few days later, she received a matchbook in the mail with that restaurant's name on it. Inside, this man had placed his monogram as the only identifying feature. A few days after that he called a very intrigued Nancy for a date.

Pass the Peanuts

The first lady of the American theater, Helen Hayes, met her husband, Charles MacArthur, at a party. She was shyly sitting alone. He approached her, gallantly handed her a bowl of peanuts, and said, "I wish they were emeralds."

Milking a Compliment

Al told Doris she looked beautiful one afternoon. She said, "Excuse me?" When he repeated himself, she said, "I heard what you said the first time. I just wanted to hear you say it again."

PREPARING TO REACH OUT

Spotting the offbeat chance waiting to happen occurs as you trust your creativity and open your heart. But as we experience more life, we have to work harder to maintain a belief in such possibilities. We are wrongly led to think that this belief maintains itself and that once it's gone, it's gone for good. Or that if we have to work at being positive, it's not worth it.

> Experiments done with monkeys and rats have shown that when they are isolated and deprived of companionship and stimulation, they become less responsive. Emotionally or physically isolated people suffer the same fate. They lessen their ability to reach out or to recognize affection when it is offered.

Only concrete things take care of themselves—your stamp collection, your signed Pittsburgh Pirates baseball—you can shut these things in a room and expect them to look the same a year later. People are not like that. People need regular workouts to stay in shape.

To start your workout simply walk out the door and . . .

- Smile at a stranger.
- Jump into his section of a revolving door when that cute guy who works in your building shows up one morning at the same time as you.
- At a bar, "accidentally" reach for her glass at the same moment she's reaching for it.
- Purchase a bunch of flowers and hand them to a complete stranger as you pass by.
- Give the UPS deliverer a can of soda for the road.
- Bring a bottle of sparkling cider into the office and share it.
- Always carry an ice scraper and help some lucky guy who forgot his.

Remember: It's hard to maintain the agility to act on impulse without regular workouts. If you aren't limber, you could wind up doubled over with cramps instead of saying hello.

In a world filled with lots of good people who are hoping that you've read this book first . . . in a world where the importance lies not in banishing your fears but in acting in spite of them . . . in a world where feeling anxious is a measure of your remarkable progress:

- Exercise your heart and mind.
- Push yourself a little further than you've gone before.
- Take pleasure in the act.
- Don't wait for the magic—go out and *make* the magic.

Epilogue
The Wisdom of Others

In the last minutes of every workshop, I ask the participants if have a few final words of wisdom that they would like to share with other members of the group. I think you'll enjoy this last-minute pep talk from your peers, so I'd like to pass their advice on to you. Some of these affirmations have been repeated elsewhere in the book, but I hope it will be encouraging and memorable to see them together at one time.

If you must have regrets, regret what you've done . . . not what you haven't done.

Keep it fun by lowering expectations.

Show, don't hide, your interest.

Make open communication and flirtation a part of your everyday life.

Never ask yourself, "What if?"

Build bridges, not walls.

Don't wait until you feel more comfortable. Embrace your discomfort and do something.

Wear sultry hats.

Do a minimum of one fun thing per week.

Set goals for improving your social life and stick to them.

Smile at people one block at a time.

Think of yourself as a ray of sunshine melting an ice cube.

Buy season tickets.

Ask your dry cleaner, your accountant, or your hairdresser to fix you up.

Respect the human courting ritual.

Try to look like a million bucks.

A sales representative makes seventeen calls to make one sale. Get those sixteen no's out of the way.

Imagine yourself at ninety-five in your rocking chair reflecting on your life. What do you want to think about? Opportunities you took or opportunities you let slip away?

Don't look to find the right person. Look to be the right person.

Use the quota system: five flirts a day.

Work toward getting rejected by a better class of person.

If you don't exceed the boundaries of decency, no one will be hurt.

Borrow the AA affirmation, "Progress, not perfection."

Once you've laughed together, everything gets easier.

The power to shift a stranger to a friend is only a hello away.

Of course you'll feel stressed (GET USED TO IT)!

Flirts make things happen. They are not content to wait passively for others to make them feel good. They know how to make themselves feel good.

You don't flirt to get something from someone. You flirt to *give* something *to* someone.

Share your gifts.

Flirt from the heart.

Prepare for success.

Finally, I'd like to leave you with one of my all-time favorite stories. It's not specifically about dating, but it captures the idea that looking for romance has its own rewards.

THE TRIP TO HANA

When Katherine's tour group departed the plane, they knew they had limited time in Maui, so they asked the residents of the island which tourist attractions they definitely shouldn't miss. The resounding answer was that no one should come to Maui and miss the trip to Hana. An old friend of Katherine's, Darius, lived on Maui and he offered to take her. The rest of the tour group got maps and rented cars.

The winding road Darius and Katherine drove along was filled with hairpin turns, gorgeous statuary, and even a breathtaking waterfall. Darius stopped frequently so that Katherine could get out of the car and take in the wonderful sights. The trip took hours, and Darius made sure Katherine didn't miss a thing. When they reached Hana, Katherine realized it was a tiny, tiny place.

When Darius returned Katherine to her tour group, she was reveling in the trip and astonished to find that everyone else was griping. They said Hana was a huge disappointment. If you blinked, you could miss it. They couldn't figure out why anyone, let alone everyone, would tell them to go there. After hearing them out, Darius explained what went wrong. They flew past the waterfall, they rushed past the statues, they hightailed it past the scenic views. It was a common mistake:

Everyone went to Hana, but no one took the trip to Hana.

As for you, you've never been better prepared to find another person to treasure and love. I hope you relish every hairpin turn on the trip.

For More Information

Guerrilla Dating Tactics relates the experiences of the thousands of people who have attended Sharyn Wolf's relationship seminars throughout the United States. Sharyn is available for speaking engagements, workshops, and conferences. She maintains a private practice in New York City offering individual consultations, psychotherapy, and support groups.

If this book helps you to feel more optimistic about your social life, if you have a personal story you'd like to share, or if you want information about other workshops in your area, please write to Sharyn at the address below.

Sharyn Wolf, C.S.W.
330 West 58th Street
Room 404
New York, NY 10019
(212) 397–7579

Index